Travel phrasebooks collection
«Everything Will Be Okay!»

T&P Books Publishing

# PHRASEBOOK

# · LITHUANIAN ·

By Andrey Taranov

## THE MOST IMPORTANT PHRASES

This phrasebook contains the most important phrases and questions for basic communication
Everything you need to survive overseas

T&P BOOKS

**Phrasebook + 3000-word dictionary**

# English-Lithuanian phrasebook & topical vocabulary

By Andrey Taranov

The collection of "Everything Will Be Okay" travel phrasebooks published by T&P Books is designed for people traveling abroad for tourism and business. The phrasebooks contain what matters most - the essentials for basic communication. This is an indispensable set of phrases to "survive" while abroad.

This book also includes a small topical vocabulary that contains roughly 3,000 of the most frequently used words. Another section of the phrasebook provides a gastronomical dictionary that may help you order food at a restaurant or buy groceries at the store.

T&P Books Publishing
www.tpbooks.com

ISBN: 978-1-78716-265-5

This book is also available in E-book formats.
Please visit www.tpbooks.com or the major online bookstores.

# FOREWORD

The collection of "Everything Will Be Okay" travel phrasebooks published by T&P Books is designed for people traveling abroad for tourism and business. The phrasebooks contain what matters most - the essentials for basic communication. This is an indispensable set of phrases to "survive" while abroad.

This phrasebook will help you in most cases where you need to ask something, get directions, find out how much something costs, etc. It can also resolve difficult communication situations where gestures just won't help.

This book contains a lot of phrases that have been grouped according to the most relevant topics. The edition also includes a small vocabulary that contains roughly 3,000 of the most frequently used words. Another section of the phrasebook provides a gastronomical dictionary that may help you order food at a restaurant or buy groceries at the store.

Take "Everything Will Be Okay" phrasebook with you on the road and you'll have an irreplaceable traveling companion who will help you find your way out of any situation and teach you to not fear speaking with foreigners.

# TABLE OF CONTENTS

**T&P Books Publishing**

# PRONUNCIATION

| Letter | Lithuanian example | T&P phonetic alphabet | English example |
|--------|--------------------|-----------------------|-----------------|
| Aa | adata | [a] | shorter than in ask |
| Ąą | ąžuolas | [aː] | calf, palm |
| Bb | badas | [b] | baby, book |
| Cc | cukrus | [ts] | cats, tsetse fly |
| Čč | česnakas | [tʃ] | church, French |
| Dd | dumblas | [d] | day, doctor |
| Ee | eglė | [æ] | chess, man |
| Ęę | vedęs | [æː] | longer than in brand |
| Ėė | ėdalas | [eː] | longer than in bell |
| Ff | fleita | [f] | face, food |
| Gg | gandras | [g] | game, gold |
| Hh | husaras | [ɣ] | between [g] and [h] |
| I i | ižas | [i] | shorter than in feet |
| Į į | mįslė | [iː] | feet, meter |
| Yy | vynas | [iː] | feet, meter |
| J j | juokas | [j] | yes, New York |
| Kk | kilpa | [k] | clock, kiss |
| L l | laisvė | [l] | lace, people |
| Mm | mama | [m] | magic, milk |
| Nn | nauda | [n] | name, normal |
| Oo | ola | [o], [oː] | floor, doctor |
| Pp | pirtis | [p] | pencil, private |
| Rr | ragana | [r] | rice, radio |
| Ss | sostinė | [s] | city, boss |
| Šš | šūvis | [ʃ] | machine, shark |
| Tt | tėvynė | [t] | tourist, trip |
| Uu | upė | [u] | book |
| Ųų | siųsti | [uː] | pool, room |
| Ūū | ūmėdė | [uː] | pool, room |
| Vv | vabalas | [ʋ] | vase, winter |
| Zz | zuikis | [z] | zebra, please |
| Žž | žiurkė | [ʒ] | forge, pleasure |

# Comments

- A macron (ū), an ogonek (ą, ę, į, ų) can all be used to mark vowel length in Modern Standard Lithuanian. Acute (Áá Ą́ą́), grave (Àà), and tilde (Ãã Ą̃ą̃) diacritics are used to indicate pitch accents. However, these pitch accents are generally not written, except in dictionaries, grammars, and where needed for clarity, such as to differentiate homonyms and dialectal use.

# LIST OF ABBREVIATIONS

## English abbreviations

| | | |
|---|---|---|
| ab. | - | about |
| adj | - | adjective |
| adv | - | adverb |
| anim. | - | animate |
| as adj | - | attributive noun used as adjective |
| e.g. | - | for example |
| etc. | - | et cetera |
| fam. | - | familiar |
| fem. | - | feminine |
| form. | - | formal |
| inanim. | - | inanimate |
| masc. | - | masculine |
| math | - | mathematics |
| mil. | - | military |
| n | - | noun |
| pl | - | plural |
| pron. | - | pronoun |
| sb | - | somebody |
| sing. | - | singular |
| sth | - | something |
| v aux | - | auxiliary verb |
| vi | - | intransitive verb |
| vi, vt | - | intransitive, transitive verb |
| vt | - | transitive verb |

## Lithuanian abbreviations

| | | |
|---|---|---|
| dgs | - | plural |
| m | - | feminine noun |
| m dgs | - | feminine plural |
| v | - | masculine noun |
| v dgs | - | masculine plural |

# LITHUANIAN PHRASEBOOK

This section contains
important phrases that may
come in handy in various
real-life situations.
The phrasebook will help
you ask for directions, clarify
a price, buy tickets, and
order food at a restaurant

**T&P Books Publishing**

# PHRASEBOOK CONTENTS

**T&P Books Publishing**

## The bare minimum

Excuse me, ...

**Atsiprašau, ...**
[atsʲɪprɑˈʃɑʊ, ...]

Hello.

**Sveikì.**
[svʲɛɪˈkʲɪ.]

Thank you.

**Ãčiū.**
[ˈaːtɕʲuː.]

Good bye.

**Ikì.**
[ɪˈkʲɪ.]

Yes.

**Taìp.**
[ˈtʌɪp.]

No.

**Nè.**
[ˈnʲɛ.]

I don't know.

**Nežinaũ.**
[nʲɛʒʲɪˈnɑʊ.]

Where? | Where to? | When?

**Kuř? | Kur? | Kadà?**
[ˈkʊr? | ˈkʊr? | kaˈda?]

---

I need ...

**Màn reìkia ...**
[ˈman ˈrʲɛɪkʲɛ ...]

I want ...

**Nóriu ...**
[ˈnorʲʊ ...]

Do you have ...?

**Ar̃ tùrite ...?**
[ar ˈtʊrʲɪtʲɛ ...?]

Is there a ... here?

**Ar̃ čià yrà ...?**
[ar ˈtɕʲæ iːˈra ...?]

May I ...?

**Ar̃ galiù ...?**
[ar gaˈlʲʊ ...?]

..., please (polite request)

**Prašaũ ...**
[praˈʃɑʊ ...]

---

I'm looking for ...

**Íeškau ...**
[ˈrʲɛʃkɑʊ ...]

restroom

**tualèto**
[tʊaˈlʲɛtɔ]

ATM

**bankomãto**
[baŋkoˈmaːtɔ]

pharmacy (drugstore)

**váistinės**
[ˈvʌɪstʲɪnʲeːs]

hospital

**ligóninės**
[lʲɪˈgonʲɪnʲeːs]

police station

**polìcijos skŷriaus**
[poˈlʲɪtsɪjos ˈskʲiːrʲɛʊs]

subway

**metrò**
[mʲɛˈtro]

---

| | |
|---|---|
| taxi | **taksì** [tak'sʲɪ] |
| train station | **traukinių stotiẽs** [trɑukʲɪ'nʲu: sto'tʲɛs] |

| | |
|---|---|
| My name is … | **Mãno vaȓdas …** ['mɑːnɔ 'vardas …] |
| What's your name? | **Kuõ jũs vardù?** ['kuɑ 'juːs var'dʊ?] |
| Could you please help me? | **Atsiprašaũ, aȓ gãlite padéti?** [atsʲɪpra'ʃɑu, ar 'gaːlʲɪte pa'dʲeːtʲɪ?] |
| I've got a problem. | **Atsitìko problemà.** [atsʲɪ'tʲɪkɔ problʲɛ'ma.] |
| I don't feel well. | **Mán blogà.** ['man blʲo'ga.] |
| Call an ambulance! | **Kviẽskite greĩtają!** ['kvʲɛskʲɪtʲɛ 'grʲɛɪtaːja:!] |
| May I make a call? | **Aȓ galiù paskam̃binti?** [ar ga'lʲʊ pas'kambʲɪntʲɪ?] |

| | |
|---|---|
| I'm sorry. | **Atsiprašaũ.** [atsʲɪpra'ʃɑu.] |
| You're welcome. | **Nėrà už ką̃.** [nʲeː'ra 'uʒ ka:.] |

| | |
|---|---|
| I, me | **àš** ['aʃ] |
| you (inform.) | **tù** ['tʊ] |
| he | **jìs** [jɪs] |
| she | **jì** [jɪ] |
| they (masc.) | **jiẽ** ['jiɛ] |
| they (fem.) | **jõs** ['jɔːs] |
| we | **mẽs** ['mʲæs] |
| you (pl) | **jũs** ['juːs] |
| you (sg, form.) | **Jũs** ['juːs] |

| | |
|---|---|
| ENTRANCE | **ĮĖJÌMAS** [iːʲɛːʲjɪmas] |
| EXIT | **IŠĖJÌMAS** [ɪʃʲeːʲjɪmas] |
| OUT OF ORDER | **NEVEĨKIA** [nʲɛ'vʲɛɪkʲɛ] |
| CLOSED | **UŽDARÝTA** [uʒda'rʲiːta] |

| | |
|---|---|
| OPEN | **ATIDARYTA**<br>[atɪdaˈrʲiːta] |
| FOR WOMEN | **MÓTERŲ**<br>[ˈmotʲɛruː] |
| FOR MEN | **VÝRŲ**<br>[ˈvʲiːruː] |

# Questions

| | |
|---|---|
| Where? | **Kur̃?**<br>['kʊr?] |
| Where to? | **Į̃ kur̃?**<br>[iː 'kʊr?] |
| Where from? | **Ìš kur̃?**<br>[ɪʃ 'kʊr?] |
| Why? | **Kodė̃l?**<br>[kɔ'dʲeːlʲ?] |
| For what reason? | **Kodė̃l?**<br>[kɔ'dʲeːlʲ?] |
| When? | **Kadà?**<br>[ka'da?] |

| | |
|---|---|
| How long? | **Kíek laĩko?**<br>['kʲiɛk 'lʲʌɪko?] |
| At what time? | **Kadà?**<br>[ka'da?] |
| How much? | **Kíek?**<br>['kʲiɛk?] |
| Do you have ...? | **Ar̃ tùrite ...?**<br>[ar 'tʊrʲɪtʲɛ ...?] |
| Where is ...? | **Kur̃ yrà ...?**<br>['kʊr iː'ra ...?] |

| | |
|---|---|
| What time is it? | **Kíek dabar̃ valandų̃?**<br>['kʲiɛk da'bar valʲan'duː?] |
| May I make a call? | **Ar̃ galiù paskam̃binti?**<br>[ar ga'lʲʊ pas'kambʲɪntʲɪ?] |
| Who's there? | **Kàs teñ?**<br>['kas tʲɛn?] |
| Can I smoke here? | **Ar̃ čià galimà rūkýti?**<br>[ar 'tʂʲæ galʲɪ'ma ruː'kʲiːtʲɪ?] |
| May I ...? | **Ar̃ galiù ...?**<br>[ar ga'lʲʊ ...?] |

# Needs

| | |
|---|---|
| I'd like ... | **Norečiau ...**<br>[no'rʲe:tsʲɛʊ ...] |
| I don't want ... | **Nenoriu ...**<br>[nʲɛ'norʲʊ ...] |
| I'm thirsty. | **Noriu atsigerti.**<br>['norʲʊ atsʲɪ'gʲɛrtʲɪ.] |
| I want to sleep. | **Noriu miego.**<br>['norʲʊ 'mʲɛgɔ.] |

| | |
|---|---|
| I want ... | **Noriu ...**<br>['norʲʊ ...] |
| to wash up | **nusiprausti**<br>[nʊsʲɪ'praʊstʲɪ] |
| to brush my teeth | **issivalyti dantis**<br>[ɪʃsʲɪva'lʲi:tʲɪ dan'tʲɪs] |
| to rest a while | **truputi pailseti**<br>[trʊ'pʊtʲɪ: pʌɪlʲ'sʲe:tʲɪ] |
| to change my clothes | **persirengti**<br>['pʲɛrsʲɪrʲɛŋktʲɪ] |

| | |
|---|---|
| to go back to the hotel | **grizti i viešbuti**<br>['grʲi:ʒtʲɪ ɪ 'vʲɛʃbʊtʲi:] |
| to buy ... | **nusipirkti ...**<br>[nʊsʲɪ'pʲɪrktʲɪ ...] |
| to go to ... | **eiti į ...**<br>['ɛɪtʲɪ i: ...] |
| to visit ... | **aplankyti ...**<br>[aplʲaŋ'kʲi:tʲɪ ...] |
| to meet with ... | **susitikti su ...**<br>[sʊsʲɪ'tʲɪktʲɪ 'sʊ ...] |
| to make a call | **paskambinti**<br>[pas'kambʲɪntʲɪ] |

| | |
|---|---|
| I'm tired. | **Aš pavarges /pavargusi/.**<br>['aʃ pa'vargʲɛ:s /pa'vargʊsʲɪ/.] |
| We are tired. | **Mes pavargome.**<br>['mʲæs pa'vargomʲɛ.] |
| I'm cold. | **Man šalta.**<br>['man 'ʃalʲta.] |
| I'm hot. | **Man karšta.**<br>['man karʃ'ta.] |
| I'm OK. | **Man viskas gerai.**<br>['man 'vʲɪskas gʲɛ'rʌɪ.] |

| | |
|---|---|
| I need to make a call. | **Mán reĩkia paskam̃binti.**<br>['man 'rɛɪkʲɛ pasˈkambʲɪntʲɪ.] |
| I need to go to the restroom. | **Mán reĩkia į̃ tualė̃tą.**<br>['man rʲɛɪkʲɛ iː tʊaˈlʲɛtaː.] |
| I have to go. | **Mán reĩkia eĩti.**<br>['man 'rʲɛɪkʲɛ 'ɛɪtʲɪ.] |
| I have to go now. | **Mán jaũ reĩkia eĩti.**<br>['man jɛʊ 'rʲɛɪkʲɛ 'ɛɪtʲɪ.] |

## Asking for directions

| | |
|---|---|
| Excuse me, ... | **Atsiprašaū, ...**<br>[atsʲɪpra'ʃɑʊ, ...] |
| Where is ...? | **Kur̃ yrà ...?**<br>['kʊr iː'ra ...?] |
| Which way is ...? | **Į̃ kurią̃ pùsę yrà ...?**<br>[iː kʊ'rʲæː 'pʊsʲɛː iː'ra ...?] |
| Could you help me, please? | **Atsiprašaū, ar̃ gãlite padéti?**<br>[atsʲɪpra'ʃɑʊ, ar 'gaːlʲɪte pa'dʲeːtʲɪ?] |

| | |
|---|---|
| I'm looking for ... | **Àš íeškau ...**<br>['aʃ 'ɪɛʃkɑʊ ...] |
| I'm looking for the exit. | **Àš íeškau išėjìmo.**<br>['aʃ 'ɪɛʃkɑʊ iʃʲe:'jɪmɔ.] |

| | |
|---|---|
| I'm going to ... | **Àš einù į̃ ...**<br>['aʃ ɛɪ'nʊ iː ...] |
| Am I going the right way to ...? | **Ar̃ àš teisìngai einù į̃ ...?**<br>[ar 'aʃ tʲɛɪ'sʲɪːngʌɪ ɛɪ'nʊ iː ...?] |

| | |
|---|---|
| Is it far? | **Ar̃ tolì?**<br>[ar to'lʲɪ?] |
| Can I get there on foot? | **Ar̃ galiù nueĩti teñ pėsčiomìs?**<br>[ar ga'lʲʊ 'nʊʲɛɪtʲɪ ten pʲe:stʲsʲo'mʲɪs?] |

| | |
|---|---|
| Can you show me on the map? | **Ar̃ gãlite paródyti žemélapyje?**<br>[ar 'gaːlʲɪte pa'roːdʲiːtʲɪ ʒe'mʲe:lapʲiːje?] |
| Show me where we are right now. | **Paródykite, kur̃ dabar̃ ēsame.**<br>[pa'roːdʲiːkʲɪtʲɛ, kʊr da'bar 'ɛsamʲɛ.] |

| | |
|---|---|
| Here | **Čià**<br>['tʂʲæ] |
| There | **Teñ**<br>['tʲɛn] |
| This way | **Eimè čià**<br>[ɛɪ'mʲɛ tʂʲæ] |

| | |
|---|---|
| Turn right. | **Sùkite dešiněn.**<br>['sʊkʲɪte deʃɪ'nʲe:n.] |
| Turn left. | **Sùkite kairěn.**<br>['sʊkʲɪte kʌɪ'rʲe:n.] |
| first (second, third) turn | **pìrmas (añtras, trẽčias) pósūkis**<br>['pʲɪrmas ('antras, 'trẽtʲɕɛs) 'posu:kʲɪs] |

| | |
|---|---|
| to the right | **Į dešinę**<br>[i: 'dʲæʃɪnʲɛ:] |
| to the left | **Į kairę**<br>[i: 'kʌɪrʲɛ:] |
| Go straight ahead. | **Eikite tiesiai.**<br>['ɛɪkʲɪtʲɛ 'tʲɛsʲɛɪ.] |

# Signs

| | |
|---|---|
| WELCOME! | **SVEIKÌ ATVŸKĘ!**<br>[svʲɛɪˈkʲɪ atʲvʲiːkʲɛːlʲ] |
| ENTRANCE | **ĮÉJÌMAS**<br>[iːʲɛːˈjɪmas] |
| EXIT | **IŠÉJÌMAS**<br>[ɪʃʲeːˈjɪmas] |

| | |
|---|---|
| PUSH | **STÙMTI**<br>[ˈstʊmtʲɪ] |
| PULL | **TRAÚKTI**<br>[ˈtrɑʊktʲɪ] |
| OPEN | **ATIDARÝTA**<br>[atʲɪdaˈrʲiːta] |
| CLOSED | **UŽDARÝTA**<br>[ʊʒdaˈrʲiːta] |

| | |
|---|---|
| FOR WOMEN | **MÓTERŲ**<br>[ˈmotʲɛruː] |
| FOR MEN | **VÝRŲ**<br>[ˈvʲiːruː] |
| GENTLEMEN, GENTS (m) | **VÝRŲ**<br>[ˈvʲiːruː] |
| WOMEN (f) | **MÓTERŲ**<br>[ˈmotʲɛruː] |

| | |
|---|---|
| DISCOUNTS | **NÚOLAIDOS**<br>[ˈnʊolʲʌɪdos] |
| SALE | **IŠPARDAVÌMAS**<br>[ɪʃpardaˈvʲɪmas] |
| FREE | **NEMÓKAMAI**<br>[nʲɛˈmokamʌɪ] |
| NEW! | **NAUJÍENA!**<br>[nɑʊˈjiɛna!] |
| ATTENTION! | **DĖMESIO!**<br>[ˈdʲeːmesʲol] |

| | |
|---|---|
| NO VACANCIES | **LAISVŲ VIÊTŲ NÈRÀ**<br>[lʲʌɪsˈvuː ˈvʲɛtu: nʲeːˈra] |
| RESERVED | **REZERVÚOTA**<br>[rʲɛzʲɛrˈvʊota] |
| ADMINISTRATION | **ADMINISTRĀCIJA**<br>[admʲɪnʲɪsˈtraːtsʲɪja] |
| STAFF ONLY | **TÌK PERSONÁLUI**<br>[ˈtʲɪk pʲɛrsoˈnalʲʊi] |

| BEWARE OF THE DOG! | **ATSARGIAĬ, ŠUŎ!** |
| | [atsar'gʲɛɪ, 'ʃʊɑ!] |
| NO SMOKING! | **NERŪKÝTI!** |
| | [nʲɛru:'kʲi:tʲɪ!] |
| DO NOT TOUCH! | **NELIĖSTI!** |
| | [nʲɛ'lʲɛstʲɪ!] |
| DANGEROUS | **PAVOJÌNGA** |
| | [pavo'jɪnga] |
| DANGER | **PAVÓJUS** |
| | [pa'vo:jʊs] |
| HIGH VOLTAGE | **AUKŠTÀ ĮTAMPA** |
| | [ɑʊkʃ'ta 'i:tampa] |
| NO SWIMMING! | **NESIMÁUDYTI!** |
| | [nʲɛsʲɪ'mɑʊdʲi:tʲɪ!] |

| OUT OF ORDER | **NEVEĬKIA** |
| | [nʲɛ'vʲɛɪkʲæ] |
| FLAMMABLE | **DEGÙ** |
| | [dʲɛ'gʊ] |
| FORBIDDEN | **UŽDRAUSTÀ** |
| | [ʊʒdrɑʊs'ta] |
| NO TRESPASSING! | **PRAĖJÌMO NĖRÀ!** |
| | [praʲe:'jɪmɔ nʲe:'ra!] |
| WET PAINT | **DAŽÝTA** |
| | [da'ʒʲi:ta] |

| CLOSED FOR RENOVATIONS | **UŽDARÝTA REMÒNTUI** |
| | [ʊʒda'rʲi:ta rʲɛ'montʊi] |
| WORKS AHEAD | **KĖLIO DARBAĬ** |
| | ['kʲælʲɔ dar'bʌɪ] |
| DETOUR | **APÝLANKA** |
| | [a'pʲi:lʲaŋka] |

## Transportation. General phrases

| | |
|---|---|
| plane | **lėktuvas**<br>[lʲeːkˈtʊvas] |
| train | **traukinỹs**<br>[trɑʊkʲɪˈnʲiːs] |
| bus | **autobùsas**<br>[ɑʊtoˈbʊsas] |
| ferry | **kéltas**<br>[ˈkʲɛlʲtas] |
| taxi | **taksì**<br>[takˈsʲɪ] |
| car | **automobìlis**<br>[ɑʊtomoˈbʲɪlʲɪs] |

| | |
|---|---|
| schedule | **tvarkãraštis**<br>[tvarˈkaːraʃtʲɪs] |
| Where can I see the schedule? | **Kur̃ galiù ràsti tvarkãraštį?**<br>[ˈkʊr gaˈlʲʊ ˈrastʲɪ tvarˈkaːraʃtʲɪː?] |
| workdays (weekdays) | **dárbo dienomìs**<br>[ˈdarbɔ dʲiɛnoˈmʲɪs] |
| weekends | **savaìtgaliais**<br>[saˈvʌɪtgalʲɛɪs] |
| holidays | **šveñtinėmis dienomìs**<br>[ˈʃvɛntʲɪnʲeːmʲɪs dʲiɛnoˈmʲɪs] |

| | |
|---|---|
| DEPARTURE | **IŠVYKÌMAS**<br>[ɪʃvʲiːˈkʲɪmas] |
| ARRIVAL | **ATVYKÌMAS**<br>[atvʲiːˈkʲɪmas] |
| DELAYED | **ATIDĖTAS**<br>[atʲɪˈdʲeːtas] |
| CANCELLED | **ÀTŠAUKTAS**<br>[ˈatʃɑʊktas] |

| | |
|---|---|
| next (train, etc.) | **kìtas**<br>[ˈkʲɪtas] |
| first | **pìrmas**<br>[ˈpʲɪrmas] |
| last | **paskutìnis**<br>[paskʊˈtʲɪnʲɪs] |

| | |
|---|---|
| When is the next ...? | **Kadà kìtas ...?**<br>[kaˈda ˈkʲɪtas ...?] |
| When is the first ...? | **Kadà pìrmas ...?**<br>[kaˈda ˈpʲɪrmas ...?] |

When is the last ...?

**Kadà paskutìnis ...?**
[ka'da pasku'tʲɪnʲɪs ...?]

transfer (change of trains, etc.)

**pérsėdimas**
['pʲɛrsʲeːdʲɪmas]

to make a transfer

**pérsėsti**
['pʲɛrsʲeːstʲɪ]

Do I need to make a transfer?

**Aȓ mán reĩkia pérsėsti?**
[ar 'man 'rʲɛɪkʲɛ 'pʲæːrsʲeːstʲɪ?]

# Buying tickets

| | |
|---|---|
| Where can I buy tickets? | **Kur galiu nusipirkti bilietą?**<br>['kʊr ɡa'lʲʊ nʊsʲɪ'pʲɪrktʲɪ 'bʲɪlʲiɛta:?] |
| ticket | **bilietas**<br>['bʲɪlʲiɛtas] |
| to buy a ticket | **nusipirkti bilietą**<br>[nʊsʲɪ'pʲɪrktʲɪ 'bʲɪlʲiɛta:] |
| ticket price | **bilieto kaina**<br>['bʲɪlʲiɛtɔ 'kʌɪna] |
| Where to? | **Į kur?**<br>[i: 'kʊr?] |
| To what station? | **Į kurią stotį?**<br>[i: kʊ'rʲæ: 'stɔ:tʲɪ?] |
| I need … | **Man reikia …**<br>['man 'rɛɪkʲɛ …] |
| one ticket | **vieno bilieto**<br>['vʲiɛnɔ 'bʲɪlʲiɛtɔ] |
| two tickets | **dviejų bilietų**<br>[dvʲiɛ'ju: 'bʲɪlʲiɛtu:] |
| three tickets | **trijų bilietų**<br>[trʲɪ'ju: 'bʲɪlʲiɛtu:] |
| one-way | **Į vieną pusę**<br>[i: 'vʲiɛna: 'pʊsʲɛ:] |
| round-trip | **pirmyn - atgal**<br>[pʲɪr'mʲi:n - at'ɡalʲ] |
| first class | **pirmąja klasė**<br>[pʲɪr'ma:ja klʲa'sʲɛ] |
| second class | **antrąja klasė**<br>[ant'ra:ja klʲa'sʲɛ] |
| today | **šiandien**<br>['ʃændʲiɛn] |
| tomorrow | **rytoj**<br>[rʲi:'toj] |
| the day after tomorrow | **poryt**<br>[po'rʲi:t] |
| in the morning | **rytė**<br>[rʲi:'tʲɛ] |
| in the afternoon | **pō pietų**<br>['po: pʲiɛ'tu:] |
| in the evening | **vakarė**<br>[vaka'rʲɛ] |

| | |
|---|---|
| aisle seat | **vietà priẽ praėjìmo**<br>[vʲiɛ'ta prʲɛ praʲe:'jɪmɔ] |
| window seat | **vietà priẽ lángo**<br>[vʲiɛ'ta prʲɛ 'lʲangɔ] |
| How much? | **Kíek?**<br>['kʲiɛk?] |
| Can I pay by credit card? | **Ar̃ galiù mokéti kredìto kortelè?**<br>[ar ga'lʲʊ mo'kʲe:tʲɪ kre'dʲɪtɔ korte'lʲɛ?] |

# Bus

| | |
|---|---|
| bus | **autobùsas**<br>[ɑuto'busas] |
| intercity bus | **tarpmiestìnis autobùsas**<br>[tarpmʲiɛs'tʲɪnʲɪs ɑuto'busas] |
| bus stop | **autobùsų stotelė**<br>[ɑuto'busu: sto'tʲælʲe:] |
| Where's the nearest bus stop? | **Kur̃ yrà arčiáusia autobùsų stotelė?**<br>['kur i:'ra ar'tʂʲæusʲɛ ɑuto'busu: sto'tʲælʲe:?] |

| | |
|---|---|
| number (bus ~, etc.) | **nùmeris**<br>['numʲɛrʲɪs] |
| Which bus do I take to get to ...? | **Kuriuõ ą̃utobusù galimà nuvažiuóti į̃ ...?**<br>[ku'rʲuo: ɑutobu'su galʲɪ'ma nuva'ʒʲuotʲɪ i: ...?] |
| Does this bus go to ...? | **Ar̃ šìs autobùsas važiuója į̃ ...?**<br>[ar ʃɪ:s ɑuto'busas va'ʒʲuo:je i: ...?] |
| How frequent are the buses? | **Kàs kíek laĩko važiuója autobùsai?**<br>['kas 'kʲiɛk 'lʲʌɪko va'ʒʲuo:je ɑuto'busʌɪ?] |

| | |
|---|---|
| every 15 minutes | **kàs penkiólika minùčių**<br>['kas pʲɛŋ'kʲolʲɪka mʲɪ'nutʂʲu:] |
| every half hour | **kàs pùsvalandį**<br>['kas 'pusvalʲandʲɪ:] |
| every hour | **kàs vãlandą**<br>['kas 'va:lʲanda:] |
| several times a day | **Kelìs kartùs per̃ diẽną**<br>[kʲɛ'lʲɪs kar'tus pʲɛr 'dʲɛna:] |
| ... times a day | **... kartùs per̃ diẽną**<br>[... kar'tus pʲɛr 'dʲɛna:] |

| | |
|---|---|
| schedule | **tvarkãraštis**<br>[tvar'ka:raʃtʲɪs] |
| Where can I see the schedule? | **Kur̃ galiù ràsti tvarkãraštį?**<br>['kur ga'lʲu 'rastʲɪ tvar'ka:raʃtʲɪ:?] |
| When is the next bus? | **Kadà kìtas autobùsas?**<br>[ka'da 'kʲɪtas ɑuto'busas?] |
| When is the first bus? | **Kadà pìrmas autobùsas?**<br>[ka'da 'pʲɪrmas ɑuto'busas?] |
| When is the last bus? | **Kadà paskutìnis autobùsas?**<br>[ka'da pasku'tʲɪnʲɪs ɑuto'busas?] |

stop

**stotėlė**
[sto'tʲælʲeː]

next stop

**kita stotėlė**
[kɪ'ta sto'tʲælʲeː]

last stop (terminus)

**paskutinė maršruto stotėlė**
[paskʊ'tʲɪnʲeː marʃrʊtɔ sto'tʲælʲeː]

Stop here, please.

**Prašau, sustokite čia.**
[pra'ʃɑʊ, sʊs'tokʲɪtʲɛ tsʲæ.]

Excuse me, this is my stop.

**Atsiprašau, tai mano stotėlė.**
[atsʲɪpra'ʃɑʊ, tʌɪ 'maːnɔ sto'tʲælʲeː.]

# Train

| | |
|---|---|
| train | **traukinỹs**<br>[traʊkʲɪˈrʲnʲiːs] |
| suburban train | **priemiestìnis traukinỹs**<br>[prʲiɛmʲiɛsˈtʲɪnʲɪs traʊkʲɪˈrʲnʲiːs] |
| long-distance train | **tarpmiestìnis traukinỹs**<br>[tarpmʲiɛsˈtʲɪnʲɪs traʊkʲɪˈrʲnʲiːs] |
| train station | **traukiniũ stotìs**<br>[traʊkʲɪnʲuː stoˈtʲɪs] |
| Excuse me, where is the exit to the platform? | **Atsiprašaũ, kuř yrà išėjìmas į̃ peroną?**<br>[atsʲɪpraˈʃaʊ, kʊr iːˈra iʃeːˈjɪmas iː peˈrona:?] |

| | |
|---|---|
| Does this train go to …? | **Ar̃ šìs traukinỹs važiúoja į̃ …?**<br>[ar ʃɪːs traʊkʲɪˈrʲnʲiːs vaˈʒʲʊoːjɛ iː …?] |
| next train | **kìtas traukinỹs**<br>[ˈkʲɪtas traʊkʲɪˈrʲnʲiːs] |
| When is the next train? | **Kadà kìtas traukinỹs?**<br>[kaˈda kʲɪtas traʊkʲɪˈrʲnʲiːs?] |
| Where can I see the schedule? | **Kuř galiù ràsti tvarkãraštį?**<br>[ˈkʊr gaˈlʲʊ ˈrastʲɪ tvarˈkaːraʃtʲɪ:?] |
| From which platform? | **Ìš kuriõ peróno?**<br>[ɪʃ kʊˈrʲoː pʲɛˈrono?] |
| When does the train arrive in …? | **Kadà traukinỹs atvažiuõs į̃ …?**<br>[kaˈda traʊkʲɪˈrʲnʲɪːs atvaˈʒʲʊoːs iː …?] |

| | |
|---|---|
| Please help me. | **Prašaũ, padékite mán.**<br>[praˈʃaʊ, paˈdʲeːkʲɪte ˈman.] |
| I'm looking for my seat. | **Íeškau sàvo viẽtos.**<br>[ˈrʲɛʃkaʊ ˈsavo ˈvʲɛtos.] |
| We're looking for our seats. | **Íeškome sàvo viẽtų.**<br>[ˈrʲɛʃkomʲɛ ˈsavo ˈvʲɛtu:.] |
| My seat is taken. | **Màno vietà užimtà.**<br>[ˈmano vʲiɛˈta ʊʒˈɪmˈta.] |
| Our seats are taken. | **Mū̃sų viẽtos ùžimtos.**<br>[ˈmuːsu: ˈvʲɛtos ˈʊʒʲɪmtos.] |

| | |
|---|---|
| I'm sorry but this is my seat. | **Atsiprašaũ, bèt taĩ mãno vietà.**<br>[atsʲɪpraˈʃaʊ, bʲɛt tʌɪ ˈmano vʲiɛˈta.] |
| Is this seat taken? | **Ar̃ šì vietà užimtà?**<br>[ar ʃɪ vʲiɛˈta ʊʒˈɪmˈta?] |
| May I sit here? | **Ar̃ galiù čià atsisésti?**<br>[ar gaˈlʲʊ ˈtʂʲæ atsʲɪˈsʲeːstʲɪ?] |

## On the train. Dialogue (No ticket)

Ticket, please.

**Prašau paródyti bilietą.**
[praˈʃɒʊ paˈrodʲiːtʲɪ bʲɪlʲiɛta:.]

I don't have a ticket.

**Àš neturiù bìlieto.**
[ˈaʃ nʲɛtʊˈrʲʊ ˈbʲɪlʲiɛto.]

I lost my ticket.

**Pàmečiau sàvo bìlietą.**
[ˈpamʲɛtsʲɛʊ ˈsavɔ ˈbʲɪlʲiɛta:.]

I forgot my ticket at home.

**Pamiršaū sàvo bìlietą namuosė.**
[pamʲɪrˈʃɒʊ ˈsavɔ ˈbʲɪlʲiɛta: namʊɑˈsʲɛ.]

You can buy a ticket from me.

**Gãlite nusipìrkti bìlietą ìš manęs.**
[ˈgaːlʲɪtʲɛ nʊsʲɪˈpʲɪrktʲɪ ˈbʲɪlʲiɛta: ɪʃ maˈnʲɛ:s.]

You will also have to pay a fine.

**Taĩp pàt turėsite sumokéti baũdą.**
[ˈtʌɪp ˈpat tʊˈrʲeːsʲɪtʲɛ sʊmoˈkʲeːtʲɪ ˈbɒʊda:.]

Okay.

**Geraĩ.**
[gʲɛˈrʌɪ.]

Where are you going?

**Kuř važiúojate?**
[ˈkʊr vaˈʒʲʊoːjɛtʲɛ?]

I'm going to …

**Važiúoju į̃ …**
[vaˈʒʲʊoːjʊ iː …]

How much? I don't understand.

**Kíek? Àš nesuprantù.**
[ˈkʲiɛk? aʃ nʲɛsʊpranˈtʊ.]

Write it down, please.

**Ař gãlite užrašýti?**
[ar ˈgaːlʲɪtʲɛ ʊʒraˈʃʲɪːtʲɪ?]

Okay. Can I pay with a credit card?

**Geraĩ. Ař galiù mokéti kredìto kortelė?**
[gʲɛˈrʌɪ. ar gaˈlʲʊ moˈkʲeːtʲɪ kreˈdʲɪto korteˈlʲɛ?]

Yes, you can.

**Taĩp, gãlite.**
[ˈtʌɪp, ˈgaːlʲɪtʲɛ.]

Here's your receipt.

**Štaĩ júsų čèkis.**
[ˈʃtʌɪ ˈjuːsʊ ˈtʂʲɛkʲɪs.]

Sorry about the fine.

**Atsiprašaū dėl baudõs.**
[atsʲɪpraˈʃɒʊ dʲeːlʲ bɒʊˈdoːs.]

That's okay. It was my fault.

**Niẽko, taĩ mãno kaltė̃.**
[ˈnʲɛko, ˈtʌɪ ˈmanɔ kalʲˈtʲeː.]

Enjoy your trip.

**Gẽros kelionės.**
[ˈgʲɛroːs kʲɛˈlʲionʲɛs.]

## Taxi

| | |
|---|---|
| taxi | **taksì**<br>[tak'sʲɪ] |
| taxi driver | **taksì vairúotojas**<br>[tak'sʲɪ vʌɪ'rʋoto:jɛs] |
| to catch a taxi | **susistabdýti taksì**<br>[sʋsʲɪstab'dʲi:tʲɪ tak'sʲɪ] |
| taxi stand | **taksì stotẽlė**<br>[tak'sʲɪ sto'tʲælʲe:] |
| Where can I get a taxi? | **Kur̃ galiù išsikviẽsti taksì?**<br>['kʋr ga'lʲʋ ɪʃsʲɪk'vʲɛstʲɪ tak'sʲɪ?] |
| to call a taxi | **išsikviẽsti taksì**<br>[ɪʃsʲɪ'kvʲɛstʲɪ tak'sʲɪ] |
| I need a taxi. | **Mán reĩkia taksì.**<br>['man 'rʲɛɪkʲɛ tak'sʲɪ.] |
| Right now. | **Dabar̃.**<br>[da'bar.] |
| What is your address (location)? | **Kóks jū́sų ãdresas?**<br>['koks 'ju:su: 'a:drʲɛsas?] |
| My address is ... | **Màno ãdresas yrà...**<br>['manɔ 'a:drʲɛsas i:'ra...] |
| Your destination? | **Kur̃ važiúosite?**<br>['kʋr va'ʒʲʋosʲɪtʲɛ?] |
| Excuse me, ... | **Atsiprašaũ, ...**<br>[atsʲɪpra'ʃaʊ, ...] |
| Are you available? | **Ar̃ Jū̃s neužimtas?**<br>[ar 'ju:s 'nʲɛʊ ʒʲɪmtas?] |
| How much is it to get to ...? | **Kíek kainúotų nuvažiúoti į̃ ...?**<br>['kʲiɛk kʌɪ'nʋotu: nʋva'ʒʲʋotʲɪ i: ...?] |
| Do you know where it is? | **Ar̃ žìnote, kur̃ taĩ yrà?**<br>[ar 'ʒʲɪnotʲɛ, kʋr tʌɪ i:'ra?] |
| Airport, please. | **Į̃ óro úostą.**<br>[i: 'orɔ 'ʋasta:.] |
| Stop here, please. | **Sustókite čià, prašaũ.**<br>[sʋs'tokʲɪtʲɛ tʂʲæ, pra'ʃaʊ.] |
| It's not here. | **Taĩ nè čià.**<br>['tʌɪ nʲɛ 'tʂʲæ.] |
| This is the wrong address. | **Čià nè tàs ãdresas.**<br>['tʂʲæ nʲɛ 'tas 'a:drʲɛsas.] |
| Turn left. | **Sùkite kairẽn.**<br>['sʋkʲɪte kʌɪ'rʲe:n.] |
| Turn right. | **Sùkite dešinẽn.**<br>['sʋkʲɪte deʃʲɪ'nʲe:n.] |

How much do I owe you?

I'd like a receipt, please.

Keep the change.

**Kíek aš skolìngas/skolìnga?**
['kʲiɛk aʃ sko'lʲɪngas /sko'lʲɪnga?/]
**Noréčiau čèkio.**
[no'rʲe:tʃʲɛʊ 'tʃʲɛkʲɔ.]
**Grąžą pasilìkite.**
[gra:'ʒa: pasʲɪ'lʲɪkʲɪtʲɛ.]

---

Would you please wait for me?

five minutes

ten minutes

fifteen minutes

twenty minutes

half an hour

**Prašaũ mãnęs paláukti.**
[pra'ʃɔʊ 'ma:nʲɛ:s pa'lʲɑʊktʲɪ.]
**penkiàs minutès**
[pʲɛŋ'kʲæs mʲɪnʊ'tʲɛs]
**dẽšimt minùčių**
['dʲæʃɪmt mʲɪ'nʊtʃʲu:]
**penkiólika minùčių**
[pʲɛŋ'kʲolʲɪka mʲɪ'nʊtʃʲu:]
**dvìdešimt minùčių**
['dvʲɪdʲɛʃɪmt mʲɪ'nʊtʃʲu:]
**pùsvalandį**
['pʊsvalʲandʲɪ:]

# Hotel

| | |
|---|---|
| Hello. | **Sveikì.**<br>[svʲɛɪ'kʲɪ.] |
| My name is ... | **Màno vȧrdas ...**<br>['ma:nɔ 'vardas ...] |
| I have a reservation. | **Aš rezervavaũ kaṁbarį.**<br>['aʃ rʲɛzʲɛrva'vɑʊ 'kambarʲɪ:.] |
| I need ... | **Maṅ reìkia ...**<br>['man 'rʲɛɪkʲɛ ...] |
| a single room | **kaṁbario vienám žmógui**<br>['kambarʲɔ vʲɛ'nam 'ʒmoguɪ] |
| a double room | **kaṁbario dviems žmonéms**<br>['kambarʲɔ 'dvʲɛms ʒmo'nʲe:ms] |
| How much is that? | **Kíek taì kainuõs?**<br>['kʲɛk 'tʌɪ kʌɪ'nuɑs?] |
| That's a bit expensive. | **Trupùtį brangù.**<br>[trʊ'pʊtʲ bran'gʊ.] |
| Do you have anything else? | **Aȓ tùrite kažką̀ kìto?**<br>[ar 'tʊrʲɪtʲɛ kaʒ'ka: 'kʲɪto?] |
| I'll take it. | **Paiṁsiu.**<br>['pʌɪmsʲʊ.] |
| I'll pay in cash. | **Mokésiu grynaìs.**<br>[mo'kʲe:sʲʊ grʲɪ:'nʌɪs.] |
| I've got a problem. | **Turiù problèmą.**<br>[tʊ'rʲʊ prob'lʲɛma:.] |
| My ... is broken. | **Sulū̃žo màno ... .**<br>[sʊ'lʲu:ʒɔ 'manɔ ...] |
| My ... is out of order. | **Neveìkia màno ... .**<br>[nʲɛ'vʲɛɪkʲɛ 'manɔ ...] |
| TV | **televìzorius**<br>[tʲɛlʲɛ'vʲɪzorʲʊs] |
| air conditioner | **óro kondicioniẽrius**<br>['ɔrɔ kondʲɪtsʲɪjo'nʲɛrʲʊs] |
| tap | **čiáupas**<br>['tʂʲæʊpas] |
| shower | **dùšas**<br>['dʊʃas] |
| sink | **praustùvė**<br>[prɑʊs'tʊvʲe:] |
| safe | **seìfas**<br>['sʲɛɪfas] |

| | |
|---|---|
| door lock | **durų spyna**<br>[dʊˈru: spl'i:ˈna] |
| electrical outlet | **elektros lizdas**<br>[ɛˈlʲɛktros ˈlʲɪzdas] |
| hairdryer | **plaukų džiovintuvas**<br>[plʲɑʊˈku: dʒʲovʲɪnˈtʊvas] |

| | |
|---|---|
| I don't have ... | **Aš neturiu ...**<br>[ˈaʃ nʲɛtʊˈrʲʊ ...] |
| water | **vandens**<br>[vanˈdʲɛns] |
| light | **šviesos**<br>[ʃvʲɪɛˈso:s] |
| electricity | **elektros**<br>[ɛˈlʲɛktros] |

| | |
|---|---|
| Can you give me ...? | **Ar galite duoti ...?**<br>[ar ˈga:lʲɪtʲɛ ˈdʊotʲɪ ...?] |
| a towel | **rankšluostį**<br>[ˈraŋkʃlʲʊɑstiː] |
| a blanket | **antklodę**<br>[ˈantklʲodʲɛ:] |
| slippers | **šlepetes**<br>[ʃlʲɛpɛˈtʲɛs] |
| a robe | **chalatą**<br>[xaˈlʲa:ta:] |
| shampoo | **šampūno**<br>[ʃamˈpu:no] |
| soap | **muilo**<br>[ˈmʊɪlʲo] |

| | |
|---|---|
| I'd like to change rooms. | **Norėčiau pakeisti kambarį.**<br>[noˈrʲe:tʂʲɛʊ paˈkʲɛɪstʲɪ ˈkambarʲɪ:.] |
| I can't find my key. | **Nerandu savo rakto.**<br>[nʲɛranˈdʊ ˈsavo ˈra:kto.] |
| Could you open my room, please? | **Ar galite atrakinti mano kambarį?**<br>[ar ˈga:lʲɪtʲɛ atrakʲɪːntʲɪ ˈmano ˈkambarʲɪ:?] |
| Who's there? | **Kas ten?**<br>[ˈkas tʲɛn?] |
| Come in! | **Užeikite!**<br>[ʊˈʒʲɛɪkʲɪtʲɛ!] |
| Just a minute! | **Palaukite minutę!**<br>[paˈlʲɑʊkʲɪtʲɛ mʲɪˈnʊtʲɛ:!] |
| Not right now, please. | **Nė dabar, prašau.**<br>[ˈnʲɛ daˈbar, praˈʃɑʊ.] |

| | |
|---|---|
| Come to my room, please. | **Prašau, užeikite į mano kambarį.**<br>[praˈʃɑʊ, ʊˈʒʲɛɪkʲɪtʲɛ iː ˈmano ˈkambarʲɪ:.] |
| I'd like to order food service. | **Norėčiau užsisakyti maisto.**<br>[noˈrʲe:tʂʲɛʊ ʊʒsʲɪsaˈkʲi:tʲɪ ˈmʌɪsto.] |
| My room number is ... | **Mano kambario numeris ...**<br>[ˈma:no ˈkambarʲo ˈnʊmʲɛrʲɪs ...] |

I'm leaving ... **Àš išvykstù ...**
['aʃ iʃvʲiːksˈtʊ ...]

We're leaving ... **Mēs išvȳkstame ...**
['mʲæs iʃˈvʲiːkstamʲɛ ...]

right now **dabar̃**
[daˈbar]

this afternoon **põ pietų̃**
['poː pʲiɛˈtuː]

tonight **šiãnakt**
['ʃæːnakt]

tomorrow **rytój**
[rʲiːˈtoj]

tomorrow morning **rýt rytè**
['rʲiːt rʲiːˈtʲɛ]

tomorrow evening **rýt vakarè**
['rʲiːt vakaˈrʲɛ]

the day after tomorrow **porýt**
[poˈrʲiːt]

---

I'd like to pay. **Norė́čiau sumokė́ti.**
[noˈrʲeːtʃʲɛʊ sʊmoˈkʲeːtʲɪ.]

Everything was wonderful. **Vìskas bùvo nuostabù.**
['vʲɪskas 'bʊvɔ nʊɑstaˈbʊ.]

Where can I get a taxi? **Kur̃ galiù išsikviẽsti taksì?**
['kʊr ɡaˈlʲʊ ɪʃsʲɪkˈvʲɛstʲɪ takˈsʲɪ?]

Would you call a taxi for me, please? **Ar̃ galė́tumėte mán iškviẽsti taksì?**
[ar ɡaˈlʲeːtʊmʲeːte 'man iʃkˈvʲɛstʲɪ takˈsʲɪ?]

## Restaurant

Can I look at the menu, please?

**Ar galiù gáuti meniù?**
[ar ga'lʲʊ 'ɡɑutʲɪ mʲɛ'nʲʊ?]

Table for one.

**Stãlą vienám.**
['sta:lʲa: vʲiɛ'nam.]

There are two (three, four) of us.

**Mū́sų dù (trỹs, keturì).**
['mu:su: 'dʊ ('tryi:s, ketʊ'rʲɪ ).]

Smoking

**Rū́kantiems**
['ru:kantʲiɛms]

No smoking

**Nerū́kantiems**
[nʲɛ'ru:kantʲiɛms]

Excuse me! (addressing a waiter)

**Atsiprašaū!**
[atsʲɪpra'ʃɑu!]

menu

**meniù**
[mʲɛ'nʲʊ]

wine list

**vỹno meniù**
['vʲi:nɔ mʲɛ'nʲʊ]

The menu, please.

**Meniù, prašaū.**
[mʲɛ'nʲʊ, pra'ʃɑu.]

Are you ready to order?

**Ar jaũ norésite užsisakýti?**
[ar jɛʊ no'rʲe:sʲɪte ʊʒsʲɪsa'kʲi:tʲɪ?]

What will you have?

**Ką̃ užsisakýsite?**
[ka: ʊʒsʲɪsa'kʲi:sʲɪtʲɛ?]

I'll have ...

**Àš paimsiu ...**
['aʃ 'pʌɪmsʲʊ ...]

I'm a vegetarian.

**Àš vegetãras /vegetãrė/.**
['aʃ vege'ta:ras /vege'ta:rʲe:/.]

meat

**mė̃sos**
[mʲe:'so:s]

fish

**žuviẽs**
[ʒʊ'vʲɛs]

vegetables

**daržóvės**
[dar'ʒovʲe:s]

Do you have vegetarian dishes?

**Ar tùrite vegetãriškų patiekalų̃?**
[ar 'tʊrʲɪtʲɛ vʲɛgʲɛ'ta:rɪʃku: patʲiɛka'lʲu:?]

I don't eat pork.

**Àš neválgau kiaulíenos.**
['aʃ nʲɛ'valʲɡɑu kʲɛʊ'lʲiɛnos.]

He /she/ doesn't eat meat.

**Jìs /jì/ neválgo mė̃sos.**
[jɪs /jɪ/ ne'valʲɡɔ mʲe:'so:s.]

I am allergic to ...

**Àš alèrgiškas /alèrgiška/ ...**
['aʃ a'lʲɛrɡʲɪʃkas /a'lʲɛrɡʲɪʃka/ ...]

| | |
|---|---|
| Would you please bring me ... | **Prašau atnèšti mán ...**<br>[praˈʃɑʊ atˈnʲɛʃtʲɪ ˈman ...] |
| salt | pepper | sugar | **drùskos | pipìrų | cùkraus**<br>[ˈdrʊskos | pʲɪˈpʲɪruː | ˈtsʊkrɑʊs] |
| coffee | tea | dessert | **kavõs | arbãtos | desèrtą**<br>[kaˈvoːs | arˈbaːtos | dʲɛˈsʲɛrta] |
| water | sparkling | plain | **vandeñs | gazúoto | negazúoto**<br>[vanˈdʲɛns | gaˈzʊoto | nʲɛgaˈzʊoto] |
| a spoon | fork | knife | **šáukštą | šakùtę | peĩlį**<br>[ˈʃɑʊkʃtaː | ʃaˈkʊtʲɛː | ˈpʲɛɪlʲɪː] |
| a plate | napkin | **lẽkštę | servetẽlę**<br>[lʲeːkʃtʲɛː | serveˈtʲeːlʲɛː] |

| | |
|---|---|
| Enjoy your meal! | **Skanaũs!**<br>[skaˈnɑʊs!] |
| One more, please. | **Prašau dár víeną.**<br>[praˈʃɑʊ ˈdar ˈvʲiɛnaː] |
| It was very delicious. | **Bùvo lãbai skanù.**<br>[ˈbʊvo ˈlʲaːbaɪ skaˈnʊ] |

| | |
|---|---|
| check | change | tip | **sąskaita | grąžà | arbãtpinigiai**<br>[ˈsaːskʌɪta | graːˈʒa | arˈbaːtpʲɪnʲɪgʲɛɪ] |
| Check, please.<br>(Could I have the check, please?) | **Sąskaitą, prašau.**<br>[ˈsaːskʌɪtaː, praˈʃɑʊ] |
| Can I pay by credit card? | **Ař galiù mokéti kredìto kortelè?**<br>[ar gaˈlʲʊ moˈkʲeːtʲɪ kreˈdʲɪtɔ korteˈlʲɛ?] |
| I'm sorry, there's a mistake here. | **Atsiprašaũ, bèt jũs suklýdote.**<br>[atsʲɪpraˈʃɑʊ, bʲɛt ˈjuːs sʊkˈlʲiːdotʲɛ] |

# Shopping

Can I help you?
**Kuõ galiù padéti?**
['kʊɑ ga'lʲʊ pa'dʲe:tʲɪ?]

Do you have ...?
**Ar̃ tùrite ...?**
[ar 'tʊrʲɪtʲɛ ...?]

I'm looking for ...
**Ieškau ...**
['ɪɛʃkɑʊ ...]

I need ...
**Mán reĩkia ...**
['man 'rʲɛɪkʲɛ ...]

---

I'm just looking.
**Àš tìk apžiūrinéju.**
['aʃ tʲɪk apʒʲu:rʲɪ'nʲe:jʊ.]

We're just looking.
**Mẽs tìk apžiūrinéjame.**
['mʲæs 'tʲɪk apʒʲu:rʲɪ'nʲe:jame.]

I'll come back later.
**Sugrį̃šiu vėliaũ.**
[sʊg'rʲɪ:ʃʊ vʲe:'lʲɛʊ.]

We'll come back later.
**Sugrį̃šime vėliaũ.**
[sʊg'rʲɪ:ʃʲɪme vʲe:'lʲɛʊ.]

discounts | sale
**núolaidos | išpardavìmas**
['nʊolʲʌɪdos | iʃparda'vʲɪmas]

---

Would you please show me ...
**Paródykite mán, prašaũ, ...**
[pa'rodʲɪkʲɪtʲɛ 'man, pra'ʃɑʊ, ...]

Would you please give me ...
**Dúokite mán, prašaũ, ...**
['dʊokʲɪtʲɛ 'man, pra'ʃɑʊ, ...]

Can I try it on?
**Ar̃ galiù pasimatúoti?**
[ar ga'lʲʊ pasʲɪma'tʊotʲɪ?]

Excuse me, where's the fitting room?
**Atsiprašaũ, kur̃ yrà matãvimosi kabìnos?**
[atsʲɪpra'ʃɑʊ, kʊr i:'ra ma'ta:vʲɪmosʲɪ ka'bʲɪnos?]

Which color would you like?
**Kokiõs spalvõs norétumėte?**
[ko'kʲo:s spalʲ'vo:s no'rʲe:tumʲe:te?]

size | length
**dỹdis | ĩlgis**
['dʲi:dʲɪs | 'ilʲgʲɪs]

How does it fit?
**Ar̃ tiñka?**
[ar 'tʲɪŋka?]

---

How much is it?
**Kíek taĩ kainúoja?**
['kʲiɛk 'tʌɪ kʌɪ'nʊo:jɛ?]

That's too expensive.
**Per̃ brangù.**
['pʲɛr bran'gʊ.]

I'll take it.
**Paim̃siu.**
['pʌɪmsʲʊ.]

Excuse me, where do I pay?

**Atsiprašaū, kuř galiù sumokéti?**
[atsɪpraˈʃɑʊ, kʊr gaˈlʲʊ sʊmoˈkʲeːtʲɪ?]

Will you pay in cash or credit card?

**Mokésite grynaĩs ař kredìto kortelè?**
[moˈkʲeːsʲɪte grʲiːˈnʌɪs ar krʲɛˈdʲɪtɔ korteˈlʲɛ?]

In cash | with credit card

**grynaĩs | kredìto kortelè**
[grʲiːˈnʌɪs | krʲɛˈdʲɪtɔ kortʲɛˈlʲɛ]

---

Do you want the receipt?

**Ař reĩkia čèkio?**
[ar ˈrʲɛɪkʲɛ ˈtʃʲɛkʲo?]

Yes, please.

**Taĩp.**
[ˈtʌɪp.]

No, it's OK.

**Nè, nereĩkia.**
[ˈnʲɛ, nʲɛˈrʲɛɪkʲæ.]

Thank you. Have a nice day!

**Āčiū. Vìso gèro.**
[ˈaːtʃʲuː. ˈvʲɪsɔ ˈgʲærɔ.]

# In town

| | |
|---|---|
| Excuse me, please. | **Atsiprašau, ...**<br>[atsʲɪpraˈʃɑu.] |
| I'm looking for ... | **Íeškau ...**<br>[ˈɪɛʃkɑu ...] |

| | |
|---|---|
| the subway | **metrò**<br>[mʲɛˈtro] |
| my hotel | **sàvo viẽšbučio**<br>[ˈsavɔ ˈvʲɛʃbutsʲɔ] |
| the movie theater | **kìno teãtro**<br>[ˈkʲɪnɔ tʲɛˈaːtrɔ] |
| a taxi stand | **taksì stotẽlę**<br>[takˈsʲɪ stoˈtʲælʲɛː] |

| | |
|---|---|
| an ATM | **bankomãto**<br>[baŋkoˈmaːtɔ] |
| a foreign exchange office | **valiùtos keitỹklos**<br>[vaˈlʲʊtos kʲɛɪˈtʲiːklos] |
| an internet café | **internèto kavìnės**<br>[ɪntɛrˈnʲɛtɔ kavʲɪˈnʲeːs] |
| ... street | **... gãtvės**<br>[... gaːtˈvʲeːs] |
| this place | **šiõs viẽtos**<br>[ˈʃoːs ˈvʲɛtos] |

| | |
|---|---|
| Do you know where ... is? | **Aȓ žìnote, kuȓ yrà ...?**<br>[ar ˈʒʲɪnotʲɛ, kʊr iːˈra ...?] |
| Which street is this? | **Kokià čià gãtvė?**<br>[koˈkʲæ tʂʲæ ˈgaːtvʲeː?] |

| | |
|---|---|
| Show me where we are right now. | **Parõdykite, kuȓ dabaȓ ẽsame.**<br>[paˈrodʲiːkʲɪtʲɛ, kʊr daˈbar ˈɛsamʲɛ.] |
| Can I get there on foot? | **Aȓ galiù nueĩti teñ pėsčiomìs?**<br>[ar gaˈlʲʊ ˈnʊʲɛɪtʲɪ tɛn pʲeːstʂʲoˈmʲɪs?] |
| Do you have a map of the city? | **Aȓ tùrite miẽsto žemélapį?**<br>[ar ˈtʊrʲɪte ˈmʲɪːɛstɔ ʒeˈmʲeːlʲapʲɪ:?] |

| | |
|---|---|
| How much is a ticket to get in? | **Kíek kainúoja įėjìmo bìlietas?**<br>[ˈkʲiɛk kʌɪˈnʊɑːjɛ iːɛˈjɪmɔ ˈbʲɪlʲiɛtas?] |
| Can I take pictures here? | **Aȓ čià galimà fotografúoti?**<br>[ar ˈtʂʲæ galʲɪˈma fotograˈfʊotʲɪ?] |
| Are you open? | **Aȓ jũs veĩkiate?**<br>[ar ˈjuːs ˈvʲɛɪkʲætʲɛ?] |

When do you open?

**Kadà atsidãrote?**
[ka'da atsʲɪ'da:rotʲɛ?]

When do you close?

**Kadà užsidãrote?**
[ka'da ʊʒsʲɪ'da:rotʲɛ?]

# Money

| | |
|---|---|
| money | **pinigai**<br>[pʲɪnʲɪˈgʌɪ] |
| cash | **grynieji**<br>[grʲiːˈnʲiɛjɪ] |
| paper money | **banknotai**<br>[baŋkˈnotʌɪ] |
| loose change | **monetos**<br>[moˈnʲɛtos] |
| check \| change \| tip | **sąskaita \| grąžà \| arbãtpinigiai**<br>[ˈsaːskʌɪta \| graːˈʒa \| arˈbaːtpʲɪnʲɪgʲɛɪ] |

| | |
|---|---|
| credit card | **kredito kortelė**<br>[krʲɛˈdʲɪto korˈtʲælʲeː] |
| wallet | **piniginė**<br>[pʲɪnʲɪˈgʲɪnʲeː] |
| to buy | **pirkti**<br>[ˈpʲɪrktʲɪ] |
| to pay | **moketi**<br>[moˈkʲeːtʲɪ] |
| fine | **bauda**<br>[bɑʊˈda] |
| free | **nemokamai**<br>[nʲɛˈmokamʌɪ] |

| | |
|---|---|
| Where can I buy ...? | **Kur galiu nusipirkti ...?**<br>[ˈkʊr gaˈlʲʊ nusʲɪˈpʲɪrktʲɪ ...?] |
| Is the bank open now? | **Ar bankas jau dirba?**<br>[ar ˈbaŋkas ˈjɛʊ ˈdʲɪrba?] |
| When does it open? | **Kada atsidaro?**<br>[kaˈda atsʲɪˈdaːro?] |
| When does it close? | **Kada užsidaro?**<br>[kaˈda ʊʒsʲɪˈdaːro?] |

| | |
|---|---|
| How much? | **Kiek?**<br>[ˈkʲiɛk?] |
| How much is this? | **Kiek tai kainuoja?**<br>[ˈkʲiɛk ˈtʌɪ kʌɪˈnʊoːjɛ?] |
| That's too expensive. | **Per brangu.**<br>[ˈpʲɛr branˈgʊ.] |

| | |
|---|---|
| Excuse me, where do I pay? | **Atsiprašau, kur galiu sumoketi?**<br>[atsʲɪpraˈʃɑʊ, kʊr gaˈlʲʊ sumoˈkʲeːtʲɪ?] |
| Check, please. | **Čekį, prašau.**<br>[ˈtʃʲɛkʲɪː, praˈʃɑʊ.] |

| | |
|---|---|
| Can I pay by credit card? | **Ar galiu mokėti kredito kortele?**<br>[ar ga'lʲʊ mo'kʲe:tʲɪ kre'dʲɪtɔ korte'lʲɛ?] |
| Is there an ATM here? | **Ar čia yra bankomatas?**<br>[ar 'tʂʲæ i:'ra baŋko'ma:tas?] |
| I'm looking for an ATM. | **Ieškau bankomato.**<br>['ɪɛʃkɑʊ baŋko'ma:tɔ.] |
| I'm looking for a foreign exchange office. | **Ieškau valiutos keityklos.**<br>['ɪɛʃkɑʊ va'lʲʊtos kʲɛr'tʲi:klos.] |
| I'd like to change … | **Noriu pasikeisti …**<br>['norʲʊ pasʲɪ'kʲɛɪstʲɪ …] |
| What is the exchange rate? | **Koks valiutos kursas?**<br>['koks va'lʲʊtos 'kʊrsas?] |
| Do you need my passport? | **Ar reikia mano pasō?**<br>[ar 'rʲɛɪkʲɛ 'manɔ 'pa:sɔ?] |

# Time

| | |
|---|---|
| What time is it? | **Kíek dabar valandų?**<br>['kʲiɛk da'bar valʲan'du:?] |
| When? | **Kada?**<br>[ka'da?] |
| At what time? | **Kada?**<br>[ka'da?] |
| now \| later \| after … | **dabar \| véliaũ \| põ …**<br>[da'bar \| vʲe:'lʲɛʊ \| 'po: …] |
| one o'clock | **pìrmą vãlandą**<br>['pʲɪrma: 'va:lʲanda:] |
| one fifteen | **põ pirmõs penkiólika**<br>['po: pʲɪr'mo:s pʲɛŋ'kʲolʲɪka] |
| one thirty | **pùsė dviejų**<br>['pʊsʲe: dvʲiɛ'ju:] |
| one forty-five | **bè penkiólikos dvì**<br>['bʲɛ pʲɛŋ'kʲolʲɪkos dvʲɪ] |
| one \| two \| three | **pirmà \| antrà \| trečià**<br>[pʲɪr'ma \| an'tra \| trʲɛ'tʃʲæ] |
| four \| five \| six | **ketvirtà \| penktà \| šeštà**<br>[kʲɛtvʲɪr'ta \| pʲɛŋk'ta \| ʃɛʃ'ta] |
| seven \| eight \| nine | **septintà \| aštuntà \| devintà**<br>[sʲɛptʲɪn'ta \| aʃtʊn'ta \| dʲɛvʲɪn'ta] |
| ten \| eleven \| twelve | **dešimtà \| vienúolikta \| dvýlikta**<br>[dʲɛʃɪm'ta \| vʲiɛ'nʊolʲɪkta \| 'dvʲi:lʲɪkta] |
| in … | **ùž …**<br>['ʊʒ …] |
| five minutes | **penkių minùčių**<br>[pʲɛŋ'kʲu: mʲɪ'nʊtʂʲu:] |
| ten minutes | **dešimt minùčių**<br>['dʲæʃɪmt mʲɪ'nʊtʂʲu:] |
| fifteen minutes | **penkiólikos minùčių**<br>[pʲɛŋ'kʲolʲɪkos mʲɪ'nʊtʂʲu:] |
| twenty minutes | **dvìdešimt minùčių**<br>['dvʲɪdʲɛʃɪmt mʲɪ'nʊtʂʲu:] |
| half an hour | **pùsvalandžio**<br>['pʊsvalʲandʒʲɔ] |
| an hour | **valandõs**<br>[valʲan'do:s] |

| | |
|---|---|
| in the morning | **rytè**<br>[rʲiː'tʲɛ] |
| early in the morning | **ankstì rytè**<br>[aŋk'stʲɪ rʲiː'tʲɛ] |
| this morning | **šį̃ryt**<br>['ʃɪːrʲɪːt] |
| tomorrow morning | **rýt rytè**<br>['rʲiːt rʲiː'tʲɛ] |

| | |
|---|---|
| in the middle of the day | **per̃ pietùs**<br>['pʲɛr pʲiɛ'tʊs] |
| in the afternoon | **põ pietų̃**<br>['poː pʲiɛ'tuː] |
| in the evening | **vakarè**<br>[vaka'rʲɛ] |
| tonight | **šią̃nakt**<br>['ʃæːnakt] |

| | |
|---|---|
| at night | **nãktį**<br>['naːktiː] |
| yesterday | **vãkar**<br>['vaːkar] |
| today | **šiañdien**<br>['ʃændʲiɛn] |
| tomorrow | **rytój**<br>[rʲiː'toj] |
| the day after tomorrow | **porýt**<br>[po'rʲiːt] |

| | |
|---|---|
| What day is it today? | **Kokià šiañdien dienà?**<br>[kɔ'kʲæ 'ʃændʲiɛn dʲiɛ'na?] |
| It's ... | **Šiañdien yrà ...**<br>['ʃændʲiɛn iː'ra ...] |
| Monday | **pirmãdienis**<br>[pʲɪr'maːdʲiɛnʲɪs] |
| Tuesday | **antrãdienis**<br>[an'traːdʲiɛnʲɪs] |
| Wednesday | **trečiãdienis**<br>[trʲɛ'tʂʲædʲiɛnʲɪs] |

| | |
|---|---|
| Thursday | **ketvirtãdienis**<br>[kʲɛtvʲɪr'taːdʲiɛnʲɪs] |
| Friday | **penktãdienis**<br>[pʲɛŋk'taːdʲiɛnʲɪs] |
| Saturday | **šeštãdienis**<br>[ʃʲɛʃ'taːdʲiɛnʲɪs] |
| Sunday | **sekmãdienis**<br>[sʲɛk'maːdʲiɛnʲɪs] |

# Greetings. Introductions

| | |
|---|---|
| Hello. | **Sveikì.** <br> [svʲɛɪˈkʲɪ.] |
| Pleased to meet you. | **Malonù susipažìnti.** <br> [malʲoˈnʊ sʊsʲɪpaˈʒʲɪntʲɪ.] |
| Me too. | **Mán ìrgi.** <br> [ˈman ˈɪrgʲɪ.] |
| I'd like you to meet … | **Nóriu, kàd susipažìntum sù …** <br> [ˈnorʲʊ, ˈkad sʊsʲɪpaˈʒʲɪntum ˈsʊ …] |
| Nice to meet you. | **Malonù susipažìnti.** <br> [malʲoˈnʊ sʊsʲɪpaˈʒʲɪntʲɪ.] |

| | |
|---|---|
| How are you? | **Kaȋp laȋkotės?** <br> [ˈkʌɪp ˈlʲʌɪkotʲeːs?] |
| My name is … | **Māno var̄das …** <br> [ˈmaːnɔ vardas …] |
| His name is … | **Jō var̄das …** <br> [jɔː ˈvardas …] |
| Her name is … | **Jì vardù …** <br> [ˈjɪ varˈdʊ …] |
| What's your name? | **Kuō jũs vardù?** <br> [ˈkʊɑ ˈjuːs varˈdʊ?] |
| What's his name? | **Kuō jìs vardù?** <br> [ˈkʊɑ jɪs varˈdʊ?] |
| What's her name? | **Kuō jì vardù?** <br> [ˈkʊɑ jɪ varˈdʊ?] |

| | |
|---|---|
| What's your last name? | **Kokià jū́sų pavardė̃?** <br> [kɔˈkʲæ ˈjuːsuː pavarˈdʲeː?] |
| You can call me … | **Gāli manè vadìnti …** <br> [ˈgaːlʲɪ maˈnʲɛ vaˈdʲɪntʲɪ …] |
| Where are you from? | **Ȋš kur̄ jũs ēsate?** <br> [ɪʃ ˈkʊr ˈjuːs ˈɛsatʲɛ?] |
| I'm from … | **Àš ìš …** <br> [ˈaʃ ɪʃ …] |
| What do you do for a living? | **Kuō užsiȋmate?** <br> [ˈkʊɑ ʊʒˈsʲɪimatʲɛ?] |

| | |
|---|---|
| Who is this? | **Kàs tàs žmogùs?** <br> [ˈkas ˈtas ʒmoˈgʊs?] |
| Who is he? | **Kàs jìs?** <br> [ˈkas ˈjɪs?] |
| Who is she? | **Kàs jì?** <br> [ˈkas jɪ?] |

| | |
|---|---|
| Who are they? | **Kàs jiē?**<br>['kas jɪɛ?] |
| This is ... | **Taì ...**<br>['tʌɪ ...] |
| my friend (masc.) | **mãno draūgas**<br>['maːnɔ 'drɑʊgas] |
| my friend (fem.) | **mãno draugě**<br>['maːnɔ drɑʊ'gʲeː] |
| my husband | **mãno výras**<br>['maːnɔ ˈvʲiːras] |
| my wife | **mãno žmonà**<br>['maːnɔ ʒmo'na] |
| my father | **màno tévas**<br>['manɔ 'tʲeːvas] |
| my mother | **mãno mamà**<br>['maːnɔ ma'ma] |
| my brother | **mãno brólis**<br>['maːnɔ 'brolʲɪs] |
| my sister | **mãno sesuō**<br>['maːnɔ sʲɛ'sʊɑ] |
| my son | **mãno sūnùs**<br>['maːnɔ suː'nʊs] |
| my daughter | **mãno dukrà**<br>['maːnɔ dʊk'ra] |
| This is our son. | **Taì mū́sų sūnùs.**<br>['tʌɪ 'muːsuː suː'nʊs.] |
| This is our daughter. | **Taì mū́sų dukrà.**<br>['tʌɪ 'muːsuː dʊk'ra.] |
| These are my children. | **Taì mãno vaikaì.**<br>['tʌɪ 'maːnɔ vʌɪ'kʌɪ.] |
| These are our children. | **Taì mū́sų vaikaì.**<br>['tʌɪ 'muːsuː vʌɪ'kʌɪ.] |

# Farewells

| | |
|---|---|
| Good bye! | **Vìso gẽro!**<br>['vɪsɔ 'gʲæːrɔ!] |
| Bye! (inform.) | **Ikì!**<br>[ɪ'kʲɪ!] |
| See you tomorrow. | **Pasimatýsim rýt.**<br>[pasʲimaˈtʲiːsʲɪm 'rʲiːt.] |
| See you soon. | **Greìtai pasimatýsime.**<br>['grʲɛɪtʌɪ pasʲimaˈtʲiːsʲɪmʲɛ.] |
| See you at seven. | **Pasimatýsime septiñtą.**<br>[pasʲimaˈtʲiːsʲɪmʲɛ sʲɛpˈtʲɪntaː.] |
| Have fun! | **Pasilìnksminkite!**<br>[pasʲɪˈlʲɪŋksmʲɪŋkʲɪtʲɛ!] |
| Talk to you later. | **Pašnekẽsim vẽliaũ.**<br>[paʃnʲɛˈkʲeːsʲɪm vʲeːˈlʲɛʊ.] |
| Have a nice weekend. | **Gẽro savaĩtgalio.**<br>['gʲæːrɔ saˈvʌɪtgalʲɔ.] |
| Good night. | **Labãnakt.**<br>[lʲaˈbaːnakt.] |
| It's time for me to go. | **Màn jaũ laĩkas eĩti.**<br>['man 'jɛʊ 'lʲʌɪkas 'ɛɪtʲɪ.] |
| I have to go. | **Màn reĩkia eĩti.**<br>['man 'rʲɛɪkʲɛ 'ɛɪtʲɪ.] |
| I will be right back. | **Tuõj grĩšiu.**<br>['tʊɔj 'grʲɪːʃʊ.] |
| It's late. | **Jaũ vẽlù.**<br>['jɛʊ vʲeːˈlʲʊ.] |
| I have to get up early. | **Màn reĩkia ankstì kéltis.**<br>['man 'rʲɛɪkʲɛ aŋkˈstʲɪ 'kʲɛlʲtʲɪs.] |
| I'm leaving tomorrow. | **Àš išvỹkstù rýt.**<br>['aʃ iʃvʲiːksˈtʊ 'rʲiːt.] |
| We're leaving tomorrow. | **Mẽs išvỹkstame rýt.**<br>['mʲæs iʃvʲiːkstamʲɛ 'rʲiːt.] |
| Have a nice trip! | **Gẽros keliõnės!**<br>[gʲæːros kʲɛˈlʲoːnʲeːs!] |
| It was nice meeting you. | **Bùvo malonù susipažìnti.**<br>['bʊvɔ malʲoˈnʊ susʲɪpaˈʒʲɪntʲɪ.] |
| It was nice talking to you. | **Bùvo malonù pasišnekéti.**<br>['bʊvɔ malʲoˈnʊ pasʲɪʃnʲɛˈkʲeːtʲɪ.] |
| Thanks for everything. | **Ãčiū ùž vìską.**<br>['aːtʃʲuː 'ʊʒ 'vʲɪskaː.] |

I had a very good time.

**Puikiai praleidau laiką.**
[puɪkʲɛɪ praˈlʲɛɪdɑu ˈlʌɪkaː.]

We had a very good time.

**Mes puikiai praleidome laiką.**
[ˈmʲæs ˈpuɪkʲɛɪ praˈlʲɛɪdomʲɛ ˈlʌɪkaː.]

It was really great.

**Buvo tikrai smagu.**
[ˈbuvɔ tʲɪkˈrʌɪ smaˈɡu.]

I'm going to miss you.

**Pasiilgsiu tavęs.**
[pasʲɪˈɪlʲɡsʲu taˈvʲɛːs.]

We're going to miss you.

**Pasiilgsime jūsų.**
[pasʲɪˈɪlʲɡsʲɪmʲɛ ˈjuːsuː.]

---

Good luck!

**Sėkmės!**
[sʲeːkˈmʲeːs!]

Say hi to …

**Perduokite linkėjimus …**
[ˈpʲɛrduɑkʲɪtʲɛ lʲɪŋˈkʲɛjɪmus …]

# Foreign language

I don't understand.
**Nesuprantù.**
[nʲɛsʊpranˈtʊ.]

Write it down, please.
**Užrašýkite, prašaũ.**
[ʊʒraˈʃiːkʲɪtʲɛ, praˈʃɑʊ.]

Do you speak ...?
**Aȓ kaĺbate ...?**
[ar ˈkalʲbatʲɛ ...?]

I speak a little bit of ...
**Trupùtį kalbù ...**
[trʊˈpʊtʲ kalʲˈbʊ ...]

English
**ángliškai**
[ˈanglʲɪʃkʌɪ]

Turkish
**tur̃kiškai**
[ˈtʊrkʲɪʃkʌɪ]

Arabic
**arãbiškai**
[aˈraːbʲɪʃkʌɪ]

French
**prancũziškai**
[pranˈtsuːzʲɪʃkʌɪ]

German
**vókiškai**
[ˈvokʲɪʃkʌɪ]

Italian
**itãliškai**
[ɪˈtaːlʲɪʃkʌɪ]

Spanish
**ispãniškai**
[ɪsˈpaːnʲɪʃkʌɪ]

Portuguese
**portugãliškai**
[portʊˈgaːlʲɪʃkʌɪ]

Chinese
**kìniškai**
[ˈkʲɪnʲɪʃkʌɪ]

Japanese
**japòniškai**
[jaˈponʲɪʃkʌɪ]

Can you repeat that, please.
**Aȓ gãlite pakartóti?**
[ar ˈgaːlʲɪtʲɛ pakarˈtotʲɪ?]

I understand.
**Suprantù.**
[sʊpranˈtʊ.]

I don't understand.
**Nesuprantù.**
[nʲɛsʊpranˈtʊ.]

Please speak more slowly.
**Aȓ gãlite kalbéti lėčiaũ?**
[ar ˈgaːlʲɪte kalʲˈbʲeːtʲɪ lʲeːˈtʂʲɛʊ?]

Is that correct? (Am I saying it right?)
**Aȓ teisìngai?**
[ar tʲɛɪsʲɪngʌɪ?]

What is this? (What does this mean?)
**Ką̃ taĩ réiškia?**
[kaː ˈtʌɪ ˈrʲɛɪʃkʲæ?]

## Apologies

| | |
|---|---|
| Excuse me, please. | **Atleiskite.**<br>[atˈlʲɛɪskʲɪtʲɛ.] |
| I'm sorry. | **Atsiprašau.**<br>[atsʲɪpraˈʃɑʊ.] |
| I'm really sorry. | **Man labai gaila.**<br>[ˈman lʲaˈbʌɪ ˈgʌɪlʲa.] |
| Sorry, it's my fault. | **Atsiprašau, tai aš kaltas /kalta/.**<br>[atsʲɪpraˈʃɑʊ, ˈtʌɪ aʃ ˈkalʲtas /kalˈta/.] |
| My mistake. | **Tai mano klaida.**<br>[ˈtʌɪ ˈmaːnɔ klʲʌɪˈda.] |

| | |
|---|---|
| May I ...? | **Ar galiu ...?**<br>[ar gaˈlʲʊ ...?] |
| Do you mind if I ...? | **Ar jūs nieko prieš, jei ...?**<br>[ar ˈjuːs ˈnʲɛkɔ ˈprʲɛʃ, jɛɪ ...?] |
| It's OK. | **Nieko tokio.**<br>[ˈnʲɛkɔ ˈtokʲɔ.] |
| It's all right. | **Viskas gerai.**<br>[ˈvʲɪskas gʲɛˈrʌɪ.] |
| Don't worry about it. | **Nesijaudinkite dėl to.**<br>[nʲɛsʲɪˈjɑʊdʲɪŋkʲɪte ˈdʲeːlʲ ˈtoː.] |

## Agreement

| | |
|---|---|
| Yes. | **Taìp.**<br>['tʌɪp.] |
| Yes, sure. | **Žìnoma.**<br>['ʒʲɪnoma.] |
| OK (Good!) | **Geraì.**<br>[gʲɛ'rʌɪ.] |
| Very well. | **Puikù.**<br>[puɪ'ku.] |
| Certainly! | **Būtinaĩ!**<br>[buːtʲɪ'nʌɪ!] |
| I agree. | **Sutinkù.**<br>[sutʲɪŋ'ku.] |

| | |
|---|---|
| That's correct. | **Tikraĩ.**<br>[tʲɪk'rʌɪ.] |
| That's right. | **Teisìngai.**<br>[tʲɛɪ'sʲɪŋgʌɪ.] |
| You're right. | **Jũs teisùs /teisì/.**<br>['juːs tʲɛɪ'sus /tʲɛɪ'sʲɪ/.] |
| I don't mind. | **Mán tiñka.**<br>['man 'tʲɪŋka.] |
| Absolutely right. | **Tikraĩ taìp.**<br>[tʲɪk'rʌɪ 'tʌɪp.] |

| | |
|---|---|
| It's possible. | **Įmãnoma.**<br>[iː'maːnoma.] |
| That's a good idea. | **Gerà mintìs.**<br>[gʲɛ'ra mʲɪn'tʲɪs.] |
| I can't say no. | **Negaliù atsisakýti.**<br>[nʲɛga'lʲu atsʲɪsa'kʲiːtʲɪ.] |
| I'd be happy to. | **Mielaĩ.**<br>[mʲɪɛ'lʲʌɪ.] |
| With pleasure. | **Sù mielu nóru.**<br>['su 'mʲɪɛlʲu 'noru.] |

## Refusal. Expressing doubt

| No. | Nè. |
| --- | --- |
| | ['nʲɛ.] |
| Certainly not. | Tikraì nè. |
| | [tʲɪk'rʌɪ nʲɛ.] |
| I don't agree. | Àš nesutinkù. |
| | ['aʃ nʲɛsʊtʲɪŋ'kʊ.] |
| I don't think so. | Nemanaũ. |
| | [nʲɛma'nɑʊ.] |
| It's not true. | Taì netiesà. |
| | ['tʌɪ nʲɛtʲiɛ'sa.] |

| You are wrong. | Jū̃s klýstate. |
| --- | --- |
| | ['ju:s 'kʲlʲi:statʲɛ.] |
| I think you are wrong. | Manaũ, jū̃s klýstate. |
| | [ma'nɑʊ, 'ju:s 'kʲlʲi:statʲɛ.] |
| I'm not sure. | Nesù tìkras /tikrà/. |
| | [nʲɛ'sʊ 'tʲɪkras /tʲɪk'ra/.] |

| It's impossible. | Neįmãnoma. |
| --- | --- |
| | [nʲɛɪ'ma:noma.] |
| Nothing of the kind (sort)! | Niẽko panašaũs! |
| | ['nʲɛkɔ pana'ʃɑʊs!] |

| The exact opposite. | Vìsiškai príešingai. |
| --- | --- |
| | ['vʲɪsʲɪʃkʌɪ 'prʲiɛʃɪŋʌɪ.] |
| I'm against it. | Àš prieštaráuju. |
| | ['aʃ prʲiɛʃta'rɑʊjʊ.] |
| I don't care. | Mán nerū̃pi. |
| | ['man nʲɛ'ru:pʲɪ.] |
| I have no idea. | Neįsivaizdúoju. |
| | [nʲɛɪ:sʲɪvʌɪz'dʊo:jʊ.] |
| I doubt it. | Abejóju. |
| | [abʲɛ'joju.] |

| Sorry, I can't. | Atsiprašaũ, bèt negaliù. |
| --- | --- |
| | [atsʲɪpra'ʃɑʊ, bʲɛt nʲɛga'lʲʊ.] |
| Sorry, I don't want to. | Atsiprašaũ, bèt nenóriu. |
| | [atsʲɪpra'ʃɑʊ, bʲɛt nʲɛ'norʲʊ.] |

| Thank you, but I don't need this. | Ãčiū, bèt mán nereĩkia. |
| --- | --- |
| | ['a:tʃʲu:, bʲɛt 'man nʲɛ'rʲɛɪkʲæ.] |
| It's getting late. | Jaũ vėlù. |
| | ['jɛʊ vʲe:'lʲʊ.] |

I have to get up early.

**Mán reĩkia ankstì kéltis.**
['man 'rɛɪkʲɛ aŋk'stʲɪ 'kʲɛlʲtʲɪs.]

I don't feel well.

**Nesijaučiù geraĩ.**
[nʲɛsʲɪ'jɛʊ'tʂʲʊ gʲɛ'rʌɪ.]

# Expressing gratitude

Thank you.
**Ãčiū.**
['aːtʃʲuː.]

Thank you very much.
**Labaĩ ãčiū.**
[lʲaˈbʌɪ 'aːtʃʲuː.]

I really appreciate it.
**Aš labaĩ dėkìngas /dėkìnga/.**
['aʃ lʲaˈbʌɪ dʲeːˈkʲɪngas /dʲeːˈkʲɪnga/.]

I'm really grateful to you.
**Labaĩ jùms dėkóju.**
[lʲaˈbʌɪ 'jums dʲeːˈkoːjʊ.]

We are really grateful to you.
**Mẽs jùms labaĩ dėkìngi.**
['mʲæs 'jums lʲaˈbʌɪ dʲeːˈkʲɪngʲɪ.]

Thank you for your time.
**Ãčiū ùž jū́sų laĩką.**
['aːtʃʲuː 'ʊʒ 'juːsu: 'lʲʌɪkaː.]

Thanks for everything.
**Ãčiū ùž vìską.**
['aːtʃʲuː 'ʊʒ 'vʲɪskaː.]

Thank you for ...
**Ãčiū ùž ...**
['aːtʃʲuː 'ʊʒ ...]

your help
**pagálbą**
[paˈgalʲbaː]

a nice time
**smagiaĩ praléistą laĩką**
[smaˈgʲɛɪ praˈlʲɛɪstaː 'lʲʌɪkaː]

a wonderful meal
**nuostãbų pãtiekalą**
[nʊɑˈstaːbu: 'paːtʲiɛkalʲaː]

a pleasant evening
**malõnų vãkarą**
[maˈlʲoːnu: 'vaːkaraː]

a wonderful day
**nuostãbią diẽną**
[nʊɑˈstaːbʲæː 'dʲɛnaː]

an amazing journey
**nuostãbią keliónę**
[nʊɑˈstaːbʲæː kʲɛˈlʲoːnʲɛː]

Don't mention it.
**Nėrà ùž ką̃.**
[nʲeːˈra 'ʊʒ kaː.]

You are welcome.
**Nedėkókite.**
[nʲɛdʲeːˈkokʲɪtɛ.]

Any time.
**Bèt kadà.**
['bʲɛt kaˈda.]

My pleasure.
**Bùvo malonù padéti.**
['bʊvɔ malʲoˈnʊ paˈdʲeːtʲɪ.]

Forget it.
**Ką̃ jū̃s, vìskas geraĩ.**
[kaː 'juːs, 'vʲɪskas gʲɛˈrʌɪ.]

Don't worry about it.
**Nesijáudinkite dė̃l tõ.**
[nʲɛsʲɪˈjɑʊdʲɪŋkʲɪtɛ 'dʲeːlʲ 'toː.]

## Congratulations. Best wishes

Congratulations!
**Sveikinu!**
['sv'ɛɪk'ɪnʊ!]

Happy birthday!
**Sù gimìmo dienà!**
['sʊ g'ɪ'm'ɪmɔ d'iɛ'na!]

Merry Christmas!
**Linksmũ Kalẽdų!**
[l'ɪŋks'mu: ka'l'e:du:!]

Happy New Year!
**Sù Naujaìsiais mẽtais!**
['sʊ nɑʊ'jʌɪs'ɛɪs 'm'æ̃tʌɪs!]

Happy Easter!
**Sù Šventóm Velýkom!**
['sʊ ʃv'ɛn'tom v'ɛ'l'i:kom!]

Happy Hanukkah!
**Sù Chanùka!**
['sʊ xa'nʊka!]

I'd like to propose a toast.
**Nóriu paskélbti tòstą.**
['nor'ʊ pas'k'ɛl'pt'ɪ 'tosta:.]

Cheers!
**Į sveikãtą!**
[i: sv'ɛɪ'ka:ta:!]

Let's drink to ...!
**Išgérkime ùž ...!**
[ɪʃ'g'ɛrk'ɪm'ɛ 'ʊʒ ...!]

To our success!
**Ùž mũsų sẽkmę!**
['ʊʒ 'mu:su: 's'e:km'ɛ:!]

To your success!
**Ùž jũsų sẽkmę!**
['ʊʒ 'ju:su: 's'e:km'ɛ:!]

Good luck!
**Sẽkmẽs!**
[s'e:k'm'e:s!]

Have a nice day!
**Gẽros diẽnos!**
['g'ɛros 'd'ɛnos!]

Have a good holiday!
**Gerũ atóstogų!**
[g'ɛ'ru: a'tostogu:!]

Have a safe journey!
**Saũgios keliõnės!**
['sɑʊg'os ke'l'o:n'e:s!]

I hope you get better soon!
**Lìnkiu greìtai pasveìkti!**
['l'ɪŋk'ʊ 'gr'ɛɪtʌɪ pas'v'ɛɪkt'ɪ!]

## Socializing

| | |
|---|---|
| Why are you sad? | **Kodėl táu liūdna?**<br>[kɔ'dʲeːl 'taʊ lʲuːd'na?] |
| Smile! Cheer up! | **Nusišypsók! Pralinksmék!**<br>[nʊsʲɪʃɪːp'sok! pralʲɪŋk'smʲeːk!] |
| Are you free tonight? | **Ar jūs šiandien neužsiėmę?**<br>[ar 'juːs 'ʃændʲiɛn neʊʒ'sʲiɛːmʲɛ:?] |
| May I offer you a drink? | **Ar galiù táu pasiūlyti išgérti?**<br>[ar ga'lʲʊ 'taʊ pa'sʲuːlʲiːtʲɪ ɪʃɡʲɛrtʲɪ?] |
| Would you like to dance? | **Ar norétum pašókti?**<br>[ar noʲrʲeːtʊm pa'ʃoktʲɪ?] |
| Let's go to the movies. | **Gál eikime į kiną?**<br>['galʲ 'ɛɪkʲɪmʲɛ iː 'kʲɪːna:?] |
| May I invite you to ...? | **Ar galiù tavè pakviẽsti ...?**<br>[ar ga'lʲʊ ta'vʲɛ pak'vʲɛstʲɪ ...?] |
| a restaurant | **į restoraną**<br>[iː rʲɛsto'raːna:] |
| the movies | **į kiną**<br>[iː 'kʲɪːna:] |
| the theater | **į teãtrą**<br>[iː tʲɛ'aːtra:] |
| go for a walk | **pasivaikščioti**<br>[pasʲɪ'vʌɪkʃtʂʲotʲɪ] |
| At what time? | **Kadà?**<br>[ka'da?] |
| tonight | **šiąnakt**<br>['ʃæːnakt] |
| at six | **šẽštą**<br>['ʃæʃtaː] |
| at seven | **septiñtą**<br>[sʲɛpʲtʲɪntaː] |
| at eight | **aštuñtą**<br>[aʃ'tʊntaː] |
| at nine | **deviñtą**<br>[dʲɛ'vʲɪntaː] |
| Do you like it here? | **Ar táu čià patiñka?**<br>[ar 'taʊ tʂʲæ pa'tʲɪŋka?] |
| Are you here with someone? | **Ar tù nè víena?**<br>[ar 'tʊ nʲɛ 'vʲiɛna?] |
| I'm with my friend. | **Àš sù draugù /draugè/.**<br>['aʃ 'sʊ drɑʊ'gʊ /drɑʊ'gʲɛ/.] |

I'm with my friends.

**Aš su draugaìs /draugémìs/.**
[ˈaʃ ˈsʊ drɑʊˈgʌɪs /drɑʊgʲeˈmʲɪs/.]

No, I'm alone.

**Nè, àš víena.**
[ˈnʲɛ, aʃ ˈvʲiɛna.]

Do you have a boyfriend?

**Ar tùri vaikìną?**
[ar ˈtʊrʲɪ vʌɪˈkʲɪnaː?]

I have a boyfriend.

**Turiù vaikìną.**
[tʊˈrʲʊ vʌɪˈkʲɪnaː.]

Do you have a girlfriend?

**Ar tùri mergìną?**
[ar ˈtʊrʲɪ mʲɛrˈgʲɪnaː?]

I have a girlfriend.

**Turiù mergìną.**
[tʊˈrʲʊ mʲɛrˈgʲɪnaː.]

Can I see you again?

**Ar gãlime dár kadà pasimatýti?**
[ar ˈgaːlʲɪmʲɛ ˈdar kaˈda pasʲɪmaˈtʲiːtʲɪ?]

Can I call you?

**Ar galiù táu paskaṁbinti?**
[ar gaˈlʲʊ ˈtɑʊ pasˈkambʲɪntʲɪ?]

Call me. (Give me a call.)

**Paskaṁbink mán.**
[pasˈkambʲɪŋk ˈman.]

What's your number?

**Kóks tàvo nùmeris?**
[ˈkoks ˈtavɔ ˈnʊmʲɛrʲɪs?]

I miss you.

**Pasìlgau tavę́s.**
[pasʲɪˈlʲɡɑʊ taˈvʲɛːs.]

You have a beautiful name.

**Tàvo gražùs vãrdas.**
[ˈtavɔ graˈʒʊs ˈvardas.]

I love you.

**Mýliu tavè.**
[ˈmʲiːlʲʊ taˈvʲɛ.]

Will you marry me?

**Ar tekési ùž manę́s?**
[ar teˈkʲeːsʲɪ ˈʊʒ maˈnʲɛːs?]

You're kidding!

**Tù juokáuji!**
[ˈtʊ jʊɑˈkɑʊjɪ!]

I'm just kidding.

**Aš juokáuju.**
[ˈaʃ jʊɑˈkɑʊjʊ.]

Are you serious?

**Ar tù rimtaì?**
[ar ˈtʊ rʲɪmˈtʌɪ?]

I'm serious.

**Aš rimtaì.**
[ˈaʃ rʲɪmˈtʌɪ.]

Really?!

**Tikraì?**
[tʲɪkˈrʌɪ?]

It's unbelievable!

**Neįtikétina!**
[nʲɛɪˈtʲɪˈkʲeːtʲɪna!]

I don't believe you.

**Nètikiu.**
[ˈnʲɛtʲɪkʲʊ.]

I can't.

**Aš negaliù.**
[ˈaʃ nʲɛgaˈlʲʊ.]

I don't know.

**Nežinaũ.**
[nʲɛʒʲɪˈnɑʊ.]

I don't understand you.

**Nesuprantù tavę́s.**
[nʲɛsʊpranˈtʊ taˈvʲɛːs.]

Please go away.

**Prašau atstók.**
[pra'ʃɑu ats'tok.]

Leave me alone!

**Palìk manè víeną!**
[pa'lʲɪk ma'nʲɛ 'vʲiɛnaː!]

I can't stand him.

**Àš negaliù jõ pakęst.**
['aʃ nʲɛga'lʲiʊ jɔː pa'kʲɛːst.]

You are disgusting!

**Tù šlykštùs!**
['tʊ ʃlʲiːkʃtʊs!]

I'll call the police!

**Àš iškviẽsiu polìciją!**
['aʃ iʃk'vʲɛsʲʊ po'lʲɪtsʲɪjaː!]

# Sharing impressions. Emotions

| I like it. | **Mán patiñka.** |
| | ['man pa'tʲɪŋka.] |
| Very nice. | **Labaì gražù.** |
| | [lʲa'bʌɪ gra'ʒʊ.] |
| That's great! | **Puikù!** |
| | [pʊi'kʊ!] |
| It's not bad. | **Neblogaì.** |
| | [nʲɛblʲo'gʌɪ.] |

| I don't like it. | **Mán nepatiñka.** |
| | ['man nʲɛpa'tʲɪŋka.] |
| It's not good. | **Taì nèrà geraì.** |
| | ['tʌɪ nʲeː'ra ge'rʌɪ.] |
| It's bad. | **Taì blogaì.** |
| | ['tʌɪ blʲogʌɪ.] |
| It's very bad. | **Taì labaì blogaì.** |
| | ['tʌɪ lʲa'bʌɪ blʲo'gʌɪ.] |
| It's disgusting. | **Taì šlykštù.** |
| | [tʌɪ ʃlʲiːkʃtʊ.] |

| I'm happy. | **Àš laimìngas /laimìnga/.** |
| | ['aʃ lʲʌɪ'mʲɪngas /lʲʌɪ'mʲɪnga/.] |
| I'm content. | **Àš paténkintas /paténkinta/.** |
| | ['aʃ pa'tʲɛŋkʲɪntas /patʲɛŋkʲɪnta/.] |
| I'm in love. | **Àš įsimyléjęs /įsimyléjusi/.** |
| | ['aʃ iːsʲɪmʲɪː'lʲeːjɛːs /iːsʲɪmʲɪː'lʲeːjʊsʲɪ/.] |
| I'm calm. | **Àš ramùs /ramì/.** |
| | ['aʃ ra'mʊs /ra'mʲɪ/.] |
| I'm bored. | **Mán nuobodù.** |
| | ['man nʊɑbo'dʊ.] |

| I'm tired. | **Àš pavar̃gęs /pavar̃gusi/.** |
| | ['aʃ pa'vargʲɛːs /pa'vargʊsʲɪ/.] |
| I'm sad. | **Mán liūdnà.** |
| | ['man 'lʲuːd'na.] |
| I'm frightened. | **Àš išsigañdęs /išsigañdusi/.** |
| | ['aʃ iʃsʲɪ'gandʲɛːs /iʃsʲɪ'gandʊsʲɪ/.] |
| I'm angry. | **Àš supỹkęs /supỹkusi/.** |
| | ['aʃ sʊ'pʲiːkʲɛːs /sʊ'pʲiːkʊsʲɪ/.] |

| I'm worried. | **Àš susirū́pinęs /susirū́pinusi/.** |
| | ['aʃ sʊsʲɪ'ruːpʲɪnʲɛːs /sʊsʲɪ'ruːpʲɪnʊsʲɪ/.] |
| I'm nervous. | **Àš susinèrvinęs /susinèrvinusi/.** |
| | ['aʃ sʊsʲɪ'nʲɛrvʲɪnʲɛːs /sʊsʲɪ'nʲɛrvʲɪnʊsʲɪ/.] |

I'm jealous. (envious)

**Àš pavýdžiu.**
['aʃ pa'vʲiːdʑʊ.]

I'm surprised.

**Àš nustēbęs /nustēbusi/.**
['aʃ nʊstʲæbʲɛːs /nʊstʲæbʊsʲɪ/.]

I'm perplexed.

**Àš sumìšęs /sumìšusi/.**
['aʃ sʊ'mʲɪʃɛːs /sʊ'mʲɪʃʊsʲɪ/.]

## Problems. Accidents

| | |
|---|---|
| I've got a problem. | **Atsitiko problema.** [atsɪ'tʲɪkɔ probl'ɛ'ma.] |
| We've got a problem. | **Mes turime problema.** ['mʲæs 'turʲɪmʲɛ probl'ɛ'ma.] |
| I'm lost. | **Aš pasiklydau.** ['aʃ pasʲɪk'lʲiːdɑʊ.] |
| I missed the last bus (train). | **Nespėjau į paskutinį autobusą (traukinį).** [nʲɛs'pʲeːjɛʊ i: paskʊ'tʲiːnʲɪ ɑʊto'busaː ('trɑʊkʲɪnʲɪː).] |
| I don't have any money left. | **Nebeturiu pinigų.** [nʲɛbʲɛtʊ'rʲʊ pʲɪnʲɪ'guː.] |

| | |
|---|---|
| I've lost my ... | **Aš pamečiau ...** ['aʃ 'pamʲɛtʃɛʊ ...] |
| Someone stole my ... | **Kažkas pavogė mano ...** [kaʒ'kas 'pavogʲeː 'manɔ ...] |

| | |
|---|---|
| passport | **pasą** ['paːsaː] |
| wallet | **pinigìnę** [pʲɪnʲɪ'gʲɪnʲɛː] |
| papers | **dokumentùs** [dokʊmʲɛn'tʊs] |
| ticket | **bilietą** ['bʲɪlʲiɛtaː] |

| | |
|---|---|
| money | **pinigus** ['pʲɪnʲɪgʊs] |
| handbag | **rankinę** ['rankʲɪnʲɛː] |
| camera | **fotoaparatą** [fotoapa'raːtaː] |
| laptop | **nešiojamąjį kompiuterį** [nʲɛ'ʃojamaːjiː kom'pʲʊtʲɛrʲɪː] |
| tablet computer | **planšetinį kompiuterį** [plʲan'ʃɛtʲɪnʲɪː kom'pʲʊtʲɛrʲiː] |
| mobile phone | **mobiluji telefoną** [mo'bʲɪluːjiː tʲɛlʲɛ'fonaː] |

| | |
|---|---|
| Help me! | **Padėkite man!** [pa'dʲeːkʲɪte 'man!] |
| What's happened? | **Kas atsitiko?** ['kas atsɪ'tʲɪkɔ?] |

| | |
|---|---|
| fire | **gaĩsras**<br>['gʌɪsras] |
| shooting | **kažkàs šáudė**<br>[kaʒ'kas 'ʃaʊdⁱeː] |
| murder | **žmogžudỹstė**<br>[ʒmogʒʊ'dⁱiːstⁱeː] |
| explosion | **sprogìmas**<br>[spro'gⁱɪmas] |
| fight | **muštỹnės**<br>[mʊʃˈtⁱiːnⁱeːs] |

| | |
|---|---|
| Call the police! | **Kviẽskite polìciją!**<br>['kvⁱɛskⁱɪtⁱɛ po'lⁱɪtsⁱɪjaː!] |
| Please hurry up! | **Prašaũ, paskubékite!**<br>[pra'ʃaʊ, paskʊ'bⁱeːkⁱɪte!] |
| I'm looking for the police station. | **Ieškau polìcijos skỹriaus.**<br>['ⁱɛʃkaʊ po'lⁱɪtsⁱɪjos 'skⁱiːrⁱɛʊs.] |
| I need to make a call. | **Mán reĩkia paskam̃binti.**<br>['man 'rⁱɛɪkⁱɛ pas'kambⁱɪntⁱɪ.] |
| May I use your phone? | **Ar̃ galiù pasinaudóti jū́sų telefonù?**<br>[ar ga'lⁱʊ pasⁱɪnaʊ'dotⁱɪ 'juːsu: tⁱɛlⁱɛfo'nʊ?] |

| | |
|---|---|
| I've been … | **Manè …**<br>[ma'nⁱɛ …] |
| mugged | **apiplė́šė**<br>[apⁱɪ'plⁱeːʃeː] |
| robbed | **àpvogė**<br>['apvogⁱeː] |
| raped | **išprievartãvo**<br>[ɪʃprⁱɪɛvar'taːvɔ] |
| attacked (beaten up) | **užpúolė**<br>[ʊʒ'puolⁱeː] |

| | |
|---|---|
| Are you all right? | **Ar̃ vìskas geraĩ?**<br>[ar 'vⁱɪskas gⁱɛ'rʌɪ?] |
| Did you see who it was? | **Ar̃ mãtėte, kàs taĩ bùvo?**<br>[ar 'maːtⁱeːte, 'kas tʌɪ 'bʊvo?] |
| Would you be able to recognize the person? | **Ar̃ sugebétumėte atpažìnti tą̃ žmõgų?**<br>[ar sʊge'bⁱeːtʊmⁱeːte atpa'ʒⁱɪntⁱɪ taː: 'ʒmogu:?] |
| Are you sure? | **Ar̃ jū̃s tìkras /tikrà/?**<br>[ar 'juːs tⁱɪkras /tⁱɪk'ra/?] |

| | |
|---|---|
| Please calm down. | **Prašaũ, nurìmkite.**<br>[pra'ʃaʊ, nʊ'rⁱɪmkⁱɪtⁱɛ.] |
| Take it easy! | **Ramiaũ!**<br>[ra'mⁱɛʊ!] |
| Don't worry! | **Nesijáudinkite!**<br>[nⁱɛsⁱɪ'jaʊdⁱɪŋkⁱɪtⁱɛ!] |
| Everything will be fine. | **Vìskas bùs geraĩ.**<br>['vⁱɪskas 'bʊs gⁱɛ'rʌɪ.] |

| | |
|---|---|
| Everything's all right. | **Vìskas geraì.**<br>['vʲɪskas gʲɛ'rʌɪ.] |
| Come here, please. | **Prašaũ, ateìkite čià.**<br>[pra'ʃɑʊ, a'tʲɛɪkʲɪtʲɛ tʃʲæ.] |
| I have some questions for you. | **Turiù jùms kẽletą kláusimų.**<br>[tʊ'rʲʊ 'jʊms 'kʲælʲɛta: 'klɑʊsʲɪmu:.] |
| Wait a moment, please. | **Prašaũ trupùtį paláukti.**<br>[pra'ʃɑʊ trʊ'pʊtʲɪ: pa'lʲɑʊktʲɪ.] |
| Do you have any I.D.? | **Aȓ tùrite kokiùs nórs asmeñs dokumentùs?**<br>[ar 'tʊrʲɪtʲɛ ko'kʲʊs 'nors as'mʲɛns dokʊmʲɛn'tʊs?] |
| Thanks. You can leave now. | **Āčiū. Gãlite eĩti.**<br>['a:tʃʲu:. 'ga:lʲɪtʲɛ 'ɛɪtʲɪ.] |
| Hands behind your head! | **Rankàs ùž galvõs!**<br>[raŋ'kas 'ʊʒ galʲvo:s!] |
| You're under arrest! | **Jū̃s suimamas!**<br>['ju:s 'sʊimamas!] |

# Health problems

| | |
|---|---|
| Please help me. | **Prašau, padėkite mán.**<br>[pra'ʃɑʊ, padʲeːkʲɪte 'man.] |
| I don't feel well. | **Mán blogà.**<br>['man blʲoˈga.] |
| My husband doesn't feel well. | **Máno výrui blogà.**<br>['maːnɔ 'vʲiːrʊɪ blʲoˈga.] |
| My son ... | **Màno sūnui ...**<br>['manɔ 'suːnʊɪ ...] |
| My father ... | **Màno tévui ...**<br>['manɔ 'tʲeːvʊɪ ...] |

| | |
|---|---|
| My wife doesn't feel well. | **Màno žmónai blogà.**<br>['manɔ 'ʒmonʌɪ blʲoˈga.] |
| My daughter ... | **Màno dùkrai ...**<br>['manɔ 'dʊkrʌɪ ...] |
| My mother ... | **Màno mãmai ...**<br>['manɔ 'maːmʌɪ ...] |

| | |
|---|---|
| I've got a ... | **Mán ...**<br>['man ...] |
| headache | **skaūda gálvą**<br>['skɑʊda 'galʲva:] |
| sore throat | **skaūda gérklę**<br>['skɑʊda 'gʲɛrklʲɛ:] |
| stomach ache | **skaūda skrañdį**<br>['skɑʊda 'skrandʲiː] |
| toothache | **skaūda dañtį**<br>['skɑʊda 'dantiː] |

| | |
|---|---|
| I feel dizzy. | **Mán svaĩgsta galvà.**<br>['man 'svʌɪgsta galʲˈva.] |
| He has a fever. | **Jìs karščiúoja.**<br>[jɪs karʃˈtʂʲʊoːjɛ.] |
| She has a fever. | **Jì karščiúoja.**<br>[jɪ karʃˈtʂʲʊoːjɛ.] |
| I can't breathe. | **Negaliù kvėpúoti.**<br>[nʲɛgaˈlʲʊ kvʲeːˈpʊotʲɪ.] |

| | |
|---|---|
| I'm short of breath. | **Mán sunkù kvėpúoti.**<br>['man sʊŋˈkʊ kvʲeːˈpʊotʲɪ.] |
| I am asthmatic. | **Sergù astmà.**<br>[sʲɛrˈgʊ astˈma.] |
| I am diabetic. | **Sergù diabetù.**<br>[sʲɛrˈgʊ dʲæbʲɛˈtʊ.] |

| | |
|---|---|
| I can't sleep. | **Negaliu užmigti.**<br>[nʲɛga'lʲʊ ʊʒ'mʲɪktʲɪ.] |
| food poisoning | **apsinuõdijimas maistù**<br>[apsʲɪ'nʊadʲɪjimas mʌɪs'tʊ] |

| | |
|---|---|
| It hurts here. | **Skaũda čià.**<br>['skɑʊda 'tʂʲæ.] |
| Help me! | **Padékite màn!**<br>[pa'dʲeːkʲɪte 'man!] |
| I am here! | **Àš čià!**<br>['aʃ tʂʲæ!] |
| We are here! | **Mẽs čià!**<br>['mʲæs tʂʲæ!] |
| Get me out of here! | **Ištráukite manè ìš čià!**<br>[ɪʃ'trɑʊkʲɪtʲɛ ma'nʲɛ ɪʃ tʂʲæ!] |
| I need a doctor. | **Màn reĩkia dãktaro.**<br>['man 'rʲɛɪkʲɛ 'daːktarɔ.] |
| I can't move. | **Negaliu pajudéti.**<br>[nʲɛga'lʲʊ pajʊ'dʲeːtʲɪ.] |
| I can't move my legs. | **Negaliu pajùdinti kójų.**<br>[nʲɛga'lʲʊ pa'jʊdʲɪntʲɪ 'kojuː.] |

| | |
|---|---|
| I have a wound. | **Àš sužeĩstas /sužeistà/.**<br>['aʃ 'sʊʒʲɛɪstas /sʊʒʲɛɪs'ta/.] |
| Is it serious? | **Ar̃ žaizdà sunkì?**<br>[ar ʒʌɪz'da sʊŋ'kʲɪ?] |
| My documents are in my pocket. | **Mãno dokumeñtai kišenéje.**<br>['maːnɔ dokʊ'mentʌɪ kʲɪ'ʃænʲeːje.] |
| Calm down! | **Nurìmkite!**<br>[nʊrʲ'ɪmkʲɪtʲɛ!] |
| May I use your phone? | **Ar̃ galiù pasinaudóti jū́sų telefonù?**<br>[ar ga'lʲʊ pasʲɪnɑʊ'dotʲɪ 'juːsu: tʲɛlʲɛfo'nʊ?] |

| | |
|---|---|
| Call an ambulance! | **Kviẽskite greĩtają!**<br>['kvʲɛskʲɪtʲɛ 'grʲɛɪtaːjaː!] |
| It's urgent! | **Taĩ skubù!**<br>['tʌɪ skʊ'bʊ!] |
| It's an emergency! | **Taĩ skubùs ãtvejis!**<br>['tʌɪ skʊ'bʊs 'aːtvʲɛjis!] |
| Please hurry up! | **Prašaũ, paskubékite!**<br>[pra'ʃɑʊ, paskʊ'bʲeːkʲɪte!] |
| Would you please call a doctor? | **Ar̃ gãlite iškviẽsti dãktarą?**<br>[ar 'gaːlʲɪtʲɛ iʃk'vʲɛstʲɪ 'daːktaraː?] |
| Where is the hospital? | **Kur̃ ligóninė?**<br>['kʊr lʲɪ'gonʲɪnʲeː?] |

| | |
|---|---|
| How are you feeling? | **Kaĩp jaũčiatės?**<br>['kʌɪp 'jɛʊtʂʲætʲeːs?] |
| Are you all right? | **Ar̃ vìskas geraĩ?**<br>[ar 'vʲɪskas gʲɛ'rʌɪ?] |
| What's happened? | **Kàs atsitìko?**<br>['kas atsʲɪ'tʲɪko?] |

I feel better now.

**Jaučiúosi geriaũ.**
[jɛu'tʂʲuosʲɪ gʲɛ'rʲɛu.]

It's OK.

**Vìskas tvarkojè.**
['vʲɪskas tvarko'jæ.]

It's all right.

**Vìskas geraĩ.**
['vʲɪskas gʲɛ'rʌɪ.]

# At the pharmacy

| pharmacy (drugstore) | vaistinė<br>['vʌɪstʲɪnʲeː] |
|---|---|
| 24-hour pharmacy | vìsą parą dìrbanti vaistinė<br>['vʲɪsa: 'pa:ra: 'dʲɪrbantʲɪ 'vʌɪstʲɪnʲeː] |
| Where is the closest pharmacy? | Kuř yrà artimiáusia vaistinė?<br>['kʊr iː'ra artʲɪ'mʲæʊsʲɛ 'vʌɪstʲɪnʲeː?] |

| Is it open now? | Ař jì dabař dìrba?<br>[ar jɪ da'bar 'dʲɪrba?] |
|---|---|
| At what time does it open? | Kadà jì atsidãro?<br>[ka'da jɪ atsʲɪ'da:ro?] |
| At what time does it close? | Kadà jì užsidãro?<br>[ka'da jɪ ʊʒsʲɪ'da:ro?] |

| Is it far? | Ař jì tõli?<br>[ar jɪ 'to:lʲɪ?] |
|---|---|
| Can I get there on foot? | Ař galiù nueĩti teñ pėsčiomìs?<br>[ar ga'lʲʊ 'nʊʲɛɪtʲɪ ten pʲeːstʲɔ'mʲɪs?] |
| Can you show me on the map? | Ař gãlite parõdyti žemėlapyje?<br>[ar 'ga:lʲɪte pa'rodʲiːtʲɪ ʒeʲmʲeːlapʲiːje?] |

| Please give me something for ... | Dúokite mán kažką̃ nuõ ...<br>['dʊokʲɪtʲɛ 'man kaʒ'ka: nʊa ...] |
|---|---|
| a headache | galvõs skaũsmo<br>[galʲ'voːs 'skaʊsmɔ] |
| a cough | kosùlio<br>[kɔ'sʊlʲɔ] |
| a cold | péršalimo<br>['pʲɛrʃalʲɪmɔ] |
| the flu | grìpo<br>['grʲɪpɔ] |

| a fever | karščiãvimo<br>[karʃ'tsʲævʲɪmɔ] |
|---|---|
| a stomach ache | skrañdžio skaũsmo<br>['skrandʒʲɔ 'skaʊsmɔ] |
| nausea | pỹkinimo<br>['pʲiːkʲɪnʲɪmɔ] |
| diarrhea | viduriãvimo<br>[vʲɪdʊ'rʲævʲɪmɔ] |
| constipation | vidurių̃ užkietėjimo<br>[vʲɪdʊ'rʲu: ʊʒkʲɪɛ'tʲɛjɪmɔ] |
| pain in the back | nùgaros skaũsmo<br>['nʊgarɔs 'skaʊsmɔ] |

| | |
|---|---|
| chest pain | **krutinės skaũsmo**<br>[krʊtɪrˈnʲeːs ˈskaʊsmɔ] |
| side stitch | **šóno diegìmo**<br>[ˈʃonɔ dʲiɛˈgʲɪmɔ] |
| abdominal pain | **pílvo skaũsmo**<br>[ˈpʲɪlʲvɔ ˈskaʊsmɔ] |

| | |
|---|---|
| pill | **tabletė**<br>[tabˈlʲɛtʲeː] |
| ointment, cream | **tẽpalas, krẽmas**<br>[ˈtʲæpalʲas, ˈkrʲɛmas] |
| syrup | **sìrupas**<br>[ˈsʲɪrʊpas] |
| spray | **purškalas**<br>[ˈpʊrʃkalʲas] |
| drops | **lašaĩ**<br>[lʲaˈʃʌɪ] |

| | |
|---|---|
| You need to go to the hospital. | **Jùms reĩkia į̃ ligóninę.**<br>[ˈjʊms ˈrʲɛɪkʲɛ iː lʲɪˈgonʲɪnʲɛː.] |
| health insurance | **sveikãtos draudìmas**<br>[svʲɛɪˈkaːtos draʊˈdʲɪmas] |
| prescription | **váisto recẽptas**<br>[ˈvʌɪstɔ rʲɛˈtsʲɛptas] |
| insect repellant | **vabzdžių̃ repeleñtas**<br>[vabzˈdʒʲuː rʲɛpʲɛˈlʲɛntas] |
| Band Aid | **pleĩstras**<br>[ˈplʲɛɪstras] |

# The bare minimum

| | |
|---|---|
| Excuse me, ... | **Atsiprašaū, ...**<br>[atsʲɪpraˈʃɑʊ, ...] |
| Hello. | **Sveikì.**<br>[svʲɛɪˈkʲɪ.] |
| Thank you. | **Āčiū.**<br>[ˈaːtʂʲuː.] |
| Good bye. | **Ikì.**<br>[ɪˈkʲɪ.] |
| Yes. | **Taìp.**<br>[ˈtʌɪp.] |
| No. | **Nè.**<br>[ˈnʲɛ.] |
| I don't know. | **Nežinaū.**<br>[nʲɛʒɪˈnɑʊ.] |
| Where? \| Where to? \| When? | **Kuȓ? \| Kur? \| Kadà?**<br>[ˈkʊr? \| ˈkʊr? \| kaˈda?] |
| I need ... | **Mán reìkia ...**<br>[ˈman ˈrʲɛɪkʲɛ ...] |
| I want ... | **Nóriu ...**<br>[ˈnorʲʊ ...] |
| Do you have ...? | **Aȓ tùrite ...?**<br>[ar ˈtʊrʲɪtʲɛ ...?] |
| Is there a ... here? | **Aȓ čià yrà ...?**<br>[ar ˈtʂʲæ iːˈra ...?] |
| May I ...? | **Aȓ galiù ...?**<br>[ar gaˈlʲʊ ...?] |
| ..., please (polite request) | **Prašaū ...**<br>[praˈʃɑʊ ...] |
| I'm looking for ... | **Íeškau ...**<br>[ˈɪʲɛʃkɑʊ ...] |
| restroom | **tualèto**<br>[tʊaˈlʲɛtɔ] |
| ATM | **bankomāto**<br>[baŋkoˈmaːtɔ] |
| pharmacy (drugstore) | **váistinės**<br>[ˈvʌɪstʲɪnʲeːs] |
| hospital | **ligóninės**<br>[lʲɪˈgonʲɪnʲeːs] |
| police station | **polìcijos skýriaus**<br>[poˈlʲɪtsɪjos ˈskʲiːrʲɛʊs] |
| subway | **metrò**<br>[mʲɛˈtro] |

| | |
|---|---|
| taxi | **taksi**<br>[tak'sʲɪ] |
| train station | **traukinių stotiẽs**<br>[trɑʊkʲɪ'nʲu: sto'tʲɛs] |

| | |
|---|---|
| My name is ... | **Mãno vaŕdas ...**<br>['ma:nɔ 'vardas ...] |
| What's your name? | **Kuõ jũs vardù?**<br>['kʊɑ 'ju:s var'dʊ?] |
| Could you please help me? | **Atsiprašaũ, aŕ gãlite padéti?**<br>[atsʲɪpra'ʃɑʊ, ar 'ga:lʲɪte pa'dʲe:tʲɪ?] |
| I've got a problem. | **Atsitìko problemà.**<br>[atsʲɪ'tʲɪkɔ problʲɛ'ma.] |
| I don't feel well. | **Mán blogà.**<br>['man blʲo'ga.] |
| Call an ambulance! | **Kviẽskite greĩtają!**<br>['kvʲɛskʲɪtʲɛ 'grʲɛɪta:ja:!] |
| May I make a call? | **Aŕ galiù paskambinti?**<br>[ar ga'lʲʊ pas'kambʲɪntʲɪ?] |

| | |
|---|---|
| I'm sorry. | **Atsiprašaũ.**<br>[atsʲɪpra'ʃɑʊ.] |
| You're welcome. | **Nėrà ùž ką̃.**<br>[nʲe:'ra 'ʊʒ ka:.] |

| | |
|---|---|
| I, me | **àš**<br>['aʃ] |
| you (inform.) | **tù**<br>['tʊ] |
| he | **jìs**<br>[jɪs] |
| she | **jì**<br>[jɪ] |
| they (masc.) | **jiẽ**<br>['jiɛ] |
| they (fem.) | **jõs**<br>['jo:s] |
| we | **mẽs**<br>['mʲæs] |
| you (pl) | **jũs**<br>['ju:s] |
| you (sg, form.) | **Jũs**<br>['ju:s] |

| | |
|---|---|
| ENTRANCE | **ĮĖJÌMAS**<br>[i:'ɛ:'jɪmas] |
| EXIT | **IŠĖJÌMAS**<br>[ɪʃʲe:'jɪmas] |
| OUT OF ORDER | **NEVEĨKIA**<br>[nʲɛ'vʲɛɪkʲɛ] |
| CLOSED | **UŽDARÝTA**<br>[ʊʒda'rʲi:ta] |

| | |
|---|---|
| OPEN | **ATIDARYTA**<br>[atɪda'riːta] |
| FOR WOMEN | **MÓTERŲ**<br>['motʲɛruː] |
| FOR MEN | **VYRŲ**<br>['vʲiːruː] |

# TOPICAL
# VOCABULARY

This section contains more
than 3,000 of the most
important words.
The dictionary will provide
invaluable assistance while
traveling abroad, because
frequently individual words
are enough for you to be
understood.
The dictionary includes a
convenient transcription of
each foreign word

**T&P Books Publishing**

# VOCABULARY CONTENTS

**T&P Books Publishing**

# BASIC CONCEPTS

**T&P Books Publishing**

## 1. Pronouns

| | | |
|---|---|---|
| I, me | aš | ['aʃ] |
| you | tù | ['tu] |
| he | jìs | [jɪs] |
| she | jì | [jɪ] |
| we | mẽs | ['mʲæs] |
| you (to a group) | jũs | ['ju:s] |
| they | jiẽ | ['jiɛ] |

## 2. Greetings. Salutations

| | | |
|---|---|---|
| Hello! (fam.) | Sveìkas! | ['svʲɛɪkas!] |
| Hello! (form.) | Sveikì! | [svʲɛɪ'kʲɪ!] |
| Good morning! | Lãbas rýtas! | ['lʲa:bas 'rʲi:tas!] |
| Good afternoon! | Labà dienà! | [lʲa'ba dʲiɛ'na!] |
| Good evening! | Lãbas vãkaras! | ['lʲa:bas 'va:karas!] |
| to say hello | sveĩkintis | ['svʲɛɪkʲɪntʲɪs] |
| Hi! (hello) | Lãbas! | ['lʲa:bas!] |
| greeting (n) | linkéjimas (v) | [lʲɪŋ'kʲejɪmas] |
| to greet (vt) | sveĩkinti | ['svʲɛɪkʲɪntʲɪ] |
| How are you? | Kaĩp sẽkasi? | ['kʌɪp 'sʲækasʲɪ?] |
| What's new? | Kàs naũjo? | ['kas 'nɑʊjo?] |
| Bye-Bye! Goodbye! | Ikì pasimãtymo! | [ɪkʲɪ pasʲɪmatʲi:mo!] |
| See you soon! | Ikì greĩto susìtikimo! | [ɪ'kʲɪ 'grʲɛɪto susʲɪtʲɪ'kʲɪmo!] |
| Farewell! | Lìkite sveikì! | ['lʲɪkʲɪtʲɛ svʲɛɪ'kʲɪ!] |
| to say goodbye | atsisveĩkinti | [atsʲɪ'svʲɛɪkʲɪntʲɪ] |
| So long! | Ikì! | [ɪ'kʲɪ!] |
| Thank you! | Ãčiū! | ['a:tʂʲu:!] |
| Thank you very much! | Labaĩ ãčiū! | [lʲa'bʌɪ 'a:tʂʲu:!] |
| You're welcome | Prãšom. | ['pra:ʃom] |
| Don't mention it! | Nevertà padėkõs. | [nʲever'ta padʲe:'ko:s] |
| It was nothing | Nėrà ùž kã. | [nʲe:'ra 'ʊʒ ka:] |
| Excuse me! (fam.) | Atleìsk! | [at'lʲɛɪsk!] |
| Excuse me! (form.) | Atleìskite! | [at'lʲɛɪskʲɪtʲɛ!] |
| to excuse (forgive) | atleĩsti | [at'lʲɛɪstʲɪ] |
| to apologize (vi) | atsiprašýti | [atsʲɪpra'ʃɪːtʲɪ] |
| My apologies | Mãno atsiprãšymas. | ['ma:nɔ atsʲɪ'pra:ʃɪːmas] |

| I'm sorry! | Atleiskite! | [at'lʲɛɪskʲɪtʲɛ!] |
| to forgive (vt) | atleisti | [at'lʲɛɪstʲɪ] |
| It's okay! (that's all right) | Nieko baisaus. | ['nʲɛkɔ bʌɪ'sɑʊs] |
| please (adv) | prašom | ['pra:ʃom] |

| Don't forget! | Nepamiřškite! | [nʲɛpa'mʲɪrʃkʲɪtʲɛ!] |
| Certainly! | Žìnoma! | ['ʒʲɪnoma!] |
| Of course not! | Žìnoma nè! | ['ʒʲɪnoma nʲɛ!] |
| Okay! (I agree) | Sutinkù! | [sʊtʲɪŋ'kʊ!] |
| That's enough! | Užteks! | [ʊʒ'tʲɛks!] |

## 3. Questions

| Who? | Kàs? | ['kas?] |
| What? | Ką̃? | ['ka:?] |
| Where? (at, in) | Kuř? | ['kʊr?] |
| Where (to)? | Kuř? | ['kʊr?] |
| From where? | Ìš kuř? | [ɪʃ 'kʊr?] |
| When? | Kadà? | [ka'da?] |
| Why? (What for?) | Kám? | ['kam?] |
| Why? (~ are you crying?) | Kodėl? | [kɔ'dʲe:lʲ?] |

| What for? | Kám? | ['kam?] |
| How? (in what way) | Kaĩp? | ['kʌɪp?] |
| What? (What kind of ...?) | Kóks? | ['koks?] |
| Which? | Kurìs? | [kʊ'rʲɪs?] |

| To whom? | Kám? | ['kam?] |
| About whom? | Apiẽ ką̃? | [a'pʲɛ 'ka:?] |
| About what? | Apiẽ ką̃? | [a'pʲɛ 'ka:?] |
| With whom? | Sù kuõ? | ['sʊ 'kʊɑ?] |

| How many? How much? | Kíek? | ['kʲiɛk?] |
| Whose? | Kienõ? | [kʲiɛ'no:?] |

## 4. Prepositions

| with (accompanied by) | sù ... | ['sʊ ...] |
| without | bè | ['bʲɛ] |
| to (indicating direction) | ̀ | [i:] |
| about (talking ~ ...) | apiẽ | [a'pʲɛ] |
| before (in time) | ikì | [ɪ'kʲɪ] |
| in front of ... | priẽš | ['prʲɛʃ] |

| under (beneath, below) | põ | ['po:] |
| above (over) | viřš | ['vʲɪrʃ] |
| on (atop) | añt | ['ant] |
| from (off, out of) | ìš | [ɪʃ] |

| | | |
|---|---|---|
| of (made from) | iš | [ɪʃ] |
| in (e.g., ~ ten minutes) | põ ..., už ... | ['po: ...], ['ʊʒ ...] |
| over (across the top of) | per̃ | ['pʲɛr] |

## 5. Function words. Adverbs. Part 1

| | | |
|---|---|---|
| Where? (at, in) | Kur̃? | ['kʊr?] |
| here (adv) | čià | ['tsʲæ] |
| there (adv) | teñ | ['tʲɛn] |
| | | |
| somewhere (to be) | kažkur̃ | [kaʒ'kʊr] |
| nowhere (not anywhere) | niẽkur | ['nʲɛkʊr] |
| | | |
| by (near, beside) | priẽ ... | ['prʲɛ ...] |
| by the window | priẽ lángo | ['prʲɛ 'lʲangɔ] |
| | | |
| Where (to)? | Kur̃? | ['kʊr?] |
| here (e.g., come ~!) | čià | ['tsʲæ] |
| there (e.g., to go ~) | teñ | ['tʲɛn] |
| from here (adv) | iš čià | [ɪʃ tsʲæ] |
| from there (adv) | iš teñ | [ɪʃ tʲɛn] |
| | | |
| close (adv) | šalià | [ʃa'lʲæ] |
| far (adv) | tolì | [to'lʲɪ] |
| | | |
| near (e.g., ~ Paris) | šalià | [ʃa'lʲæ] |
| nearby (adv) | artì | [ar'tʲɪ] |
| not far (adv) | netolì | [nʲɛ'tolʲɪ] |
| | | |
| left (adj) | kairỹs | [kʌɪ'rʲiːs] |
| on the left | iš kair̃ės | [ɪʃ kʌɪ'rʲeːs] |
| to the left | į̃ kaĩrę | [iː 'kʌɪrʲɛː] |
| | | |
| right (adj) | dešinỹs | [dʲɛʃɪ'nʲiːs] |
| on the right | iš dešiñės | [ɪʃ deʃɪ'nʲeːs] |
| to the right | į̃ dẽšinę | [iː 'dʲæʃʲɪnʲɛː] |
| | | |
| in front (adv) | príekyje | ['prʲɛkʲiːjɛ] |
| front (as adj) | príekinis | ['prʲɛkʲɪnʲɪs] |
| ahead (the kids ran ~) | pirmỹn | [pʲɪr'mʲiːn] |
| | | |
| behind (adv) | galè | [ga'lʲɛ] |
| from behind | iš gãlo | [ɪʃ 'ga:lɔ] |
| back (towards the rear) | atgal̃ | [at'galʲ] |
| | | |
| middle | vidurỹs (v) | [vʲɪdu'rʲiːs] |
| in the middle | per̃ vìdurį | ['pʲɛr 'vʲɪːdurʲɪː] |
| | | |
| at the side | šóne | ['ʃonʲɛ] |
| everywhere (adv) | visur̃ | [vʲɪ'sʊr] |

| around (in all directions) | aplinkui | [ap'lʲɪŋkʊi] |
| from inside | iš vidaus | [ɪʃ vʲɪ'dɑʊs] |
| somewhere (to go) | kažkur | [kaʒ'kʊr] |
| straight (directly) | tiesiai | ['tʲɛsʲɛɪ] |
| back (e.g., come ~) | atgal | [at'galʲ] |

| from anywhere | iš kur nors | [ɪʃ 'kʊr 'nors] |
| from somewhere | iš kažkur | [ɪʃ kaʒ'kʊr] |

| firstly (adv) | pirma | ['pʲɪrma] |
| secondly (adv) | antra | ['antra] |
| thirdly (adv) | trečia | ['trʲætʂʲæ] |

| suddenly (adv) | staiga | [stʌɪ'ga] |
| at first (in the beginning) | pradžioj | [prad'ʒʲoːj] |
| for the first time | pirmą kartą | ['pʲɪrma: 'karta:] |
| long before ... | daug laiko prieš ... | ['dɑʊg 'lʲʌɪkɔ 'prʲɛʃ ...] |
| anew (over again) | iš naujo | [ɪʃ 'nɑʊjɔ] |
| for good (adv) | visám laikui | [vʲɪ'sam 'lʲʌɪkʊi] |

| never (adv) | niekada | [nʲiɛkad'a] |
| again (adv) | vėl | ['vʲeːlʲ] |
| now (adv) | dabar | [da'bar] |
| often (adv) | dažnai | [daʒ'nʌɪ] |
| then (adv) | tada | [ta'da] |
| urgently (quickly) | skubiai | [skʊ'bʲɛɪ] |
| usually (adv) | įprastai | [iːpras'tʌɪ] |

| by the way, ... | beje, ... | [bɛ'jæ, ...] |
| possible (that is ~) | įmanoma | [iː'ma:noma] |
| probably (adv) | tikėtina | [tʲɪ'kʲeːtʲɪna] |
| maybe (adv) | gali būti | ['ga:lʲɪ 'buːtʲɪ] |
| besides ... | be to, ... | ['bʲɛ toː, ...] |
| that's why ... | todėl ... | [to'dʲeːlʲ ...] |
| in spite of ... | nepaisant ... | [nʲɛ'pʌɪsant ...] |
| thanks to ... | ... dėka | [... dʲeː'ka] |

| what (pron.) | kas | ['kas] |
| that (conj.) | kas | ['kas] |
| something | kažkas | [kaʒ'kas] |
| anything (something) | kažkas | [kaʒ'kas] |
| nothing | nieko | ['nʲɛkɔ] |

| who (pron.) | kas | ['kas] |
| someone | kažkas | [kaʒ'kas] |
| somebody | kažkas | [kaʒ'kas] |

| nobody | niekas | ['nʲɛkas] |
| nowhere (a voyage to ~) | niekur | ['nʲɛkʊr] |
| nobody's | niekieno | ['nʲɛ'kʲiɛnɔ] |
| somebody's | kažkieno | [kaʒkʲiɛ'noː] |
| so (I'm ~ glad) | taip | ['tʌɪp] |

| | | |
|---|---|---|
| also (as well) | taìp pàt | ['tʌɪp 'pat] |
| too (as well) | ìrgi | ['ɪrgʲɪ] |

## 6. Function words. Adverbs. Part 2

| | | |
|---|---|---|
| Why? | Kodėl? | [kɔ'dʲeːlʲ?] |
| for some reason | kažkodėl | [kaʒkɔ'dʲeːlʲ] |
| because ... | ... todėl, kàd | [... to'dʲeːlʲ, 'kad] |
| for some purpose | kažkodėl | [kaʒkɔ'dʲeːlʲ] |

| | | |
|---|---|---|
| and | ìr | [ɪr] |
| or | arbà | [ar'ba] |
| but | bèt | ['bʲɛt] |

| | | |
|---|---|---|
| too (~ many people) | pernelýg | [pʲɛrnʲɛ'lʲiːg] |
| only (exclusively) | tiktaì | [tʲɪk'tʌɪ] |
| exactly (adv) | tiksliaì | [tʲɪksʲ'lʲɛɪ] |
| about (more or less) | maždaūg | [maʒ'dɑʊg] |

| | | |
|---|---|---|
| approximately (adv) | apýtikriai | [a'pʲiːtʲɪkrʲɛɪ] |
| approximate (adj) | apýtikriai | [a'pʲiːtʲɪkrʲɛɪ] |
| almost (adv) | beveìk | [bʲɛ'vʲɛɪk] |
| the rest | vìsa kìta (m) | ['vʲɪsa 'kʲɪta] |

| | | |
|---|---|---|
| each (adj) | kiekvíenas | [kʲiɛk'vʲiɛnas] |
| any (no matter which) | bèt kurìs | ['bʲɛt kʊ'rʲɪs] |
| many, much (a lot of) | daūg | ['dɑʊg] |
| many people | daūgelis | ['dɑʊgʲɛlʲɪs] |
| all (everyone) | visì | [vʲɪ'sʲɪ] |

| | | |
|---|---|---|
| in return for ... | mainaìs į̇̃ ... | [mʌɪ'nʌɪs iː ..] |
| in exchange (adv) | mainaìs | [mʌɪ'nʌɪs] |
| by hand (made) | rañkiniu būdù | ['raŋkʲɪnʲʊ buː'dʊ] |
| hardly (negative opinion) | kažì | [ka'ʒʲɪ] |

| | | |
|---|---|---|
| probably (adv) | tikriáusiai | [tʲɪk'rʲæʊsʲɛɪ] |
| on purpose (intentionally) | týčia | ['tʲiːtʂʲæ] |
| by accident (adv) | netýčia | [nʲɛ'tʲiːtʂʲæ] |

| | | |
|---|---|---|
| very (adv) | labaì | [lʲa'bʌɪ] |
| for example (adv) | pãvyzdžiui | ['pɑːvʲiːzdʒʲʊi] |
| between | tãrp | ['tarp] |
| among | tãrp | ['tarp] |
| so much (such a lot) | tiẽk | ['tʲɛk] |
| especially (adv) | ýpač | ['ɪːpatʂ] |

# NUMBERS.
# MISCELLANEOUS

**T&P Books Publishing**

## 7. Cardinal numbers. Part 1

| | | |
|---|---|---|
| 0 zero | nùlis | ['nʊlʲɪs] |
| 1 one | víenas | ['vʲiɛnas] |
| 2 two | dù | ['dʊ] |
| 3 three | trìs | ['trʲɪs] |
| 4 four | keturì | [kʲɛtʊ'rʲɪ] |
| 5 five | penkì | [pʲɛŋ'kʲɪ] |
| 6 six | šešì | [ʃɛ'ʃʲɪ] |
| 7 seven | septynì | [sʲɛptʲi:'nʲɪ] |
| 8 eight | aštuonì | [aʃtʊɑ'nʲɪ] |
| 9 nine | devynì | [dʲɛvʲi:'nʲɪ] |
| 10 ten | dešimt | ['dʲæʃɪmt] |
| 11 eleven | vienúolika | [vʲiɛ'nʊɑlʲɪka] |
| 12 twelve | dvýlika | ['dvʲi:lʲɪka] |
| 13 thirteen | trýlika | ['trʲi:lʲɪka] |
| 14 fourteen | keturiólika | [kʲɛtʊ'rʲolʲɪka] |
| 15 fifteen | penkiólika | [pʲɛŋ'kʲolʲɪka] |
| 16 sixteen | šešiólika | [ʃɛ'ʃolʲɪka] |
| 17 seventeen | septyniólika | [sʲɛptʲi:'nʲolʲɪka] |
| 18 eighteen | aštuoniólika | [aʃtʊɑ'nʲolʲɪka] |
| 19 nineteen | devyniólika | [dʲɛvʲi:'nʲolʲɪka] |
| 20 twenty | dvìdešimt | ['dvʲɪdʲɛʃɪmt] |
| 21 twenty-one | dvìdešimt víenas | ['dvʲɪdʲɛʃɪmt 'vʲiɛnas] |
| 22 twenty-two | dvìdešimt dù | ['dvʲɪdʲɛʃɪmt 'dʊ] |
| 23 twenty-three | dvìdešimt trìs | ['dvʲɪdʲɛʃɪmt 'trʲɪs] |
| 30 thirty | trìsdešimt | ['trʲɪsdʲɛʃɪmt] |
| 31 thirty-one | trìsdešimt víenas | ['trʲɪsdʲɛʃɪmt 'vʲiɛnas] |
| 32 thirty-two | trìsdešimt dù | ['trʲɪsdʲɛʃɪmt 'dʊ] |
| 33 thirty-three | trìsdešimt trìs | ['trʲɪsdʲɛʃɪmt 'trʲɪs] |
| 40 forty | kėturiasdešimt | ['kʲætʊrʲæsdʲɛʃɪmt] |
| 41 forty-one | kėturiasdešimt víenas | ['kʲætʊrʲæsdʲɛʃɪmt 'vʲiɛnas] |
| 42 forty-two | kėturiasdešimt dù | ['kʲætʊrʲæsdʲɛʃɪmt 'dʊ] |
| 43 forty-three | kėturiasdešimt trìs | ['kʲætʊrʲæsdʲɛʃɪmt 'trʲɪs] |
| 50 fifty | peñkiasdešimt | ['pʲɛŋkʲæsdʲɛʃɪmt] |
| 51 fifty-one | peñkiasdešimt víenas | ['pʲɛŋkʲæsdʲɛʃɪmt 'vʲiɛnas] |
| 52 fifty-two | peñkiasdešimt dù | ['pʲɛŋkʲæsdʲɛʃɪmt 'dʊ] |
| 53 fifty-three | peñkiasdešimt trìs | ['pʲɛŋkʲæsdʲɛʃɪmt 'trʲɪs] |
| 60 sixty | šėšiasdešimt | ['ʃæʃæsdʲɛʃɪmt] |

| 61 sixty-one | šešiasdešimt víenas | [ˈʃæʃæsdʲɛʃɪmt ˈvʲiɛnas] |
| 62 sixty-two | šešiasdešimt dù | [ˈʃæʃæsdʲɛʃɪmt ˈdʊ] |
| 63 sixty-three | šešiasdešimt trìs | [ˈʃæʃæsdʲɛʃɪmt ˈtrʲɪs] |

| 70 seventy | septýniasdešimt | [sʲɛpˈtʲiːnʲæsdʲɛʃɪmt] |
| 71 seventy-one | septýniasdešimt víenas | [sʲɛpˈtʲiːnʲæsdʲɛʃɪmt ˈvʲiɛnas] |
| 72 seventy-two | septýniasdešimt dù | [sʲɛpˈtʲiːnʲæsdʲɛʃɪmt ˈdʊ] |
| 73 seventy-three | septýniasdešimt trìs | [sʲɛpˈtʲiːnʲæsdʲɛʃɪmt ˈtrʲɪs] |

| 80 eighty | aštúoniasdešimt | [aʃˈtʊɑnʲæsdʲɛʃɪmt] |
| 81 eighty-one | aštúoniasdešimt víenas | [aʃˈtʊɑnʲæsdʲɛʃɪmt ˈvʲiɛnas] |
| 82 eighty-two | aštúoniasdešimt dù | [aʃˈtʊɑnʲæsdʲɛʃɪmt ˈdʊ] |
| 83 eighty-three | aštúoniasdešimt trìs | [aʃˈtʊɑnʲæsdʲɛʃɪmt ˈtrʲɪs] |

| 90 ninety | devýniasdešimt | [dʲɛˈvʲiːnʲæsdʲɛʃɪmt] |
| 91 ninety-one | devýniasdešimt víenas | [dʲɛˈvʲiːnʲæsdʲɛʃɪmt ˈvʲiɛnas] |
| 92 ninety-two | devýniasdešimt dù | [dʲɛˈvʲiːnʲæsdʲɛʃɪmt ˈdʊ] |
| 93 ninety-three | devýniasdešimt trìs | [dʲɛˈvʲiːnʲæsdʲɛʃɪmt ˈtrʲɪs] |

## 8. Cardinal numbers. Part 2

| 100 one hundred | šimtas | [ˈʃɪmtas] |
| 200 two hundred | dù šimtaì | [ˈdʊ ʃɪmˈtʌɪ] |
| 300 three hundred | trìs šimtaì | [ˈtrʲɪs ʃɪmˈtʌɪ] |
| 400 four hundred | keturì šimtaì | [kʲɛtʊˈrʲɪ ʃɪmˈtʌɪ] |
| 500 five hundred | penkì šimtaì | [pʲɛŋˈkʲɪ ʃɪmˈtʌɪ] |

| 600 six hundred | šešì šimtaì | [ʃɛˈʃʲɪ ʃɪmˈtʌɪ] |
| 700 seven hundred | septynì šimtaì | [sʲɛptʲiˈnʲɪ ˈʃɪmtʌɪ] |
| 800 eight hundred | aštuonì šimtaì | [aʃtʊɑˈnʲɪ ʃɪmˈtʌɪ] |
| 900 nine hundred | devynì šimtaì | [dʲɛvʲiːˈnʲɪ ʃɪmˈtʌɪ] |

| 1000 one thousand | tū́kstantis | [ˈtuːkstantʲɪs] |
| 2000 two thousand | dù tū́kstančiai | [ˈdʊ ˈtuːkstantʃʲɛɪ] |
| 3000 three thousand | trỹs tū́kstančiai | [ˈtrʲiːs ˈtuːkstantʃʲɛɪ] |
| 10000 ten thousand | dešimt tū́kstančių | [ˈdʲæʃɪmt ˈtuːkstantʃʲuː] |
| one hundred thousand | šimtas tū́kstančių | [ˈʃɪmtas ˈtuːkstantʃʲuː] |
| million | milijõnas (v) | [mʲɪlʲɪˈjɔːnas] |
| billion | milijárdas (v) | [mʲɪlʲɪˈjardas] |

## 9. Ordinal numbers

| first (adj) | pìrmas | [ˈpʲɪrmas] |
| second (adj) | añtras | [ˈantras] |
| third (adj) | trẽčias | [ˈtrʲætʃʲæs] |
| fourth (adj) | ketvìrtas | [kʲɛtˈvʲɪrtas] |
| fifth (adj) | peñktas | [ˈpʲɛŋktas] |
| sixth (adj) | šẽštas | [ˈʃæʃtas] |

| seventh (adj) | septiñtas | [sʲɛp'tʲɪntas] |
| eighth (adj) | aštuñtas | [aʃ'tuntas] |
| ninth (adj) | deviñtas | [dʲɛ'vʲɪntas] |
| tenth (adj) | dešiṁtas | [dʲɛ'ʃɪmtas] |

# COLOURS. UNITS OF MEASUREMENT

**T&P Books Publishing**

## 10. Colors

| | | |
|---|---|---|
| color | spalvà (m) | [spalʲˈva] |
| shade (tint) | àtspalvis (v) | [ˈaːtspalʲvʲɪs] |
| hue | tònas (v) | [ˈtonas] |
| rainbow | vaivórykštė (m) | [vʌɪˈvorʲiːkʃtʲeː] |
| | | |
| white (adj) | baltà | [balʲˈta] |
| black (adj) | juodà | [jʊɑˈda] |
| gray (adj) | pilkà | [pʲɪlʲˈka] |
| | | |
| green (adj) | žalià | [ʒaˈlʲæ] |
| yellow (adj) | geltóna | [gʲɛlʲˈtona] |
| red (adj) | raudóna | [rɑʊˈdona] |
| blue (adj) | mėlyna | [ˈmʲeːlʲiːna] |
| light blue (adj) | žydrà | [ʒʲiːdˈra] |
| pink (adj) | rõžinė | [ˈroːʒʲɪnʲeː] |
| orange (adj) | oránžinė | [oˈranʒʲɪnʲeː] |
| violet (adj) | violètinė | [vʲɪjoˈlʲɛtʲɪnʲeː] |
| brown (adj) | rudà | [rʊˈda] |
| | | |
| golden (adj) | auksìnis | [ɑʊkˈsʲɪnʲɪs] |
| silvery (adj) | sidabrìnis | [sʲɪdaˈbrʲɪnʲɪs] |
| beige (adj) | smėlio spalvõs | [ˈsmʲeːlʲɔ spalʲˈvoːs] |
| cream (adj) | krėmìnės spalvõs | [ˈkrʲɛmʲɪnʲeːs spalʲˈvoːs] |
| turquoise (adj) | tùrkio spalvõs | [ˈtʊrkʲɔ spalʲˈvoːs] |
| cherry red (adj) | vyšnių spalvõs | [vʲiːʃnʲu spalʲˈvoːs] |
| lilac (adj) | alývų spalvõs | [aˈlʲiːvu spalʲˈvoːs] |
| crimson (adj) | aviẽtinės spalvõs | [aˈvʲɛtʲɪnʲeːs spalʲˈvoːs] |
| | | |
| light (adj) | šviesì | [ʃvʲɛˈsʲɪ] |
| dark (adj) | tamsì | [tamˈsʲɪ] |
| bright, vivid (adj) | ryškì | [rʲiːʃˈkʲɪ] |
| | | |
| colored (pencils) | spalvótas | [spalʲˈvotas] |
| color (e.g., ~ film) | spalvótas | [spalʲˈvotas] |
| black-and-white (adj) | juodaì báltas | [jʊɑˈdʌɪ ˈbalʲtas] |
| plain (one-colored) | vienspálvis | [vʲɪɛnsˈpalʲvʲɪs] |
| multicolored (adj) | įvairiaspálvis | [iːvʌɪrʲæsˈpalʲvʲɪs] |

## 11. Units of measurement

| | | |
|---|---|---|
| weight | svõris (v) | [ˈsvoːrʲɪs] |
| length | ìlgis (v) | [iˈlʲgʲɪs] |

| width | plõtis (v) | ['pl⁰oːt⁰ɪs] |
|---|---|---|
| height | aũkštis (v) | ['ɑʊkʃt⁰ɪs] |
| depth | gỹlis (v) | ['g⁰iːl⁰ɪs] |
| volume | tũris (v) | ['tuːr⁰ɪs] |
| area | plõtas (v) | ['pl⁰otas] |

| gram | grãmas (v) | ['graːmas] |
|---|---|---|
| milligram | miligrãmas (v) | [m⁰ɪl⁰ɪ'graːmas] |
| kilogram | kilogrãmas (v) | [k⁰ɪl⁰o'graːmas] |
| ton | tonà (m) | [to'na] |
| pound | svãras (v) | ['svaːras] |
| ounce | ùncija (m) | ['ʊnts⁰ɪjɛ] |

| meter | mètras (v) | ['m⁰ɛtras] |
|---|---|---|
| millimeter | milimètras (v) | [m⁰ɪl⁰ɪ'm⁰ɛtras] |
| centimeter | centimètras (v) | [ts⁰ɛnt⁰ɪ'm⁰ɛtras] |
| kilometer | kilomètras (v) | [k⁰ɪl⁰o'm⁰ɛtras] |
| mile | mylià (m) | [m⁰iːl⁰æ] |
| inch | cõlis (v) | ['tsol⁰ɪs] |
| foot | pėdà (m) | [p⁰e'da] |
| yard | járdas (v) | [jardas] |

| square meter | kvadrãtinis mètras (v) | [kvad'raːt⁰ɪn⁰ɪs 'm⁰ɛtras] |
|---|---|---|
| hectare | hektãras (v) | [ɣ⁰ɛk'taːras] |
| liter | lìtras (v) | ['l⁰ɪtras] |
| degree | láipsnis (v) | ['l⁰ʌɪpsn⁰ɪs] |
| volt | vòltas (v) | ['vol⁰tas] |
| ampere | ampèras (v) | [am'p⁰ɛras] |
| horsepower | árklio galià (m) | ['arkl⁰ɔ ga'l⁰æ] |

| quantity | kiẽkis (v) | ['k⁰ɛk⁰ɪs] |
|---|---|---|
| a little bit of … | nedaũg … | [n⁰ɛ'dɑʊg …] |
| half | pùsė (m) | ['pʊs⁰eː] |
| dozen | tùzinas (v) | ['tʊz⁰ɪnas] |
| piece (item) | víenetas (v) | ['v⁰ɪɛn⁰ɛtas] |

| size | dỹdis (v), išmatãvimai (v dgs) | ['d⁰iːd⁰ɪs], [iʃma'taːv⁰ɪmʌɪ] |
|---|---|---|
| scale (map ~) | mastēlis (v) | [mas't⁰æl⁰ɪs] |

| minimal (adj) | minimalùs | [m⁰ɪn⁰ɪma'l⁰ʊs] |
|---|---|---|
| the smallest (adj) | mažiáusias | [ma'ʒ⁰æʊs⁰æs] |
| medium (adj) | vidutìnis | [v⁰ɪdu't⁰ɪn⁰ɪs] |
| maximal (adj) | maksimalùs | [maks⁰ɪma'l⁰ʊs] |
| the largest (adj) | didžiáusias | [d⁰ɪ'dʒ⁰æʊs⁰æs] |

## 12. Containers

| canning jar (glass ~) | stiklaĩnis (v) | [st⁰ɪk'l⁰ʌɪn⁰ɪs] |
|---|---|---|
| can | skardìnė (m) | [skar'd⁰ɪn⁰eː] |

| | | |
|---|---|---|
| bucket | **kìbiras** (v) | ['kʲɪbʲɪras] |
| barrel | **statìnė** (m) | [sta'tʲɪnʲe:] |
| | | |
| wash basin (e.g., plastic ~) | **dubenĕlis** (v) | [dʊbe'nʲe:lʲɪs] |
| tank (100L water ~) | **bãkas** (v) | ['ba:kas] |
| hip flask | **kòlba** (m) | ['kolʲba] |
| jerrycan | **kanìstras** (v) | [ka'nʲɪstras] |
| tank (e.g., tank car) | **bãkas** (v) | ['ba:kas] |
| | | |
| mug | **puodĕlis** (v) | [pʊɑ'dʲælʲɪs] |
| cup (of coffee, etc.) | **puodĕlis** (v) | [pʊɑ'dʲælʲɪs] |
| saucer | **lėkštĕlė** (m) | [lʲe:kʃtʲælʲe:] |
| glass (tumbler) | **stìklas** (v) | ['stʲɪklʲas] |
| wine glass | **taurĕ̃** (m) | [taʊ'rʲe:] |
| stock pot (soup pot) | **púodas** (v) | ['pʊɑdas] |
| | | |
| bottle (~ of wine) | **bùtelis** (v) | ['bʊtʲɛlʲɪs] |
| neck (of the bottle, etc.) | **kãklas** (v) | ['ka:klʲas] |
| | | |
| carafe (decanter) | **grafìnas** (v) | [gra'fʲɪnas] |
| pitcher | **ąsõtis** (v) | [a:'so:tʲɪs] |
| vessel (container) | **ìndas** (v) | ['ɪndas] |
| pot (crock, stoneware ~) | **púodas** (v) | ['pʊɑdas] |
| vase | **vazà** (m) | [va'za] |
| | | |
| bottle (perfume ~) | **bùtelis** (v) | ['bʊtʲɛlʲɪs] |
| vial, small bottle | **buteliùkas** (v) | [bʊtʲɛ'lʲʊkas] |
| tube (of toothpaste) | **tūbà** (m) | [tu:'ba] |
| | | |
| sack (bag) | **maĩšas** (v) | ['mʌɪʃas] |
| bag (paper ~, plastic ~) | **pakètas** (v) | [pa'kʲɛtas] |
| pack (of cigarettes, etc.) | **plúoštas** (v) | ['plʲʊɑʃtas] |
| | | |
| box (e.g., shoebox) | **dėžĕ̃** (m) | [dʲe:'ʒʲe:] |
| crate | **dėžĕ̃** (m) | [dʲe:'ʒʲe:] |
| basket | **krepšỹs** (v) | [krʲɛp'ʃʲɪːs] |

# MAIN VERBS

**T&P Books Publishing**

## 13. The most important verbs. Part 1

| | | |
|---|---|---|
| to advise (vt) | patarinéti | [patarˈɪˈnʲeːtʲɪ] |
| to agree (say yes) | sutìkti | [suˈtʲɪktʲɪ] |
| to answer (vi, vt) | atsakýti | [atsaˈkʲiːtʲɪ] |
| to apologize (vi) | atsiprašinéti | [atsʲɪpraʃɪˈnʲeːtʲɪ] |
| to arrive (vi) | atvažiúoti | [atvaˈʒʲuɑtʲɪ] |
| | | |
| to ask (~ oneself) | kláusti | [ˈklʲaʊstʲɪ] |
| to ask (~ sb to do sth) | prašýti | [praˈʃɪːtʲɪ] |
| to be (vi) | bũti | [ˈbuːtʲɪ] |
| | | |
| to be afraid | bijóti | [bʲɪˈjotʲɪ] |
| to be hungry | noréti válgyti | [noˈrʲeːtʲɪ ˈvalʲgʲiːtʲɪ] |
| to be interested in ... | domẽtis | [doˈmʲeːtʲɪs] |
| to be needed | bũti reikalìngu | [ˈbuːtʲɪ rʲɛɪkaˈlʲɪŋgu] |
| to be surprised | stebẽtis | [stɛˈbʲeːtʲɪs] |
| | | |
| to be thirsty | noréti gérti | [noˈrʲeːtʲɪ ˈgʲærtʲɪ] |
| to begin (vt) | pradẽti | [praˈdʲeːtʲɪ] |
| to belong to ... | priklausýti | [prʲɪklʲaʊˈsʲiːtʲɪ] |
| | | |
| to boast (vi) | gìrtis | [ˈgʲɪrtʲɪs] |
| to break (split into pieces) | láužyti | [ˈlʲaʊʒʲiːtʲɪ] |
| | | |
| to call (~ for help) | kviẽsti | [ˈkvʲɛstʲɪ] |
| can (v aux) | galẽti | [gaˈlʲeːtʲɪ] |
| to catch (vt) | gáudyti | [ˈgaʊdʲiːtʲɪ] |
| | | |
| to change (vt) | pakeĩsti | [paˈkʲɛɪstʲɪ] |
| to choose (select) | išsirìnkti | [ɪʃsʲɪˈrʲɪŋktʲɪ] |
| | | |
| to come down (the stairs) | léistis | [ˈlʲɛɪstʲɪs] |
| to compare (vt) | lýginti | [ˈlʲiːgʲɪntʲɪ] |
| to complain (vi, vt) | skùstis | [ˈskuːstʲɪs] |
| to confuse (mix up) | suklýsti | [suˈklʲiːstʲɪ] |
| | | |
| to continue (vt) | tẽsti | [ˈtʲɛːstʲɪ] |
| to control (vt) | kontroliúoti | [kontroˈlʲuɑtʲɪ] |
| | | |
| to cook (dinner) | gamìnti | [gaˈmʲɪntʲɪ] |
| to cost (vt) | kainúoti | [kʌɪˈnuɑtʲɪ] |
| to count (add up) | skaičiúoti | [skʌɪˈtʂʲuɑtʲɪ] |
| to count on ... | tikétis ... | [tʲɪˈkʲeːtʲɪs ...] |
| to create (vt) | sukùrti | [suˈkurtʲɪ] |
| to cry (weep) | ver̃kti | [ˈvʲɛrktʲɪ] |

## 14. The most important verbs. Part 2

| to deceive (vi, vt) | apgaudinéti | [apgaud'ı'n'e:t'ı] |
| to decorate (tree, street) | puóšti | ['puaʃt'ı] |
| to defend (a country, etc.) | gìnti | ['g'ınt'ı] |
| to demand (request firmly) | reikaláuti | [r'ɛıka'l'aut'ı] |
| to dig (vt) | raũsti | ['raust'ı] |

| to discuss (vt) | aptarinéti | [aptar'ı'n'æt'ı] |
| to do (vt) | darýti | [da'r'i:t'ı] |
| to doubt (have doubts) | abejóti | [ab'ɛ'jot'ı] |
| to drop (let fall) | numèsti | [nu'm'ɛst'ı] |
| to enter (room, house, etc.) | įeĩti | [i:'ɛıt'ı] |

| to excuse (forgive) | atléisti | [at'l'ɛıst'ı] |
| to exist (vi) | egzistúoti | [ɛgz'ıs'tuat'ı] |
| to expect (foresee) | numatýti | [numa't'i:t'ı] |

| to explain (vt) | paaĩškinti | [pa'ʌıʃk'ınt'ı] |
| to fall (vi) | krìsti | ['kr'ıst'ı] |

| to find (vt) | ràsti | ['rast'ı] |
| to finish (vt) | užbaĩgti | [uʒ'bʌıkt'ı] |
| to fly (vi) | skrìsti | ['skr'ıst'ı] |

| to follow ... (come after) | sèkti ... | ['s'ɛkt'ı ...] |
| to forget (vi, vt) | užmĩršti | [uʒ'm'ırʃt'ı] |

| to forgive (vt) | atléisti | [at'l'ɛıst'ı] |
| to give (vt) | dúoti | ['duat'ı] |

| to give a hint | užsimiñti | [uʒs'ı'm'ınt'ı] |
| to go (on foot) | eĩti | ['ɛıt'ı] |

| to go for a swim | máudytis | ['maud'i:t'ıs] |
| to go out (for dinner, etc.) | išeĩti | [ı'ʃɛıt'ı] |
| to guess (the answer) | atspéti | [at'sp'e:t'ı] |

| to have (vt) | turéti | [tu'r'e:t'ı] |
| to have breakfast | pùsryčiauti | ['pusr'ı:tʃ'ɛut'ı] |
| to have dinner | vakarieniáuti | [vakar'ıɛ'n'æut'ı] |

| to have lunch | pietáuti | [p'ıɛ'taut'ı] |
| to hear (vt) | girdéti | [g'ır'd'e:t'ı] |

| to help (vt) | padéti | [pa'd'e:t'ı] |
| to hide (vt) | slépti | ['sl'e:pt'ı] |
| to hope (vi, vt) | tikétis | [t'ı'k'e:t'ıs] |
| to hunt (vi, vt) | medžióti | [m'ɛ'dʒ'ot'ı] |
| to hurry (vi) | skubéti | [sku'b'e:t'ı] |

## 15. The most important verbs. Part 3

| | | |
|---|---|---|
| to inform (vt) | informúoti | [ɪnfor'muɑtʲɪ] |
| to insist (vi, vt) | reikaláuti | [rʲɛɪka'lʲɑutʲɪ] |
| to insult (vt) | įžeidinéti | [i:ʒʲɛɪdʲɪ'nʲe:tʲɪ] |
| to invite (vt) | kviẽsti | ['kvʲɛstʲɪ] |
| to joke (vi) | juokáuti | [juɑ'kɑutʲɪ] |
| | | |
| to keep (vt) | sáugoti | ['sɑugotʲɪ] |
| to keep silent | tyléti | [tʲi:'lʲe:tʲɪ] |
| to kill (vt) | žudýti | [ʒu'dʲi:tʲɪ] |
| to know (sb) | pažinóti | [paʒɪ'notʲɪ] |
| to know (sth) | žinóti | [ʒɪ'notʲɪ] |
| to laugh (vi) | juõktis | ['juɑktʲɪs] |
| | | |
| to liberate (city, etc.) | išláisvinti | [ɪʃʲlʲʌɪsvʲɪntʲɪ] |
| to like (I like ...) | patìkti | [pa'tʲɪktʲɪ] |
| to look for ... (search) | ieškóti | [ɪɛʃ'kotʲɪ] |
| to love (sb) | myléti | [mʲi:'lʲe:tʲɪ] |
| to make a mistake | klýsti | ['klʲi:stʲɪ] |
| to manage, to run | vadováuti | [vado'vɑutʲɪ] |
| to mean (signify) | reĩkšti | ['rʲɛɪkʃtʲɪ] |
| to mention (talk about) | minéti | [mʲɪ'nʲe:tʲɪ] |
| to miss (school, etc.) | praleidinéti | [pralʲɛɪdʲɪ'nʲe:tʲɪ] |
| to notice (see) | pastebéti | [paste'bʲe:tʲɪ] |
| | | |
| to object (vi, vt) | prieštaráuti | [prʲɪɛʃta'rɑutʲɪ] |
| to observe (see) | stebéti | [ste'bʲe:tʲɪ] |
| to open (vt) | atidarýti | [atɪda'rʲi:tʲɪ] |
| to order (meal, etc.) | užsakinéti | [uʒsakʲɪ'nʲe:tʲɪ] |
| to order (mil.) | nurodinéti | [nurodʲɪ'nʲe:tʲɪ] |
| to own (possess) | mokéti | [mo'kʲe:tʲɪ] |
| to participate (vi) | dalyváuti | [dalʲi:'vɑutʲɪ] |
| to pay (vi, vt) | mokéti | [mo'kʲe:tʲɪ] |
| to permit (vt) | léisti | ['lʲɛɪstʲɪ] |
| to plan (vt) | planúoti | [plʲa'nuɑtʲɪ] |
| to play (children) | žaĩsti | ['ʒʌɪstʲɪ] |
| | | |
| to pray (vi, vt) | meĩstis | ['mʲɛɪ̃stʲɪs] |
| to prefer (vt) | teĩkti pirmenýbę | ['tʲɛɪktʲɪ pʲɪrmʲɛ'nʲi:bʲɛ:] |
| to promise (vt) | žadéti | [ʒa'dʲe:tʲɪ] |
| to pronounce (vt) | ištãrti | [ɪʃ'tartʲɪ] |
| to propose (vt) | siúlyti | ['sʲu:lʲi:tʲɪ] |
| to punish (vt) | baũsti | ['bɑustʲɪ] |

## 16. The most important verbs. Part 4

| | | |
|---|---|---|
| to read (vi, vt) | skaitýti | [skʌɪ'tʲi:tʲɪ] |
| to recommend (vt) | rekomendúoti | [rʲɛkomʲɛn'duɑtʲɪ] |

| | | |
|---|---|---|
| to refuse (vi, vt) | atsisakýti | [atsʲɪsaˈkʲiːtʲɪ] |
| to regret (be sorry) | gailétis | [gʌɪˈlʲeːtʲɪs] |
| to rent (sth from sb) | núomotis | [ˈnʊɑmotʲɪs] |
| | | |
| to repeat (say again) | kartóti | [karˈtotʲɪ] |
| to reserve, to book | rezervúoti | [rʲɛzʲɛrˈvʊɑtʲɪ] |
| to run (vi) | bégti | [ˈbʲeːktʲɪ] |
| to save (rescue) | gélbéti | [ˈgʲælʲbʲeːtʲɪ] |
| to say (~ thank you) | pasakýti | [pasaˈkʲiːtʲɪ] |
| | | |
| to scold (vt) | bárti | [ˈbartʲɪ] |
| to see (vt) | matýti | [maˈtʲiːtʲɪ] |
| to sell (vt) | pardavinéti | [pardavʲɪˈnʲeːtʲɪ] |
| to send (vt) | išsiųsti | [ɪʃˈsʲuːstʲɪ] |
| to shoot (vi) | šáudyti | [ˈʃɑʊdʲiːtʲɪ] |
| | | |
| to shout (vi) | šaūkti | [ˈʃɑʊktʲɪ] |
| to show (vt) | ródyti | [ˈrodʲiːtʲɪ] |
| to sign (document) | pasirašinéti | [pasʲɪraʃʲɪˈnʲeːtʲɪ] |
| to sit down (vi) | séstis | [ˈsʲeːstʲɪs] |
| | | |
| to smile (vi) | šypsótis | [ʃɪːpˈsotʲɪs] |
| to speak (vi, vt) | sakýti | [saˈkʲiːtʲɪ] |
| to steal (money, etc.) | võgti | [ˈvoːktʲɪ] |
| to stop (for pause, etc.) | sustóti | [sʊsˈtotʲɪ] |
| to stop (please ~ calling me) | nustóti | [nʊˈstotʲɪ] |
| | | |
| to study (vt) | studijúoti | [stʊdʲɪˈjʊɑtʲɪ] |
| to swim (vi) | plaūkti | [ˈplʲɑʊktʲɪ] |
| to take (vt) | imti | [ˈɪmtʲɪ] |
| to think (vi, vt) | galvóti | [galʲˈvotʲɪ] |
| to threaten (vt) | grasinti | [graˈsʲɪntʲɪ] |
| | | |
| to touch (with hands) | čiupinéti | [tʃʲʊpʲɪˈnʲeːtʲɪ] |
| to translate (vt) | versti | [ˈvʲɛrstʲɪ] |
| to trust (vt) | pasitikéti | [pasʲɪtʲɪˈkʲeːtʲɪ] |
| to try (attempt) | bandýti | [banˈdʲiːtʲɪ] |
| to turn (e.g., ~ left) | sùkti | [ˈsʊktʲɪ] |
| | | |
| to underestimate (vt) | neįvértinti | [nʲɛɪːˈvʲɛrtʲɪntʲɪ] |
| to understand (vt) | supràsti | [sʊpˈrastʲɪ] |
| to unite (vt) | apjùngti | [aˈpjʊŋktʲɪ] |
| to wait (vt) | laukti | [ˈlʲɑʊktʲɪ] |
| | | |
| to want (wish, desire) | noréti | [noˈrʲeːtʲɪ] |
| to warn (vt) | pérspéti | [ˈpʲɛrspʲeːtʲɪ] |
| to work (vi) | dìrbti | [ˈdʲɪrptʲɪ] |
| to write (vt) | rašýti | [raˈʃɪːtʲɪ] |
| to write down | užrašinéti | [ʊʒraʃʲɪˈnʲeːtʲɪ] |

# TIME. CALENDAR

**T&P Books Publishing**

| Monday | **pirmãdienis** (v) | [pʲɪrˈmaːdʲiɛnʲɪs] |
| Tuesday | **antrãdienis** (v) | [anˈtraːdʲiɛnʲɪs] |
| Wednesday | **trečiãdienis** (v) | [trʲɛˈtʂʲædʲiɛnʲɪs] |
| Thursday | **ketvirtãdienis** (v) | [kʲɛtvʲɪrˈtaːdʲiɛnʲɪs] |
| Friday | **penktãdienis** (v) | [pʲɛŋkˈtaːdʲiɛnʲɪs] |
| Saturday | **šeštãdienis** (v) | [ʃɛʃˈtaːdʲiɛnʲɪs] |
| Sunday | **sekmãdienis** (v) | [sʲɛkˈmaːdʲiɛnʲɪs] |

| today (adv) | **šiañdien** | [ˈʃændʲiɛn] |
| tomorrow (adv) | **rytój** | [rʲiːˈtoj] |
| the day after tomorrow | **porýt** | [poˈrʲiːt] |
| yesterday (adv) | **vãkar** | [ˈvaːkar] |
| the day before yesterday | **ùžvakar** | [ˈʊʒvakar] |

| day | **dienà** (m) | [dʲiɛˈna] |
| working day | **dárbo dienà** (m) | [ˈdarbo dʲiɛˈna] |
| public holiday | **šveñtinė dienà** (m) | [ˈʃvʲɛntʲɪnʲeː dʲiɛˈna] |
| day off | **išeiginė dienà** (m) | [ɪʃɛɪˈgʲɪnʲeː dʲiɛˈna] |
| weekend | **savaitgalis** (v) | [saˈvʌɪtgalʲɪs] |

| all day long | **vìsą diẽną** | [ˈvʲɪsa ˈdʲɛna] |
| the next day (adv) | **sẽkančią diẽną** | [ˈsʲɛkantʂʲæ ˈdʲɛna] |
| two days ago | **priẽš dvì dienàs** | [ˈprʲɛʃ ˈdvʲɪ dʲiɛˈnas] |
| the day before | **išvakarėse** | [ˈɪʃvakarʲeˑse] |
| daily (adj) | **kasdiẽnis** | [kasˈdʲɛnʲɪs] |
| every day (adv) | **kasdiẽn** | [kasˈdʲɛn] |

| week | **savaĩtė** (m) | [saˈvʌɪtʲeˑ] |
| last week (adv) | **prãeitą savaĩtę** | [ˈpraˈɛɪta saˈvʌɪtʲɛ] |
| next week (adv) | **ateĩnančią savaĩtę** | [aˈtʲɛɪnantʂʲæ saˈvʌɪtʲɛ] |
| weekly (adj) | **kassavaĩtinis** | [kassaˈvʌɪtʲɪnʲɪs] |
| every week (adv) | **kàs savaĩtę** | [ˈkas saˈvʌɪtʲɛ] |
| twice a week | **dù kartùs peŕ savaĩtę** | [ˈdʊ karˈtʊs pʲɛr saˈvʌɪtʲɛ] |
| every Tuesday | **kiekvíeną antrãdienį** | [kʲiɛkˈvʲiɛna anˈtraːdʲɪːɛnʲɪː] |

| morning | **rýtas** (v) | [ˈrʲiːtas] |
| in the morning | **rytè** | [rʲiːˈtʲɛ] |
| noon, midday | **vidùrdienis** (v) | [vʲɪˈdurdʲiɛnʲɪs] |
| in the afternoon | **popiẽt** | [poˈpʲɛt] |
| evening | **vãkaras** (v) | [ˈvaːkaras] |

| in the evening | vakarė | [vaka'rʲɛ] |
| night | naktìs (m) | [nak'tʲɪs] |
| at night | nãktį | ['na:kti:] |
| midnight | vidùrnaktis (v) | [vʲɪ'dʊrnaktʲɪs] |

| second | sekùndė (m) | [sʲɛ'kʊndʲe:] |
| minute | minùtė (m) | [mʲɪ'nʊtʲe:] |
| hour | valandà (m) | [valʲan'da] |
| half an hour | pùsvalandis (v) | ['pʊsvalʲandʲɪs] |
| a quarter-hour | ketvìrtis valandõs | [kʲɛt'vʲɪrtʲɪs valʲan'do:s] |
| fifteen minutes | penkiólika minùčių | [pʲɛŋ'kʲɔlʲɪka mʲɪ'nʊtʂʲuːʲ] |
| 24 hours | parà (m) | [pa'ra] |

| sunrise | sáulės patekėjimas (v) | ['sɑulʲe:s patʲɛ'kʲɛjɪmas] |
| dawn | aušrà (m) | [ɑuʃ'ra] |
| early morning | ankstývas rýtas (v) | [aŋk'stʲi:vas 'rʲi:tas] |
| sunset | saulėlydis (v) | [sɑu'lʲe:lʲi:dʲɪs] |

| early in the morning | ankstì rytè | [aŋk'stʲɪ rʲi:'tʲɛ] |
| this morning | šiañdien rytè | ['ʃændʲiɛn rʲi:'tʲɛ] |
| tomorrow morning | rytój rytè | [rʲi:'toj rʲi:'tʲɛ] |

| this afternoon | šiañdien diẽną | ['ʃæn'dʲɛn 'dʲiɛna:] |
| in the afternoon | popiẽt | [po'pʲɛt] |
| tomorrow afternoon | rytój popiẽt | [rʲi:'toj po'pʲɛt] |

| tonight (this evening) | šiañdien vakarè | ['ʃændʲiɛn vaka'rʲɛ] |
| tomorrow night | rytój vakarè | [rʲi:'toj vaka'rʲɛ] |

| at 3 o'clock sharp | lýgiai trẽčią vãlandą | ['lʲi:gʲɛɪ 'trʲætʂʲæ: 'va:landa:] |
| about 4 o'clock | apiẽ ketvìrtą vãlandą | [a'pʲɛ kʲɛtvʲɪrta: va:lʲanda:] |
| by 12 o'clock | dvýliktai vãlandai | ['dvʲi:lʲɪktʌɪ 'va:landʌɪ] |

| in 20 minutes | ùž dvìdešimtiẽs minùčių | ['ʊʒ dvʲɪdʲɛʃɪm'tʲɛs mʲɪ'nʊtʂʲuː] |

| in an hour | ùž valandõs | ['ʊʒ valʲan'do:s] |
| on time (adv) | laikù | [lʲʌɪ'kʊ] |

| a quarter of … | bè ketvìrčio | ['bʲɛ 'kʲɛtvʲɪrtʂʲɔ] |
| within an hour | valandõs bė́gyje | [valʲan'do:s 'bʲɛ:gʲi:je] |
| every 15 minutes | kàs penkiólika minùčių | ['kas pʲɛŋ'kʲɔlʲɪka mʲɪ'nʊtʂʲuː] |

| round the clock | vìsą pãrą (m) | ['vʲɪsa: 'pa:ra:] |

## 19. Months. Seasons

| January | saũsis (v) | ['sɑusʲɪs] |
| February | vasãris (v) | [va'sa:rʲɪs] |
| March | kovàs (v) | [kɔ'vas] |
| April | balañdis (v) | [ba'lʲandʲɪs] |

| May | **gegužė** (m) | [gʲɛgʊ'ʒʲeː] |
| June | **birželis** (v) | [bʲɪr'ʒʲælʲɪs] |

| July | **líepa** (m) | ['lʲiɛpa] |
| August | **rugpjūtis** (v) | [rʊg'pjuːtʲɪs] |
| September | **rugsėjis** (v) | [rʊg'sʲɛjɪs] |
| October | **spãlis** (v) | ['spa:lʲɪs] |
| November | **lãpkritis** (v) | ['lʲa:pkrʲɪtʲɪs] |
| December | **grúodis** (v) | ['grʊadʲɪs] |

| spring | **pavãsaris** (v) | [pa'va:sarʲɪs] |
| in spring | **pavãsarį** | [pa'va:sarʲɪː] |
| spring (as adj) | **pavasarìnis** | [pavasa'rʲɪnʲɪs] |

| summer | **vãsara** (m) | ['va:sara] |
| in summer | **vãsarą** | ['va:sara:] |
| summer (as adj) | **vasarìnis** | [vasa'rʲɪnʲɪs] |

| fall | **ruduõ** (v) | [rʊ'dʊɑ] |
| in fall | **rùdenį** | ['rʊdʲɛnʲɪː] |
| fall (as adj) | **rudenìnis** | [rʊdʲɛ'nʲɪnʲɪs] |

| winter | **žiemà** (m) | [ʒʲiɛ'ma] |
| in winter | **žiẽmą** | ['ʒʲɛma:] |
| winter (as adj) | **žiemìnis** | [ʒʲiɛ'mʲɪnʲɪs] |

| month | **ménuo** (v) | ['mʲe:nʊɑ] |
| this month | **šį̃ ménesį** | [ʃɪː 'mʲe:nesʲɪː] |
| next month | **kìtą ménesį** | ['kʲɪːta: 'mʲe:nesʲɪː] |
| last month | **praèitą ménesį** | ['pra:ɛɪta: 'mʲe:nesʲɪː] |

| a month ago | **priẽš ménesį** | ['prʲɪːɛʃ 'mʲe:nesʲɪː] |
| in a month (a month later) | **už ménesio** | ['ʊʒ 'mʲe:nesʲɔ] |
| in 2 months (2 months later) | **už dvejų̃ ménesių** | ['ʊʒ dve'ju: 'mʲe:nesʲu:] |
| the whole month | **vìsą ménesį** | ['vʲɪsa: 'mʲe:nesʲɪː] |
| all month long | **vìsą ménesį** | ['vʲɪsa: 'mʲe:nesʲɪː] |

| monthly (~ magazine) | **kasménesìnis** | [kasmʲe:ne'sʲɪnʲɪs] |
| monthly (adv) | **kàs ménesį** | ['kas 'mʲe:nesʲɪː] |
| every month | **kiekvíeną ménesį** | [kʲiɛk'vʲiːɛna: 'mʲe:nesʲɪː] |
| twice a month | **dù kartùs peř ménesį** | ['dʊ kar'tʊs per 'mʲe:nesʲɪː] |

| year | **métai** (v dgs) | ['mʲætʌɪ] |
| this year | **šiaĩs métais** | ['ʃʲɛɪs 'mʲætʌɪs] |
| next year | **kitaĩs métais** | [kʲɪ'tʌɪs 'mʲætʌɪs] |
| last year | **praeitaĩs métais** | [pra:ɛɪ'tʌɪs 'mʲætʌɪs] |

| a year ago | **priẽš metùs** | ['prʲɛʃ mʲɛ'tʊs] |
| in a year | **už métų** | ['ʊʒ 'mʲætu:] |
| in two years | **už dvejų̃ métų** | ['ʊʒ dvʲɛ'ju: 'mʲætu:] |
| the whole year | **visùs metùs** | [vʲɪ'sʊs mʲɛ'tʊs] |

| | | |
|---|---|---|
| all year long | **visus metus** | [vʲɪ'sʊs mʲɛ'tʊs] |
| every year | **kas metus** | ['kas mʲɛ'tʊs] |
| annual (adj) | **kasmetinis** | [kasmʲɛ'tʲɪnʲɪs] |
| annually (adv) | **kas metus** | ['kas mʲɛ'tʊs] |
| 4 times a year | **keturis kartus** **per metus** | ['kʲætʊrʲɪs kar'tʊs pʲɛr mʲɛ'tʊs] |
| date (e.g., today's ~) | **diena** (m) | [dʲiɛ'na] |
| date (e.g., ~ of birth) | **data** (m) | [da'ta] |
| calendar | **kalendorius** (v) | [kalʲɛn'doːrʲʊs] |
| half a year | **pusė metų** | ['pʊsʲɛ: 'mʲætuː] |
| six months | **pusmetis** (v) | ['pʊsmʲɛtʲɪs] |
| season (summer, etc.) | **sezonas** (v) | [sʲɛ'zonas] |
| century | **amžius** (v) | ['amʒʲʊs] |

# TRAVEL. HOTEL

**T&P Books Publishing**

| | | |
|---|---|---|
| tourism, travel | turizmas (v) | [tʊ'rʲɪzmas] |
| tourist | turistas (v) | [tʊ'rʲɪstas] |
| trip, voyage | kelionė (m) | [kʲɛ'lʲoːnʲeː] |
| adventure | nuotykis (v) | ['nʊatʲiːkʲɪs] |
| trip, journey | išvyka (m) | ['ɪʃvʲiːka] |
| | | |
| vacation | atostogos (m dgs) | [a'tostogos] |
| to be on vacation | atostogauti | [atosto'gaʊtʲɪ] |
| rest | poilsis (v) | ['poɪlʲsʲɪs] |
| | | |
| train | traukinỹs (v) | [traʊkʲɪ'nʲiːs] |
| by train | traukiniu | ['traʊkʲɪnʲʊ] |
| airplane | lėktuvas (v) | [lʲeːk'tʊvas] |
| by airplane | lėktuvu | [lʲeːktʊ'vʊ] |
| by car | automobiliu | [aʊtomobʲɪ'lʲʊ] |
| by ship | laivu | [lʲʌɪ'vʊ] |
| | | |
| luggage | bagažas (v) | [ba'gaːʒas] |
| suitcase | lagaminas (v) | [lʲaga'mʲɪnas] |
| luggage cart | bagažo vežimėlis (v) | [ba'gaːʒɔ veʒʲɪ'mʲeːlʲɪs] |
| passport | pasas (v) | ['paːsas] |
| visa | viza (m) | [vʲɪ'za] |
| ticket | bilietas (v) | ['bʲɪlʲiɛtas] |
| air ticket | lėktuvo bilietas (v) | [lʲeːk'tʊvɔ 'bʲɪlʲiɛtas] |
| | | |
| guidebook | vadovas (v) | [va'doːvas] |
| map (tourist ~) | žemėlapis (v) | [ʒe'mʲeːlʲapʲɪs] |
| area (rural ~) | vietovė (m) | [vʲiɛ'tovʲeː] |
| place, site | vieta (m) | [vʲiɛ'ta] |
| | | |
| exotica (n) | egzotika (m) | [ɛg'zotʲɪka] |
| exotic (adj) | egzotinis | [ɛg'zotʲɪnʲɪs] |
| amazing (adj) | nuostabus | [nʊasta'bʊs] |
| | | |
| group | grupė (m) | ['grʊpʲeː] |
| excursion, sightseeing tour | ekskursija (m) | [ɛks'kʊrsʲɪjɛ] |
| guide (person) | ekskursijos vadovas (v) | [ɛks'kʊrsʲɪjɔs va'doːvas] |

| | | |
|---|---|---|
| hotel | viešbutis (v) | ['vʲɛʃbʊtʲɪs] |
| motel | motelis (v) | [mo'tʲɛlʲɪs] |

| | | |
|---|---|---|
| three-star (~ hotel) | **3 žvaigždùtės** | ['trʲɪs ʒvʌɪgʒ'dutʲe:s] |
| five-star | **5 žvaigždùtės** | ['penʲkʲos ʒvʌɪgʒ'dutʲe:s] |
| to stay (in a hotel, etc.) | **apsistóti** | [apsʲɪs'totʲɪ] |

| | | |
|---|---|---|
| room | **kambarỹs** (v) | [kamba'rʲi:s] |
| single room | **vienviẽtis kambarỹs** (v) | ['vʲiɛn'vʲɛtʲɪs kamba'rʲi:s] |
| double room | **dviviẽtis kambarỹs** (v) | [dvʲɪ'vʲɛtʲɪs kamba'rʲi:s] |
| to book a room | **rezervúoti kam̃barį** | [rʲɛzʲɛr'vuɑtʲɪ 'kambarʲɪ:] |

| | | |
|---|---|---|
| half board | **pusiáu pensiònas** (v) | [pusʲæʊ pʲɛnsʲɪ'jɔnas] |
| full board | **pensiònas** (v) | [pʲɛnsʲɪ'jɔnas] |

| | | |
|---|---|---|
| with bath | **sù vonià** | ['su vo'nʲæ] |
| with shower | **sù dušù** | ['su du'ʃu] |
| satellite television | **palydóvinė televìzija** (m) | [palʲi:'do:vʲɪnʲe: tʲɛlʲɛ'vʲɪzʲɪjɛ] |
| air-conditioner | **kondicioniẽrius** (v) | [kɔndʲɪtsʲɪjo'nʲɛrʲus] |
| towel | **rañkšluostis** (v) | ['raŋkʃlʲuɑstʲɪs] |
| key | **rãktas** (v) | ['ra:ktas] |

| | | |
|---|---|---|
| administrator | **administrãtorius** (v) | [admʲɪnʲɪs'tra:torʲus] |
| chambermaid | **kambarìnė** (m) | [kamba'rʲɪnʲe:] |
| porter, bellboy | **nešìkas** (v) | [nʲɛ'ʃɪkas] |
| doorman | **registrãtorius** (v) | [rʲɛgʲɪs'tra:torʲus] |

| | | |
|---|---|---|
| restaurant | **restorãnas** (v) | [rʲɛsto'ra:nas] |
| pub, bar | **bãras** (v) | ['ba:ras] |
| breakfast | **pùsryčiai** (v dgs) | ['pusrʲi:tʂʲɛɪ] |
| dinner | **vakariẽnė** (m) | [vaka'rʲɛnʲe:] |
| buffet | **švẽdiškas stãlas** (v) | ['ʃvʲɛdʲɪʃkas 'sta:lʲas] |

| | | |
|---|---|---|
| lobby | **vestibiùlis** (v) | [vʲɛstʲɪ'bʲulʲɪs] |
| elevator | **lìftas** (v) | ['lʲɪftas] |

| | | |
|---|---|---|
| DO NOT DISTURB | **NETRUKDÝTI** | [nʲɛtrʊk'dʲi:tʲɪ] |
| NO SMOKING | **NERŪKÝTI!** | [nʲɛru:'kʲi:tʲɪ] |

## 22. Sightseeing

| | | |
|---|---|---|
| monument | **pamiñklas** (v) | [pa'mʲɪŋklʲas] |
| fortress | **tvirtóvė** (m) | [tvʲɪr'tovʲe:] |
| palace | **rū́mai** (v) | ['ru:mʌɪ] |
| castle | **pilìs** (m) | [pʲɪ'lʲɪs] |
| tower | **bókštas** (v) | ['bokʃtas] |
| mausoleum | **mauzoliẽjus** (v) | [mɑʊzo'lʲɛjus] |

| | | |
|---|---|---|
| architecture | **architektū́ra** (m) | [arxʲɪtʲɛktu:'ra] |
| medieval (adj) | **vidùramžių** | [vʲɪ'durɑmʒʲu:] |
| ancient (adj) | **senóvinis** | [sʲɛ'novʲɪnʲɪs] |
| national (adj) | **nacionãlinis** | [natsʲɪjo'na:lʲɪnʲɪs] |
| famous (monument, etc.) | **žymùs** | [ʒʲi:'mus] |

| | | |
|---|---|---|
| tourist | **turìstas** (v) | [tʊˈrʲɪstas] |
| guide (person) | **gìdas** (v) | [ˈɡʲɪdas] |
| excursion, sightseeing tour | **ekskùrsija** (m) | [ɛksˈkʊrsʲɪjɛ] |
| to show (vt) | **ródyti** | [ˈrodʲiːtʲɪ] |
| to tell (vt) | **pãsakoti** | [ˈpaːsakotʲɪ] |
| | | |
| to find (vt) | **ràsti** | [ˈrastʲɪ] |
| to get lost (lose one's way) | **pasiklýsti** | [pasʲɪˈklʲiːstʲɪ] |
| map (e.g., subway ~) | **schemà** (m) | [sxʲɛˈma] |
| map (e.g., city ~) | **plãnas** (v) | [ˈplʲaːnas] |
| | | |
| souvenir, gift | **suvenỹras** (v) | [sʊvʲɛˈnʲiːras] |
| gift shop | **suvenỹrų parduotùvė** (m) | [sʊveˈnʲiːruː pardʊɑˈtʊvʲeː] |
| to take pictures | **fotografúoti** | [fotograˈfʊɑtʲɪ] |
| to have one's picture taken | **fotografúotis** | [fotograˈfʊɑtʲɪs] |

# TRANSPORTATION

**T&P Books Publishing**

| | | |
|---|---|---|
| airport | óro úostas (v) | ['orɔ 'ʊastas] |
| airplane | lėktùvas (v) | [lʲe:k'tʊvas] |
| airline | aviakompãnija (m) | [avʲæːkom'paːnʲɪjɛ] |
| air traffic controller | dispèčeris (v) | [dʲɪs'pʲɛtʂʲɛrʲɪs] |
| departure | išskridìmas (v) | [ɪʃskrʲɪ'dʲɪmas] |
| arrival | atskridìmas (v) | [atskrʲɪ'dʲɪmas] |
| to arrive (by plane) | atskrìsti | [ats'krʲɪstʲɪ] |
| departure time | išvykìmo laĩkas (v) | [ɪʃvʲi:'kʲɪmɔ 'lʲʌɪkas] |
| arrival time | atvykìmo laĩkas (v) | [atvʲi:'kʲɪmɔ 'lʲʌɪkas] |
| to be delayed | vėlúoti | [vʲe:'lʲʊatʲɪ] |
| flight delay | skrỹdžio atidėjìmas (v) | ['skrʲiːdʒʲɔ atʲɪdʲe:'jɪmas] |
| information board | informãcinė šviēslentė (m) | [ɪnfor'maːtsʲɪnʲe: 'ʃvʲɛslʲɛntʲe:] |
| information | informãcija (m) | [ɪnfor'maːtsʲɪjɛ] |
| to announce (vt) | paskélbti | [pas'kʲɛlʲptʲɪ] |
| flight (e.g., next ~) | reĩsas (v) | ['rʲɛɪsas] |
| customs | muĩtinė (m) | ['mʊɪtʲɪnʲe:] |
| customs officer | muĩtininkas (v) | ['mʊɪtʲɪnʲɪŋkas] |
| customs declaration | deklarãcija (m) | [dʲɛklʲa'raːtsʲɪjɛ] |
| to fill out (vt) | užpìldyti | [ʊʒ'pʲɪlʲdʲiːtʲɪ] |
| to fill out the declaration | užpìldyti deklarãciją | [ʊʒ'pʲɪlʲdʲiːtʲɪ dʲɛklʲa'raːtsɪjaː] |
| passport control | pasų̃ kontrolė (m) | [pa'suː kon'trolʲe:] |
| luggage | bagãžas (v) | [ba'gaːʒas] |
| hand luggage | rañkinis bagãžas (v) | ['raŋkʲɪnʲɪs ba'gaːʒas] |
| luggage cart | vežimė̃lis (v) | [vʲɛʒʲɪ'mʲe:lʲɪs] |
| landing | įlaipìnimas (v) | [i:lʲʌɪ'pʲɪːnʲɪmas] |
| landing strip | nusileidìmo tãkas (v) | [nʊsʲɪlʲɛɪ'dʲɪmɔ taːkas] |
| to land (vi) | léistis | ['lʲɛɪstʲɪs] |
| airstairs | laiptẽliai (v dgs) | [lʌɪp'tʲælʲɛɪ] |
| check-in | registrãcija (m) | [rʲɛgʲɪs'traːtsʲɪjɛ] |
| check-in counter | registrãcijos stãlas (v) | [rʲɛgʲɪs'traːtsʲɪjɔs 'staːlʲas] |
| to check-in (vi) | užsiregistrúoti | [ʊʒsʲɪrʲɛgʲɪs'trʊatʲɪ] |
| boarding pass | įlipìmo talõnas (v) | [i:lʲɪ'pʲɪːmɔ ta'lonas] |
| departure gate | išėjìmas (v) | [ɪʃe:'jɪmas] |
| transit | tranzìtas (v) | [tran'zʲɪtas] |

| to wait (vt) | láukti | ['lʲaʊktʲɪ] |
| departure lounge | laukiamàsis (v) | [lʲaʊkʲæ'masʲɪs] |
| to see off | lydéti | [lʲiː'dʲeːtʲɪ] |
| to say goodbye | atsisvéikinti | [atsʲɪ'svʲɛɪkʲɪntʲɪ] |

## 24. Airplane

| airplane | léktùvas (v) | [lʲeːk'tʊvas] |
| air ticket | léktùvo bìlietas (v) | [lʲeːk'tʊvo 'bʲɪlʲiɛtas] |
| airline | aviakompãnija (m) | [avʲækom'paːnʲɪjɛ] |
| airport | óro úostas (v) | ['orɔ 'ʊastas] |
| supersonic (adj) | viršgarsìnis | [vʲɪrʃgar'sʲɪnʲɪs] |

| captain | órlaivio kapitõnas (v) | ['orlʲʌɪvʲɔ kapʲɪ'toːnas] |
| crew | ekipãžas (v) | [ɛkʲɪ'paːʒas] |
| pilot | pilòtas (v) | [pʲɪ'lʲotas] |
| flight attendant (fem.) | stiuardésé (m) | [stʲʊar'dʲɛsʲeː] |
| navigator | štùrmanas (v) | ['ʃtʊrmanas] |

| wings | sparnaî (v dgs) | [spar'nʌɪ] |
| tail | gãlas (v) | ['gaːlʲas] |
| cockpit | kabinà (m) | [kabʲɪ'na] |
| engine | varìklis (v) | [va'rʲɪklʲɪs] |
| undercarriage | važiuõklé (m) | [vaʒʲʊ'oːklʲeː] |
| (landing gear) | | |
| turbine | turbinà (m) | [tʊrbʲɪ'na] |

| propeller | propèleris (v) | [pro'pʲɛlʲɛrʲɪs] |
| black box | juodà dèžé (m) | [jʊa'da dʲeːʒʲeː] |
| yoke (control column) | vairãratis (v) | [vʌɪ'raːratʲɪs] |
| fuel | degalaî (v dgs) | [dʲɛga'lʲʌɪ] |

| safety card | instrùkcija (m) | [ɪns'trʊktsʲɪjɛ] |
| oxygen mask | deguõnies káuké (m) | [dʲɛgʊa'nʲiɛs 'kaʊkʲeː] |
| uniform | unifórma (m) | [ʊnʲɪ'forma] |
| life vest | gélbéjimosi liemèné (m) | ['gʲælʲbʲeːjimosʲɪ lʲiɛ'mʲænʲeː] |

| parachute | parašiùtas (v) | [para'ʃʊtas] |

| takeoff | kilìmas (v) | [kʲɪ'lʲɪmas] |
| to take off (vi) | kìlti | ['kʲɪlʲtʲɪ] |
| runway | kilìmo tãkas (v) | [kʲɪ'lʲɪmɔ 'taːkas] |

| visibility | matomùmas (v) | [mato'mʊmas] |
| flight (act of flying) | skrŷdis (v) | ['skrʲiːdʲɪs] |
| altitude | aũkštis (v) | ['aʊkʃtʲɪs] |
| air pocket | óro duobé (m) | ['orɔ dʊa'bʲeː] |

| seat | vietà (m) | [vʲiɛ'ta] |
| headphones | ausìnés (m dgs) | [aʊ'sʲɪnʲeːs] |

| folding tray (tray table) | atverčiamàsis staliùkas (v) | [atvʲɛrtsʲæ'masʲɪs sta'lʲʊkas] |
| airplane window | iliuminãtorius (v) | [ɪlʲʊmʲɪ'na:torʲʊs] |
| aisle | praėjìmas (v) | [prae:'jɪmas] |

## 25. Train

| train | traukinỹs (v) | [trɑʊkʲɪ'nʲiːs] |
| commuter train | elektrìnis traukinỹs (v) | [ɛlʲɛk'trʲɪnʲɪs trɑʊkʲɪ'nʲiːs] |
| express train | greitàsis traukinỹs (v) | [grʲɛɪ'tasʲɪs trɑʊkʲɪ'nʲiːs] |
| diesel locomotive | motòrvežis (v) | [mo'torvʲɛʒʲɪs] |
| steam locomotive | garvežỹs (v) | [garvʲɛ'ʒʲiːs] |

| passenger car | vagònas (v) | [va'gonas] |
| dining car | vagònas restorãnas (v) | [va'gonas rʲɛsto'raːnas] |

| rails | bėgiai (v dgs) | ['bʲeːgʲɛɪ] |
| railroad | geležìnkelis (v) | [gʲɛlʲɛ'ʒʲɪŋkʲɛlʲɪs] |
| railway tie | pãbėgis (v) | ['paːbʲeːgʲɪs] |

| platform (railway ~) | platfòrma (m) | [plʲat'forma] |
| track (~ 1, 2, etc.) | kẽlias (v) | ['kʲælʲæs] |
| semaphore | semafòras (v) | [sʲɛma'foras] |
| station | stotìs (m) | [sto'tʲɪs] |

| engineer (train driver) | mašinìstas (v) | [maʃɪ'nʲɪstas] |
| porter (of luggage) | nešìkas (v) | [nʲɛ'ʃɪkas] |
| car attendant | kondùktorius (v) | [kɔn'dʊktorʲʊs] |
| passenger | keleìvis (v) | [kʲɛ'lʲɛɪvʲɪs] |
| conductor (ticket inspector) | kontroliẽrius (v) | [kɔntro'lʲɛrʲʊs] |

| corridor (in train) | korìdorius (v) | [ko'rʲɪdorʲʊs] |
| emergency brake | stãbdymo krãnas (v) | ['staːbdʲiːmo 'kraːnas] |

| compartment | kupė̃ (m) | [kʊ'pʲeː] |
| berth | lentýna (m) | [lʲɛn'tʲiːna] |
| upper berth | viršutìnė lentýna (m) | [vʲɪrʃʊ'tʲɪnʲeː lʲɛn'tʲiːna] |
| lower berth | apatìnė lentýna (m) | [apa'tʲɪnʲeː lʲɛn'tʲiːna] |
| bed linen, bedding | pãtalynė (m) | ['paːtalʲɪnʲeː] |

| ticket | bìlietas (v) | ['bʲɪlʲiɛtas] |
| schedule | tvarkãraštis (v) | [tvar'ka:raʃtʲɪs] |
| information display | šviẽslentė (m) | ['ʃvʲɛslʲɛntʲeː] |

| to leave, to depart | išvỹkti | [ɪʃ'vʲiːktʲɪ] |
| departure (of train) | išvykìmas (v) | [ɪʃvʲiː'kɪmas] |
| to arrive (ab. train) | atvỹkti | [at'vʲiːktʲɪ] |
| arrival | atvykìmas (v) | [atvʲiː'kɪmas] |
| to arrive by train | atvažiúoti tráukiniu | [atva'ʒʲʊatʲɪ 'trɑʊkʲɪnʲʊ] |

| to get on the train | įlipti į tráukinį | [i:'lʲɪ:ptʲɪ i: 'traʊkʲɪnʲɪ:] |
| to get off the train | išlipti iš tráukinio | [ɪʃˈlʲɪptʲɪ ɪʃ 'traʊkʲɪnʲɔ] |
| | | |
| train wreck | katastrofà (m) | [katastro'fa] |
| to derail (vi) | nulėkti nuõ bėgių | [nʊˈlʲe:ktʲɪ 'nʊɑ 'bʲe:gʲu:] |
| | | |
| steam locomotive | garvežỹs (v) | [garvʲɛ'ʒʲi:s] |
| stoker, fireman | kūrìkas (v) | [ku:'rʲɪkas] |
| firebox | kūryklà (m) | [ku:rʲi:k'lʲa] |
| coal | anglìs (m) | [ang'lʲɪs] |

## 26. Ship

| ship | laĩvas (v) | ['lʲʌɪvas] |
| vessel | laĩvas (v) | ['lʲʌɪvas] |
| | | |
| steamship | gárlaivis (v) | ['garlʲʌɪvʲɪs] |
| riverboat | motòrlaivis (v) | [mo'torlʲʌɪvʲɪs] |
| cruise ship | láineris (v) | ['lʲʌɪnʲɛrʲɪs] |
| cruiser | kreĩseris (v) | ['krʲɛɪsʲɛrʲɪs] |
| | | |
| yacht | jachtà (m) | [jax'ta] |
| tugboat | vilkìkas (v) | [vʲɪlʲ'kʲɪkas] |
| barge | bárža (m) | ['barʒa] |
| ferry | kéltas (v) | ['kʲɛlʲtas] |
| | | |
| sailing ship | bùrinis laĩvas (v) | ['bʊrʲɪnʲɪs 'lʲʌɪvas] |
| brigantine | brigantinà (m) | [brʲɪgantʲɪ'na] |
| | | |
| ice breaker | lẽdlaužis (v) | ['lʲædlɑʊʒʲɪs] |
| submarine | povandenìnis laĩvas (v) | [povandʲɛ'nʲɪnʲɪs 'lʲʌɪvas] |
| | | |
| boat (flat-bottomed ~) | váltis (m) | ['valʲtʲɪs] |
| dinghy | váltis (m) | ['valʲtʲɪs] |
| lifeboat | gélbėjimo váltis (m) | ['gʲælʲbʲe:jɪmo 'valʲtʲɪs] |
| motorboat | kãteris (v) | ['ka:tʲɛrʲɪs] |
| | | |
| captain | kapitõnas (v) | [kapʲɪ'to:nas] |
| seaman | jūreĩvis (v) | [ju:'rʲɛɪvʲɪs] |
| sailor | jūrininkas (v) | ['ju:rʲɪnʲɪŋkas] |
| crew | ekipãžas (v) | [ɛkʲɪ'pa:ʒas] |
| | | |
| boatswain | bòcmanas (v) | ['botsmanas] |
| ship's boy | jùnga (m) | ['junga] |
| cook | viréjas (v) | [vʲɪ'rʲe:jas] |
| ship's doctor | laĩvo gýdytojas (v) | ['lʲʌɪvo 'gʲi:dʲi:to:jɛs] |
| | | |
| deck | dẽnis (v) | ['dʲænʲɪs] |
| mast | stíebas (v) | ['stʲiɛbas] |
| sail | bùrė (m) | ['bʊrʲe:] |

| | | |
|---|---|---|
| hold | triùmas (v) | ['trɪ̩umas] |
| bow (prow) | laĩvo príekis (v) | ['lʲʌɪvɔ 'prʲiɛkʲɪs] |
| stern | laivãgalis (v) | [lʌɪ'va:galʲɪs] |
| oar | ìrklas (v) | ['ɪrklʲas] |
| screw propeller | sráigtas (v) | ['srʌɪktas] |

| | | |
|---|---|---|
| cabin | kajùtė (m) | [ka'jutʲe:] |
| wardroom | kajutkompãnija (m) | [kajutkom'pa:nʲɪjɛ] |
| engine room | mašìnų skýrius (v) | [ma'ʃɪnu: 'skʲi:rʲʊs] |
| bridge | kapitõno tiltēlis (v) | [kapʲɪ'to:nɔ tʲɪlʲtʲ'tʲælʲɪs] |
| radio room | rãdijo kabinà (m) | ['ra:dʲɪjɔ kabʲɪ'na] |
| wave (radio) | bangà (m) | [ban'ga] |
| logbook | laĩvo žurnãlas (v) | ['lʲʌɪvɔ ʒʊr'na:lʲas] |

| | | |
|---|---|---|
| spyglass | žiūrõnas (v) | [ʒʲu:'ro:nas] |
| bell | laĩvo skam̃balas (v) | ['lʲʌɪvɔ 'skambalʲas] |
| flag | vēliava (m) | ['vʲe:lʲæva] |

| | | |
|---|---|---|
| hawser (mooring ~) | lýnas (v) | ['lʲi:nas] |
| knot (bowline, etc.) | mãzgas (v) | ['ma:zgas] |

| | | |
|---|---|---|
| deckrails | turēklai (v dgs) | [tʊ'rʲe:klʲʌɪ] |
| gangway | trãpas (v) | ['tra:pas] |

| | | |
|---|---|---|
| anchor | iñkaras (v) | ['ɪŋkaras] |
| to weigh anchor | pakélti iñkarą | [pa'kʲɛlʲtʲɪ 'ɪŋkara:] |
| to drop anchor | nuléisti iñkarą | [nʊ'lʲɛɪstʲɪ 'ɪŋkara:] |
| anchor chain | iñkaro grandìnė (m) | ['ɪŋkarɔ gran'dʲɪnʲe:] |

| | | |
|---|---|---|
| port (harbor) | úostas (v) | ['ʊastas] |
| quay, wharf | príeplauka (m) | ['prʲiɛplʲauka] |
| to berth (moor) | prisišvartúoti | [prʲɪsʲɪʃvar'tʊatʲɪ] |
| to cast off | išplaũkti | [ɪʃplʲauktʲɪ] |

| | | |
|---|---|---|
| trip, voyage | keliõnė (m) | [kʲɛ'lʲo:nʲe:] |
| cruise (sea trip) | kruìzas (v) | [krʊ'ɪzas] |

| | | |
|---|---|---|
| course (route) | kùrsas (v) | ['kursas] |
| route (itinerary) | maršrùtas (v) | [marʃ'rutas] |

| | | |
|---|---|---|
| fairway (safe water channel) | farvãteris (v) | [far'va:tʲɛrʲɪs] |
| shallows | seklumà (m) | [sʲɛklʲʊ'ma] |
| to run aground | užplaũkti ant seklumõs | [ʊʒ'plʲauktʲɪ ant sʲɛklʲʊ'mo:s] |

| | | |
|---|---|---|
| storm | audrà (m) | [au'dra] |
| signal | signãlas (v) | [sʲɪg'na:lʲas] |
| to sink (vi) | skɛ̨̃sti | ['skʲɛ:stʲɪ] |
| Man overboard! | Žmogùs vandenyjè! | [ʒmo'gʊs vandʲɛnʲi:'jæ!] |
| SOS (distress signal) | SOS | [ɛs ɔ ɛs] |
| ring buoy | gélbėjimosi rãtas (v) | [gʲɛlʲbʲe:jimosʲɪ 'ra:tas] |

# CITY

**T&P Books Publishing**

## 27. Urban transportation

| bus | autobùsas (v) | [ɑuto'busas] |
| streetcar | tramvājus (v) | [tram'vaːjus] |
| trolley bus | troleibùsas (v) | [trolʲɛɪ'busas] |
| route (of bus, etc.) | maršrùtas (v) | [marʃrutas] |
| number (e.g., bus ~) | nùmeris (v) | ['numʲɛrʲɪs] |
| | | |
| to go by … | važiùoti … | [va'ʒʲuatʲɪ …] |
| to get on (~ the bus) | įlìpti į̃ … | [iː'lʲɪːptʲɪ iː …] |
| to get off … | išlìpti ìš … | [ɪʃˈlʲɪptʲɪ ɪʃ …] |
| | | |
| stop (e.g., bus ~) | stotēlė (m) | [sto'tʲælʲeː] |
| next stop | kità stotēlė (m) | [kʲɪ'ta sto'tʲælʲeː] |
| terminus | galutìnė stotēlė (m) | [galu'tʲɪnʲeː sto'tʲælʲeː] |
| schedule | tvarkāraštis (v) | [tvar'kaːraʃtʲɪs] |
| to wait (vt) | láukti | ['lʲɑuktʲɪ] |
| | | |
| ticket | bìlietas (v) | ['bʲɪlʲiɛtas] |
| fare | bìlieto káina (m) | ['bʲɪlʲiɛto 'kʌɪna] |
| | | |
| cashier (ticket seller) | kāsininkas (v) | ['kaːsʲɪnʲɪŋkas] |
| ticket inspection | kontrolè (m) | [kon'trolʲeː] |
| ticket inspector | kontroliērius (v) | [kontro'lʲɛrʲus] |
| | | |
| to be late (for …) | vėlúoti | [vʲeː'lʲuatʲɪ] |
| to miss (~ the train, etc.) | pavėlúoti | [pavʲeː'lʲuatʲɪ] |
| to be in a hurry | skubéti | [sku'bʲeːtʲɪ] |
| | | |
| taxi, cab | taksì (v) | [tak'sʲɪ] |
| taxi driver | taksìstas (v) | [tak'sʲɪstas] |
| by taxi | sù taksì | ['su tak'sʲɪ] |
| taxi stand | taksì stovéjimo aikštēlė | [tak'sʲɪ sto'vʲɛjɪmɔ ʌɪkʃ'tʲælʲeː] |
| | | |
| to call a taxi | iškviēsti taksì | [ɪʃk'vʲɛstʲɪ tak'sʲɪ] |
| to take a taxi | įsėstì į̃ taksì | [iːsʲes'tʲɪ iː tak'sʲɪː] |
| | | |
| traffic | gātvės judėjimas (v) | ['gaːtvʲeːs juˈdʲɛjɪmas] |
| traffic jam | kamštis (v) | ['kamʃtʲɪs] |
| rush hour | pìko vālandos (m dgs) | ['pʲɪkɔ 'vaːlʲandos] |
| to park (vi) | parkúotis | [par'kuatʲɪs] |
| to park (vt) | parkúoti | [par'kuatʲɪ] |
| parking lot | stovéjimo aikštēlė (m) | [sto'vʲɛjɪmɔ ʌɪkʃ'tʲælʲeː] |
| | | |
| subway | metrò | [mʲɛ'tro] |
| station | stotìs (m) | [sto'tʲɪs] |

| to take the subway | važiúoti metró | [va'ʒʲuɑtʲɪ mʲɛ'trɔ] |
| train | traukinỹs (v) | [trɑukʲɪ'nʲiːs] |
| train station | stotìs (m) | [sto'tʲɪs] |

## 28. City. Life in the city

| city, town | miẽstas (v) | ['mʲɛstas] |
| capital city | sóstinė (m) | ['sostʲɪnʲeː] |
| village | káimas (v) | ['kʌɪmas] |

| city map | miẽsto plãnas (v) | ['mʲɛstɔ 'plʲaːnas] |
| downtown | miẽsto ceñtras (v) | ['mʲɛstɔ 'tsʲɛntras] |
| suburb | príemiestis (v) | ['prʲɛmʲɛstʲɪs] |
| suburban (adj) | príemiesčio | ['prʲɛmʲiɛstsʲɔ] |

| outskirts | pakraštỹs (v) | [pakraʃ'tʲiːs] |
| environs (suburbs) | apýlinkės (m dgs) | [a'pʲiːlʲɪŋkʲeːs] |
| city block | kvartãlas (v) | [kvar'taːlʲas] |
| residential block (area) | gyvẽnamas kvartãlas (v) | [gʲiː'vʲænamas kvar'taːlʲas] |

| traffic | judéjimas (v) | [juˈdʲɛjɪmas] |
| traffic lights | šviesofóras (v) | [ʃvʲiɛso'foras] |
| public transportation | miẽsto transpórtas (v) | ['mʲɛstɔ trans'portas] |
| intersection | sánkryža (m) | ['saŋkrʲiːʒa] |

| crosswalk | pérėja (m) | ['pʲɛrʲeːja] |
| pedestrian underpass | požemìnė pérėja (m) | [poʒe'mʲɪnʲeː 'pʲærʲeːja] |
| to cross (~ the street) | péreiti | ['pʲɛrʲɛɪtʲɪ] |
| pedestrian | péstysis (v) | ['pʲeːstʲiːsʲɪs] |
| sidewalk | šalìgatvis (v) | [ʃa'lʲɪgatvʲɪs] |

| bridge | tìltas (v) | ['tʲɪlʲtas] |
| embankment (river walk) | krantìnė (m) | [kran'tʲɪnʲeː] |

| allée (garden walkway) | aléja (m) | [a'lʲeːja] |
| park | párkas (v) | ['parkas] |
| boulevard | bulvãras (v) | [bulʲ'vaːras] |
| square | aikštė̃ (m) | [ʌɪkʃ'tʲeː] |
| avenue (wide street) | prospèktas (v) | [pros'pʲɛktas] |
| street | gãtvė (m) | ['gaːtvʲeː] |
| side street | skérsgatvis (v) | ['skʲɛrsgatvʲɪs] |
| dead end | tupìkas (v) | [tu'pʲɪkas] |

| house | nãmas (v) | ['naːmas] |
| building | pãstatas (v) | ['paːstatas] |
| skyscraper | dangóraižis (v) | [dan'gorʌɪʒʲɪs] |

| facade | fasãdas (v) | [fa'saːdas] |
| roof | stógas (v) | ['stogas] |
| window | lángas (v) | ['lʲangas] |

| | | |
|---|---|---|
| arch | árka (m) | ['arka] |
| column | koloná (m) | [kɔlʲɔ'na] |
| corner | kam̃pas (v) | ['kampas] |

| | | |
|---|---|---|
| store window | vitriná (m) | [vʲɪtrʲɪ'na] |
| signboard (store sign, etc.) | ìškaba (m) | ['ɪʃkaba] |
| poster | afišá (m) | [afʲɪ'ʃa] |
| advertising poster | reklãminis plakãtas (v) | [rʲɛk'lʲa:mʲɪnʲɪs plʲa'ka:tas] |
| billboard | reklãminis skỹdas (v) | [rʲɛk'lʲa:mʲɪnʲɪs 'skʲi:das] |

| | | |
|---|---|---|
| garbage, trash | šiùkšlės (m dgs) | ['ʃukʃlʲe:s] |
| trashcan (public ~) | ùrna (m) | ['ʊrna] |
| to litter (vi) | šiùkšlinti | ['ʃukʃlʲɪntʲɪ] |
| garbage dump | sąvartýnas (v) | [sa:var'tʲi:nas] |

| | | |
|---|---|---|
| phone booth | telefòno bùdelė (m) | [tʲɛlʲɛ'fɔnɔ 'bʊdelʲe:] |
| lamppost | žibìnto stul̃pas (v) | [ʒʲɪ'bʲɪntɔ 'stʊlʲpas] |
| bench (park ~) | súolas (v) | ['sʊɑlʲas] |

| | | |
|---|---|---|
| police officer | policininkas (v) | [pɔ'lʲɪtsʲɪnʲɪŋkas] |
| police | policija (m) | [pɔ'lʲɪtsʲɪjɛ] |
| beggar | skur̃džius (v) | ['skʊrdʒʲʊs] |
| homeless (n) | benãmis (v) | [bʲɛ'na:mʲɪs] |

## 29. Urban institutions

| | | |
|---|---|---|
| store | parduotùvė (m) | [pardʊɑ'tʊvʲe:] |
| drugstore, pharmacy | váistinė (m) | ['vʌɪstʲɪnʲe:] |
| eyeglass store | òptika (m) | ['optʲɪka] |
| shopping mall | prekýbos centras (v) | [prʲɛ'kʲi:bos 'tsʲɛntras] |
| supermarket | supermárketas (v) | [sʊpʲɛr'markʲɛtas] |

| | | |
|---|---|---|
| bakery | bandēlių kráutuvė (m) | [ban'dʲælʲu: 'krɑʊtʊvʲe:] |
| baker | kepéjas (v) | [kʲɛ'pʲe:jas] |
| pastry shop | konditėrija (m) | [kondʲɪ'tʲɛrʲɪjɛ] |
| grocery store | bakaléja (m) | [baka'lʲe:ja] |
| butcher shop | mėsõs kráutuvė (m) | [mʲe:'soːs 'krɑʊtʊvʲe:] |

| | | |
|---|---|---|
| produce store | daržóvių kráutuvė (m) | [dar'ʒovʲu: 'krɑʊtʊvʲe:] |
| market | prekývietė (m) | [prʲɛ'kʲi:vʲiɛtʲe:] |

| | | |
|---|---|---|
| coffee house | kavìnė (m) | [ka'vʲɪnʲe:] |
| restaurant | restorãnas (v) | [rʲɛsto'ra:nas] |
| pub, bar | alùdė (m) | [a'lʲʊdʲe:] |
| pizzeria | picèrija (m) | [pʲɪ'tsʲɛrʲɪjɛ] |

| | | |
|---|---|---|
| hair salon | kirpyklà (m) | [kʲɪrpʲi:k'lʲa] |
| post office | pãštas (v) | ['pa:ʃtas] |
| dry cleaners | valyklà (m) | [valʲi:k'la] |
| photo studio | fotoateljė̃ (v) | [fotoatelʲʲje:] |

| | | |
|---|---|---|
| shoe store | **ãvalynės parduotùvė** (m) | ['a:valʲi:nʲe:s pardʊɑ'tʊvʲe:] |
| bookstore | **knygýnas** (v) | [knʲi:'gʲi:nas] |
| sporting goods store | **spòrtinių prẽkių parduotùvė** (m) | ['sportʲɪnʲu: 'prʲækʲu: pardʊɑ'tʊvʲe:] |
| clothes repair shop | **drabùžių taisyklà** (m) | [dra'bʊʒʲu: tʌɪsʲi:k'lʲa] |
| formal wear rental | **drabùžių núoma** (m) | [dra'bʊʒʲu: 'nʊɑma] |
| video rental store | **fìlmų núoma** (m) | ['fʲɪlʲmu: 'nʊɑma] |
| circus | **cìrkas** (v) | ['tsʲɪrkas] |
| zoo | **zoològijos sõdas** (v) | [zoo'lʲogʲɪjɔs 'so:das] |
| movie theater | **kìno teãtras** (v) | ['kʲɪnɔ tʲɛ'a:tras] |
| museum | **muziẽjus** (v) | [mʊ'zʲɛjʊs] |
| library | **bibliotekà** (m) | [bʲɪblʲɪjɔtʲɛ'ka] |
| theater | **teãtras** (v) | [tʲɛ'a:tras] |
| opera (opera house) | **òpera** (m) | ['opʲɛra] |
| nightclub | **naktìnis klùbas** (v) | [nak'tʲɪnʲɪs 'klʲʊbas] |
| casino | **kazinò** (v) | [kazʲɪ'no] |
| mosque | **mečètė** (m) | [mʲɛ'tʂʲɛtʲe:] |
| synagogue | **sinagogà** (m) | [sʲɪnago'ga] |
| cathedral | **kãtedra** (m) | ['ka:tʲɛdra] |
| temple | **šventyklà** (m) | [ʃvʲɛntʲi:k'lʲa] |
| church | **bažnýčia** (m) | [baʒ'nʲi:tʂʲæ] |
| college | **institùtas** (v) | [ɪnstʲɪ'tʊtas] |
| university | **universitètas** (v) | [ʊnʲɪvʲɛrsʲɪ'tʲɛtas] |
| school | **mokyklà** (m) | [mokʲi:k'lʲa] |
| prefecture | **prefektūrà** (m) | [prʲɛfʲɛk'tu:'ra] |
| city hall | **savivaldýbė** (m) | [savʲɪvalʲ'dʲi:bʲe:] |
| hotel | **viẽšbutis** (v) | ['vʲɛʃbʊtʲɪs] |
| bank | **bánkas** (v) | ['baŋkas] |
| embassy | **ambasadà** (m) | [ambasa'da] |
| travel agency | **turìzmo agentūrà** (m) | [tʊ'rʲɪzmɔ agʲɛntu:'ra] |
| information office | **informãcijos biùras** (v) | [ɪnfor'ma:tsʲɪjɔs 'bʲʊras] |
| currency exchange | **keityklà** (m) | [kʲɛɪtʲi:k'lʲa] |
| subway | **metrò** | [mʲɛ'tro] |
| hospital | **ligóninė** (m) | [lʲɪ'gonʲɪnʲe:] |
| gas station | **degalìnė** (m) | [dʲɛga'lʲɪnʲe:] |
| parking lot | **stovėjimo aikštẽlė** (m) | [sto'vʲɛjɪmɔ ʌɪkʃ'tʲælʲe:] |

## 30. Signs

| | | |
|---|---|---|
| signboard (store sign, etc.) | **ìškaba** (m) | ['ɪʃkaba] |
| notice (door sign, etc.) | **ùžrašas** (v) | ['ʊʒraʃas] |

| poster | plakãtas (v) | [plʲa'ka:tas] |
| direction sign | núoroda (m) | ['nuaroda] |
| arrow (sign) | rodỹklė (m) | [ro'dʲi:klʲe:] |

| caution | pérspėjimas (v) | ['pʲɛrspʲe:jimas] |
| warning sign | įspėjìmas (v) | [i:spʲe:'jɪmas] |
| to warn (vt) | įspéti | [i:s'pʲe:tʲɪ] |

| rest day (weekly ~) | išeigìnė dienà (m) | [ɪʃɛɪ'gʲɪnʲe: dʲiɛ'na] |
| timetable (schedule) | tvarkãraštis (v) | [tvar'ka:raʃtʲɪs] |
| opening hours | dárbo valandõs (m dgs) | ['darbɔ valʲan'do:s] |

| WELCOME! | SVEIKÌ ATVỸKĘ! | [svʲɛɪ'kʲɪ at'vʲi:kʲɛ:!] |
| ENTRANCE | ĮĖJÌMAS | [i:ʲe:'jɪmas] |
| EXIT | IŠĖJÌMAS | [ɪʃe:'jɪmas] |

| PUSH | STÙMTI | ['stumtʲɪ] |
| PULL | TRÁUKTI | ['trauktʲɪ] |
| OPEN | ATIDARÝTA | [atʲɪda'rʲi:ta] |
| CLOSED | UŽDARÝTA | [uʒda'rʲi:ta] |

| WOMEN | MÓTERIMS | ['motʲɛrʲɪms] |
| MEN | VÝRAMS | ['vʲi:rams] |

| DISCOUNTS | NÚOLAIDOS | ['nualʲʌɪdos] |
| SALE | IŠPARDAVÌMAS | [ɪʃparda'vʲɪmas] |
| NEW! | NAUJÍENA! | [nau'jiɛna!] |
| FREE | NEMÓKAMAI | [nʲɛ'mokamʌɪ] |

| ATTENTION! | DĖMESIO! | ['dʲe:mesʲɔ!] |
| NO VACANCIES | VIÉTŲ NĖRA | ['vʲɛtu: 'nʲe:ra] |
| RESERVED | REZERVÚOTA | [rʲɛzʲɛr'vuata] |

| ADMINISTRATION | ADMINISTRÃCIJA | [admʲɪnʲɪs'tratsʲɪja] |
| STAFF ONLY | TÌK PERSONÁLUI | ['tʲɪk pʲɛrso'nalʲui] |

| BEWARE OF THE DOG! | PIKTAS ŠUO | ['pʲɪktas 'ʃua] |
| NO SMOKING | RŪKÝTI DRAŨDŽIAMA | [ru:'kʲi:tʲɪ 'draudʒʲæma ] |
| DO NOT TOUCH! | NELIÉSTI! | [nʲɛ'lʲɛstʲɪ!] |

| DANGEROUS | PAVOJÌNGA | [pavo'jɪnga] |
| DANGER | PAVÕJUS | [pa'vo:jus] |
| HIGH VOLTAGE | AUKŠTÀ ĮTAMPA | [aukʃta 'i:tampa] |
| NO SWIMMING! | MÁUDYTIS DRAŨDŽIAMA | ['maudʲi:tʲɪs 'draudʒʲæma] |
| OUT OF ORDER | NEVEÌKIA | [nʲɛ'vʲɛɪkʲɛ] |

| FLAMMABLE | DEGÙ | [dʲɛ'gu] |
| FORBIDDEN | DRAŨDŽIAMA | ['draudʒʲæma] |
| NO TRESPASSING! | PRAĖJÌMAS DRAŨDŽIAMAS | [prae:'jɪmas 'draudʒʲæmas] |
| WET PAINT | NUDAŽYTA | [nuda'ʒʲi:ta] |

## 31. Shopping

| | | |
|---|---|---|
| to buy (purchase) | pirkti | ['pʲɪrktʲɪ] |
| purchase | pirkinỹs (v) | [pʲɪrkʲɪ'nʲiːs] |
| to go shopping | apsipirkti | [apsʲɪ'pʲɪrktʲɪ] |
| shopping | apsipirkìmas (v) | [apsʲɪpʲɪr'kʲɪmas] |
| | | |
| to be open (ab. store) | veĩkti | ['vʲɛɪktʲɪ] |
| to be closed | užsidarýti | [ʊʒsʲɪda'rʲiːtʲɪ] |
| | | |
| footwear, shoes | ãvalynė (m) | ['aːvalʲiːnʲeː] |
| clothes, clothing | drabùžiai (v) | [dra'bʊʒʲɛɪ] |
| cosmetics | kosmètika (m) | [kɔs'mʲɛtʲɪka] |
| food products | produktai (v) | [pro'dʊktʌɪ] |
| gift, present | dovanà (m) | [dova'na] |
| | | |
| salesman | pardavéjas (v) | [parda'vʲeːjas] |
| saleswoman | pardavéja (m) | [parda'vʲeːja] |
| | | |
| check out, cash desk | kasà (m) | [ka'sa] |
| mirror | veĩdrodis (v) | ['vʲɛɪdrodʲɪs] |
| counter (store ~) | prekýstalis (v) | [prʲɛ'kʲiːstalʲɪs] |
| fitting room | matãvimosi kabinà (m) | [ma'taːvʲɪmosʲɪ kabʲɪ'na] |
| | | |
| to try on | matúoti | [ma'tʊatʲɪ] |
| to fit (ab. dress, etc.) | tìkti | ['tʲɪktʲɪ] |
| to like (I like …) | patìkti | [pa'tʲɪktʲɪ] |
| | | |
| price | kaĩna (m) | ['kʌɪna] |
| price tag | kainýnas (v) | [kʌɪ'nʲiːnas] |
| to cost (vt) | kainúoti | [kʌɪ'nʊatʲɪ] |
| How much? | Kíek? | ['kʲiɛk?] |
| discount | núolaida (m) | ['nʊalʲʌɪda] |
| | | |
| inexpensive (adj) | nebrangùs | [nʲɛbran'gʊs] |
| cheap (adj) | pigùs | [pʲɪ'gʊs] |
| expensive (adj) | brangùs | [bran'gʊs] |
| It's expensive | Taĩ brangù. | ['tʌɪ bran'gʊ] |
| | | |
| rental (n) | núoma (m) | ['nʊama] |
| to rent (~ a tuxedo) | išsinúomoti | [ɪʃsʲɪr'nʊamotʲɪ] |
| credit (trade credit) | kredìtas (v) | [krʲɛ'dʲɪtas] |
| on credit (adv) | kreditù | [krʲɛdʲɪ'tʊ] |

# CLOTHING & ACCESSORIES

**T&P Books Publishing**

## 32. Outerwear. Coats

| clothes | **apranga** (m) | [apran'ga] |
| outerwear | **viršutiniai drabužiai** (v dgs) | [vʲɪrʃuˈtʲɪnʲɛɪ draˈbuʒʲɛɪ] |
| winter clothing | **žieminiai drabužiai** (v) | [ʒʲiɛˈmʲɪnʲɛɪ draˈbuʒʲɛɪ] |

| coat (overcoat) | **páltas** (v) | [ˈpalʲtas] |
| fur coat | **kailiniaĩ** (v dgs) | [kʌɪlʲɪˈnʲɛɪ] |
| fur jacket | **pùskailiniai** (v) | [ˈpuskʌɪlʲɪnʲɛɪ] |
| down coat | **pūkìnė** (m) | [puːˈkʲɪnʲeː] |

| jacket (e.g., leather ~) | **striùkė** (m) | [ˈstrʲukʲeː] |
| raincoat (trenchcoat, etc.) | **apsiaũstas** (v) | [apˈsʲɛustas] |
| waterproof (adj) | **nepéršlampamas** | [nʲɛˈpʲɛrʃlʲampamas] |

## 33. Men's & women's clothing

| shirt (button shirt) | **marškiniaĩ** (v dgs) | [marʃkʲɪˈnʲɛɪ] |
| pants | **kélnės** (m dgs) | [ˈkʲɛlʲnʲeːs] |
| jeans | **džìnsai** (v dgs) | [ˈdʒʲɪnsʌɪ] |
| suit jacket | **švárkas** (v) | [ˈʃvarkas] |
| suit | **kostiùmas** (v) | [kɔsˈtʲumas] |

| dress (frock) | **suknēlė** (m) | [sukˈnʲælʲeː] |
| skirt | **sijõnas** (v) | [sʲɪˈjɔːnas] |
| blouse | **palaidìnė** (m) | [palʲʌɪˈdʲɪnʲeː] |
| knitted jacket (cardigan, etc.) | **sùsegamas megztìnis** (v) | [ˈsusʲɛgamas mʲɛgzˈtʲɪnʲɪs] |
| jacket (of woman's suit) | **žakėtas, švarkẽlis** (v) | [ʒaˈkʲɛtas, ʃvarˈkʲælʲɪs] |

| T-shirt | **fùtbolininko marškiniaĩ** (v) | [ˈfutbolʲɪnʲɪŋkɔ marʃkʲɪˈnʲɛɪ] |

| shorts (short trousers) | **šórtai** (v dgs) | [ˈʃortʌɪ] |
| tracksuit | **spòrtinis kostiùmas** (v) | [ˈsportʲɪnʲɪs kɔsˈtʲumas] |
| bathrobe | **chalãtas** (v) | [xaˈlʲaːtas] |
| pajamas | **pižamà** (m) | [pʲɪʒaˈma] |

| sweater | **nertìnis** (v) | [nʲɛrˈtʲɪnʲɪs] |
| pullover | **megztìnis** (v) | [mʲɛgzˈtʲɪnʲɪs] |

| vest | **liemẽnė** (m) | [lʲiɛˈmʲænʲeː] |
| tailcoat | **frãkas** (v) | [ˈfraːkas] |
| tuxedo | **smòkingas** (v) | [ˈsmokʲɪngas] |
| uniform | **unifòrma** (m) | [unʲɪˈforma] |

| workwear | dárbo drabùžiai (v) | ['darbɔ dra'buʒʲɛɪ] |
| overalls | kombinezónas (v) | [kɔmbʲɪnʲɛ'zonas] |
| coat (e.g., doctor's smock) | chalátas (v) | [xa'lʲa:tas] |

## 34. Clothing. Underwear

| underwear | baltiniaĩ (v dgs) | [balʲtʲɪ'nʲɛɪ] |
| undershirt (A-shirt) | apatìniai | [apa'tʲɪnʲɛɪ] |
| | marškinéliai (v dgs) | marʃkʲɪ'nʲe:lʲɛɪ] |
| socks | kójinės (m dgs) | ['ko:jɪnʲe:s] |
| | | |
| nightgown | naktìniai marškiniaĩ (v dgs) | [nak'tʲɪnʲɛɪ marʃkʲɪ'nʲɛɪ] |
| bra | liemenélė (m) | [lʲiɛme'nʲe:lʲe:] |
| knee highs | gòlfai (v) | ['golʲfʌɪ] |
| (knee-high socks) | | |
| pantyhose | pédkelnės (m dgs) | ['pʲe:dkʲɛlʲnʲe:s] |
| stockings (thigh highs) | kójinės (m dgs) | ['ko:jɪnʲe:s] |
| bathing suit | máudymosi | ['maʊdʲi:mosʲɪ |
| | kostiumélis (v) | kostʲʊ'mʲe:lʲɪs] |

## 35. Headwear

| hat | kepùrė (m) | [kʲɛ'pʊrʲe:] |
| fedora | skrybélė (m) | [skrʲi:bʲe:'lʲe:] |
| baseball cap | beĩsbolo lazdà (m) | ['bʲɛɪsbolʲɔ lʲaz'da] |
| flatcap | kepùrė (m) | [kʲɛ'pʊrʲe:] |
| | | |
| beret | berètė (m) | [bʲɛ'rʲɛtʲe:] |
| hood | gobtùvas (v) | [gop'tʊvas] |
| panama hat | panamà (m) | [pana'ma] |
| knit cap (knitted hat) | megztà kepuráitė (m) | [mʲɛgz'ta kepʊ'rʌɪtʲe:] |
| | | |
| headscarf | skarà (m), skarélė (m) | [ska'ra], [ska'rʲælʲe:] |
| women's hat | skrybéláitė (m) | [skrʲi:bʲe:'lʲʌɪtʲe:] |
| | | |
| hard hat | šálmas (v) | ['ʃalʲmas] |
| garrison cap | pilòtė (m) | [pʲɪ'lʲotʲe:] |
| helmet | šálmas (v) | ['ʃalʲmas] |
| | | |
| derby | katiliùkas (v) | [katʲɪ'lʲʊkas] |
| top hat | cilìndras (v) | [tsʲɪ'lʲɪndras] |

## 36. Footwear

| footwear | ãvalynė (m) | ['a:valʲi:nʲe:] |
| shoes (men's shoes) | bãtai (v) | ['ba:tʌɪ] |

| shoes (women's shoes) | bateliai (v) | [ba'tʲælʲɛɪ] |
| boots (e.g., cowboy ~) | auliniai batai (v) | [ɑʊ'lʲɪnʲɛɪ 'ba:tʌɪ] |
| slippers | šlepetės (m dgs) | [ʃlʲɛ'pʲætʲeːs] |

| tennis shoes (e.g., Nike ~) | sportbačiai (v dgs) | ['sportbatʂʲɛɪ] |
| sneakers | sportbačiai (v dgs) | ['sportbatʂʲɛɪ] |
| (e.g., Converse ~) | | |
| sandals | sandalai (v dgs) | [san'da:lʲʌɪ] |

| cobbler (shoe repairer) | batsiuvys (v) | [batsʲʊ'vʲiːs] |
| heel | kulnas (v) | ['kʊlnas] |
| pair (of shoes) | pora (m) | [po'ra] |

| shoestring | batraištis (v) | ['ba:trʌɪʃtʲɪs] |
| to lace (vt) | varstyti | ['varstʲiːtʲɪ] |
| shoehorn | šaukštas (v) | ['ʃɑʊkʃtas] |
| shoe polish | avalynės kremas (v) | ['a:valʲiːnʲeːs 'krʲɛmas] |

## 37. Personal accessories

| gloves | pirštinės (m dgs) | ['pʲɪrʃtʲɪnʲeːs] |
| mittens | kumštinės (m dgs) | ['kʊmʃtʲɪnʲeːs] |
| scarf (muffler) | šalikas (v) | ['ʃa:lʲɪkas] |

| glasses (eyeglasses) | akiniai (dgs) | [akʲɪ'nʲɛɪ] |
| frame (eyeglass ~) | rėmėliai (v dgs) | [rʲeˑ'mʲælʲɛɪ] |
| umbrella | skėtis (v) | ['skʲeːtʲɪs] |
| walking stick | lazdelė (m) | [laz'dʲælʲeˑ] |

| hairbrush | plaukų šepetys (v) | [plʲɑʊ'ku: ʃɛpʲɛ'tʲiːs] |
| fan | vėduoklė (m) | [vʲeˑ'dʊɑklʲeˑ] |

| tie (necktie) | kaklaraištis (v) | [kak'lʲa:rʌɪʃtʲɪs] |
| bow tie | peteliškė (m) | [pʲɛtʲɛ'lʲɪʃkʲeˑ] |

| suspenders | petnešos (m dgs) | ['pʲætnʲɛʃos] |
| handkerchief | nosinė (m) | ['nosʲɪnʲeˑ] |

| comb | šukos (m dgs) | ['ʃukos] |
| barrette | segtukas (v) | [sʲɛk'tʊkas] |

| hairpin | plaukų segtukas (v) | [plʲɑʊ'ku: sʲɛk'tʊkas] |
| buckle | sagtis (m) | [sak'tʲɪs] |

| belt | diržas (v) | ['dʲɪrʒas] |
| shoulder strap | diržas (v) | ['dʲɪrʒas] |

| bag (handbag) | rankinukas (v) | [raŋkʲɪ'nʊkas] |
| purse | rankinukas (v) | [raŋkʲɪ'nʊkas] |
| backpack | kuprinė (m) | [kʊ'prʲɪnʲeˑ] |

## 38. Clothing. Miscellaneous

| | | |
|---|---|---|
| fashion | madà (m) | [ma'da] |
| in vogue (adj) | madìngas | [ma'dʲɪngas] |
| fashion designer | modeliúotojas (v) | [modʲɛ'lʲuɑto:jɛs] |
| | | |
| collar | apýkaklė (m) | [a'pʲi:kaklʲe:] |
| pocket | kišėnė (m) | [kʲɪ'ʃænʲe:] |
| pocket (as adj) | kišenìnis | [kʲɪʃɛ'nʲɪnʲɪs] |
| sleeve | rankóvė (m) | [raŋ'kovʲe:] |
| hanging loop | pakabà (m) | [paka'ba] |
| fly (on trousers) | klỹnas (v) | ['klʲi:nas] |
| | | |
| zipper (fastener) | užtrauktùkas (v) | [ʊʒtrɑuk'tukas] |
| fastener | užsegìmas (v) | [ʊʒsʲɛ'gʲɪmas] |
| button | sagà (m) | [sa'ga] |
| buttonhole | kìlpa (m) | ['kʲɪlʲpa] |
| to come off (ab. button) | atplýšti | [at'plʲi:ʃtʲɪ] |
| | | |
| to sew (vi, vt) | siúti | ['sʲu:tʲɪ] |
| to embroider (vi, vt) | siuvinéti | [sʲʊvʲɪ'nʲe:tʲɪ] |
| embroidery | siuvinéjimas (v) | [sʲʊvʲɪ'nʲɛjɪmas] |
| sewing needle | ãdata (m) | ['a:data] |
| thread | siúlas (v) | ['sʲu:lʲas] |
| seam | siúlė (m) | ['sʲu:lʲe:] |
| | | |
| to get dirty (vi) | išsitèpti | [ɪʃsʲɪ'tʲɛptʲɪ] |
| stain (mark, spot) | dėmė̃ (m) | [dʲe:'mʲe:] |
| to crease, crumple (vi) | susiglámžyti | [sʊsʲɪ'glʲa mʒʲi:tʲɪ] |
| to tear, to rip (vt) | suplėšyti | [sʊp'lʲe:ʃɪ:tʲɪ] |
| clothes moth | kandìs (v) | ['kandʲɪs] |

## 39. Personal care. Cosmetics

| | | |
|---|---|---|
| toothpaste | dantų̃ pastà (m) | [dan'tu: pas'ta] |
| toothbrush | dantų̃ šepetėlis (v) | [dan'tu: ʃepe'tʲe:lʲɪs] |
| to brush one's teeth | valýti dantìs | [va'lʲi:tʲɪ dan'tʲɪs] |
| | | |
| razor | skustùvas (v) | [skʊ'stuvas] |
| shaving cream | skutìmosi krèmas (v) | [skʊ'tʲɪmosʲɪ 'krʲɛmas] |
| to shave (vi) | skùstis | ['skʊstʲɪs] |
| | | |
| soap | muĩlas (v) | ['mʊɪlʲas] |
| shampoo | šampū̃nas (v) | [ʃam'pu:nas] |
| | | |
| scissors | žìrklės (m dgs) | ['ʒʲɪrklʲe:s] |
| nail file | dìldė (m) nagáms | ['dʲɪldʲe: na'gams] |
| nail clippers | gnybtùkai (v) | [gnʲɪ:p'tukʌɪ] |
| tweezers | pincètas (v) | [pʲɪn'tsʲɛtas] |

| cosmetics | kosmetika (m) | [kɔs'mʲɛtʲɪka] |
| face mask | kaukė (m) | ['kaʊkʲe:] |
| manicure | manikiūras (v) | [manʲɪ'kʲu:ras] |
| to have a manicure | darýti manikiūrą | [da'rʲi:tʲɪ manʲɪ'kʲu:ra:] |
| pedicure | pedikiūras (v) | [pʲɛdʲɪ'kʲu:ras] |

| make-up bag | kosmetinė (m) | [kɔs'mʲɛtʲɪnʲe:] |
| face powder | pudra (m) | [pʊd'ra] |
| powder compact | pùdrinė (m) | ['pʊdrʲɪnʲe:] |
| blusher | skaistalaì (v dgs) | [skʌɪsta'lʲāi] |

| perfume (bottled) | kvepalaì (v dgs) | [kvʲɛpa'lʲāi] |
| toilet water (lotion) | tualetinis vanduõ (v) | [tʊa'lʲɛtʲɪnʲɪs van'dʊɑ] |
| lotion | losjònas (v) | [lʲo'sjɔ nas] |
| cologne | odekolònas (v) | [odʲɛko'lʲonas] |

| eyeshadow | vokų̃ šešéliai (v) | [vo'ku: ʃeʃʲe:lʲɛɪ] |
| eyeliner | akių̃ pieštùkas (v) | [a'kʲu: pʲiɛʃ'tʊkas] |
| mascara | tùšas (v) | ['tuʃas] |

| lipstick | lū̃pų dažaì (v) | ['lʲu:pu: da'ʒʌɪ] |
| nail polish, enamel | nagų̃ lãkas (v) | [na'gu: 'lʲa:kas] |
| hair spray | plaukų̃ lãkas (v) | [plʲaʊ'ku: 'lʲa:kas] |
| deodorant | dezodorántas (v) | [dʲɛzodo'rantas] |

| cream | krèmas (v) | ['krʲɛmas] |
| face cream | veĩdo krèmas (v) | ['vʲɛɪdo 'krʲɛmas] |
| hand cream | rañkų krèmas (v) | ['raŋku: 'krʲɛmas] |
| anti-wrinkle cream | krèmas (v) nuõ raukšlių̃ | ['krʲɛmas nʊɑ raʊkʃʲlʲu:] |
| day cream | dienìnis krèmas (v) | [dʲiɛ'nʲɪnʲɪs 'krʲɛmas] |
| night cream | naktìnis krèmas (v) | [nak'tʲɪnʲɪs 'krʲɛmas] |
| day (as adj) | dienìnis | [dʲiɛ'nʲɪnʲɪs] |
| night (as adj) | naktìnis | [nak'tʲɪnʲɪs] |

| tampon | tampònas (v) | [tam'ponas] |
| toilet paper (toilet roll) | tualetinis pòpierius (v) | [tʊa'lʲɛtʲɪnʲɪs 'po:pʲiɛrʲʊs] |
| hair dryer | fènas (v) | ['fʲɛnas] |

## 40. Watches. Clocks

| watch (wristwatch) | laĩkrodis (v) | ['lʲʌɪkrodʲɪs] |
| dial | ciferblãtas (v) | [tsʲɪfʲɛr'blʲa:tas] |
| hand (of clock, watch) | rodýklė (m) | [ro'dʲi:klʲe:] |
| metal watch band | apýrankė (m) | [a'pʲi:raŋkʲe:] |
| watch strap | dirželis (v) | [dʲɪr'ʒʲælʲɪs] |

| battery | elemeñtas (v) | [ɛlʲɛ'mʲɛntas] |
| to be dead (battery) | išsikráuti | [ɪʃsʲɪ'kraʊtʲɪ] |
| to change a battery | pakeĩsti elemeñtą | [pa'kʲɛɪstʲɪ ɛlʲɛ'mʲɛnta:] |
| to run fast | skubéti | [skʊ'bʲe:tʲɪ] |

| to run slow | atsilìkti | [atsʲɪ'lʲɪktʲɪ] |
| wall clock | síeninis laîkrodis (v) | ['sʲɛnʲɪnʲɪs 'lʲʌɪkrodʲɪs] |
| hourglass | smě̃lio laîkrodis (v) | ['smʲeːlʲɔ 'lʌɪkrodʲɪs] |
| sundial | sáulės laîkrodis (v) | ['sɑʊlʲeːs 'lʌɪkrodʲɪs] |
| alarm clock | žadintùvas (v) | [ʒadʲɪn'tʊvas] |
| watchmaker | laîkrodininkas (v) | ['lʲʌɪkrodʲɪnʲɪŋkas] |
| to repair (vt) | taisýti | [tʌɪ'sʲiːtʲɪ] |

# EVERYDAY EXPERIENCE

**T&P Books Publishing**

| | | |
|---|---|---|
| money | **pinigai** (v) | [p<sup>j</sup>ɪn<sup>j</sup>ɪ'gʌɪ] |
| currency exchange | **keitìmas** (v) | [k<sup>j</sup>ɛɪ't<sup>j</sup>ɪmas] |
| exchange rate | **kùrsas** (v) | ['kʊrsas] |
| ATM | **bankomãtas** (v) | [baŋko'maːtas] |
| coin | **monetà** (m) | [mon<sup>j</sup>ɛ'ta] |
| | | |
| dollar | **dòleris** (v) | ['dol<sup>j</sup>ɛr<sup>j</sup>ɪs] |
| euro | **eùras** (v) | ['ɛʊras] |
| | | |
| lira | **lirà** (m) | [l<sup>j</sup>ɪ'ra] |
| Deutschmark | **márkė** (m) | ['mark<sup>j</sup>eː] |
| franc | **fránkas** (v) | ['fraŋkas] |
| pound sterling | **svãras** (v) | ['svaːras] |
| yen | **jenà** (m) | [jɛ'na] |
| | | |
| debt | **skolà** (m) | [sko'l<sup>j</sup>a] |
| debtor | **skòlininkas** (v) | ['sko:l<sup>j</sup>ɪn<sup>j</sup>ɪŋkas] |
| to lend (money) | **dúoti į skõlą** | ['dʊɑt<sup>j</sup>ɪ iː 'sko:l<sup>j</sup>aː] |
| to borrow (vi, vt) | **im̃ti į skõlą** | ['ɪmt<sup>j</sup>ɪ iː 'sko:l<sup>j</sup>a:] |
| | | |
| bank | **bánkas** (v) | ['baŋkas] |
| account | **sáskaita** (m) | ['sa:skʌɪta] |
| to deposit into the account | **déti į sáskaitą** | ['d<sup>j</sup>e:t<sup>j</sup>ɪ iː 'sa:skʌɪta:] |
| to withdraw (vt) | **im̃ti iš sáskaitos** | ['ɪmt<sup>j</sup>ɪ ɪʃ 'sa:skʌɪtos] |
| | | |
| credit card | **kredìtinė kortẽlė** (m) | [kr<sup>j</sup>ɛ'd<sup>j</sup>ɪt<sup>j</sup>ɪn<sup>j</sup>e: kor't<sup>j</sup>æl<sup>j</sup>e:] |
| cash | **gryníeji pinigai** (v) | [gr<sup>j</sup>i:'n<sup>j</sup>iɛjɪ p<sup>j</sup>ɪn<sup>j</sup>ɪ'gʌɪ] |
| check | **čèkis** (v) | ['tʂ<sup>j</sup>ɛk<sup>j</sup>ɪs] |
| to write a check | **išrašýti čèkį** | [ɪʃra'ʃ<sup>j</sup>ɪːt<sup>j</sup>ɪ 'tʂ<sup>j</sup>ɛk<sup>j</sup>ɪː] |
| checkbook | **čẽkių knygẽlė** (m) | ['tʂ<sup>j</sup>ɛk<sup>j</sup>u: kn<sup>j</sup>i:'g<sup>j</sup>æl<sup>j</sup>e:] |
| | | |
| wallet | **piniginė** (m) | [p<sup>j</sup>ɪn<sup>j</sup>ɪ'g<sup>j</sup>ɪn<sup>j</sup>e:] |
| change purse | **piniginė** (m) | [p<sup>j</sup>ɪn<sup>j</sup>ɪ'g<sup>j</sup>ɪn<sup>j</sup>e:] |
| safe | **seĩfas** (v) | ['s<sup>j</sup>ɛɪfas] |
| | | |
| heir | **paveldétojas** (v) | [pavel<sup>j</sup>'d<sup>j</sup>e:to:jɛs] |
| inheritance | **palikìmas** (v) | [pal<sup>j</sup>ɪ'k<sup>j</sup>ɪmas] |
| fortune (wealth) | **tùrtas** (v) | ['tʊrtas] |
| | | |
| lease | **núoma** (m) | ['nʊama] |
| rent (money) | **bùto mókestis** (v) | ['bʊtɔ 'mok<sup>j</sup>ɛst<sup>j</sup>ɪs] |
| to rent (sth from sb) | **núomotis** | ['nʊamot<sup>j</sup>ɪs] |
| price | **káina** (m) | ['kʌɪna] |
| cost | **káina** (m) | ['kʌɪna] |

| sum | sumà (m) | [sʊˈma] |
| to spend (vt) | léisti | [ˈlʲɛɪstʲɪ] |
| expenses | sánaudos (m dgs) | [ˈsaːnɑʊdos] |
| to economize (vi, vt) | taupýti | [tɑʊˈpʲiːtʲɪ] |
| economical | taupùs | [tɑʊˈpʊs] |

| to pay (vi, vt) | mokéti | [moˈkʲeːtʲɪ] |
| payment | apmokéjimas (v) | [apmoˈkʲɛjɪmas] |
| change (give the ~) | grąžà (m) | [graːˈʒa] |

| tax | mókestis (v) | [ˈmokʲɛstʲɪs] |
| fine | baudà (m) | [bɑʊˈda] |
| to fine (vt) | baũsti | [ˈbɑʊstʲɪ] |

## 42. Post. Postal service

| post office | pãštas (v) | [ˈpaːʃtas] |
| mail (letters, etc.) | pãštas (v) | [ˈpaːʃtas] |
| mailman | pãštininkas (v) | [ˈpaːʃtʲɪnʲɪŋkas] |
| opening hours | dárbo valandõs (m dgs) | [ˈdarbɔ valʲanˈdoːs] |

| letter | láiškas (v) | [ˈlʲʌɪʃkas] |
| registered letter | užsakýtas láiškas (v) | [ʊʒsaˈkʲiːtas ˈlʲʌɪʃkas] |
| postcard | atvirùtė (m) | [atvʲɪˈrutʲeː] |
| telegram | telegramà (m) | [tʲɛlʲɛgraˈma] |

| package (parcel) | siuntinỹs (v) | [sʲʊntʲɪˈnʲiːs] |
| money transfer | pinigìnis pavedìmas (v) | [pʲɪnʲɪˈgʲɪnʲɪs pavʲɛˈdʲɪmas] |

| to receive (vt) | gáuti | [ˈgɑʊtʲɪ] |
| to send (vt) | išsiũsti | [ɪʃsʲʊːstʲɪ] |
| sending | išsiuntìmas (v) | [ɪʃsʲʊnˈtʲɪmas] |

| address | ãdresas (v) | [ˈaːdrʲɛsas] |
| ZIP code | iñdeksas (v) | [ˈɪndʲɛksas] |

| sender | siuntéjas (v) | [sʲʊnˈtʲeːjas] |
| receiver | gavéjas (v) | [gaˈvʲeːjas] |

| name (first name) | var̃das (v) | [ˈvardas] |
| surname (last name) | pavardė̃ (m) | [pavarˈdʲeː] |

| postage rate | tarìfas (v) | [taˈrʲɪfas] |
| standard (adj) | į̃prastas | [ˈiːprastas] |
| economical (adj) | taupùs | [tɑʊˈpʊs] |

| weight | svõris (v) | [ˈsvoːrʲɪs] |
| to weigh (~ letters) | sver̃ti | [ˈsvʲɛrtʲɪ] |
| envelope | võkas (v) | [ˈvoːkas] |
| postage stamp | markùtė (m) | [marˈkutʲeː] |

## 43. Banking

| bank | bánkas (v) | ['baŋkas] |
| branch (of bank, etc.) | skỹrius (v) | ['skʲi:rʲʊs] |

| bank clerk, consultant | konsultántas (v) | [kɔnsʊlʲ'tantas] |
| manager (director) | valdýtojas (v) | [valʲ'dʲi:to:jɛs] |

| bank account | sąskaita (m) | ['sa:skʌɪta] |
| account number | sąskaitos númeris (v) | ['sa:skʌɪtos 'nʊmʲɛrʲɪs] |
| checking account | einamóji sąskaita (m) | [ɛɪna'mo:jɪ 'sa:skʌɪta] |
| savings account | kaupiamóji sąskaita (m) | [kaʊpʲæ'mo:jɪ 'sa:skʌɪta] |

| to open an account | atidarýti sąskaitą | [atʲɪda'rʲi:tʲɪ 'sa:skʌɪta:] |
| to close the account | uždarýti sąskaitą | [ʊʒda'rʲi:tʲɪ 'sa:skʌɪta:] |
| to deposit into the account | padéti į sąskaitą | [pa'dʲe:tʲɪ i: 'sa:skʌɪta:] |
| to withdraw (vt) | paimti iš sąskaitos | ['pʌɪmtʲɪ ɪʃ 'sa:skʌɪtos] |

| deposit | iñdėlis (v) | ['ɪndʲe:lʲɪs] |
| to make a deposit | įnešti iñdėlį | [i:'nʲɛʃtʲɪ 'ɪndʲe:lʲɪ:] |
| wire transfer | pavedìmas (v) | [pavʲɛ'dʲɪmas] |
| to wire, to transfer | atlìkti pavedìmą | [at'lʲɪktʲɪ pavʲɛ'dʲɪma:] |

| sum | sumà (m) | [sʊ'ma] |
| How much? | Kíek? | ['kʲɪɛk?] |

| signature | pãrašas (v) | ['pa:raʃas] |
| to sign (vt) | pasirašýti | [pasʲɪra'ʃɪ:tʲɪ] |

| credit card | kredìtinė kortėlė (m) | [krʲɛ'dʲɪtʲɪnʲe: kor'tʲælʲe:] |
| code (PIN code) | kòdas (v) | ['kodas] |
| credit card number | kredìtinės kortėlės númeris (v) | [krʲɛ'dʲɪtʲɪnʲe:s kor'tʲælʲe:s 'nʊmʲɛrʲɪs] |

| ATM | bankomãtas (v) | [baŋko'ma:tas] |

| check | kvìtas (v) | ['kvʲɪtas] |
| to write a check | išrašýti kvìtą | [ɪʃra'ʃɪ:tʲɪ 'kvʲɪta:] |
| checkbook | čėkių knygėlė (m) | ['tʃʲɛkʲu: knʲɪ:'gʲælʲe:] |

| loan (bank ~) | kredìtas (v) | [krʲɛ'dʲɪtas] |
| to apply for a loan | kreìptis dėl kredìto | ['krʲɛɪptʲɪs dʲe:lʲ krʲɛ'dʲɪto] |
| to get a loan | im̃ti kredìtą | ['ɪmtʲɪ krʲɛ'dʲɪta:] |
| to give a loan | suteìkti kredìtą | [sʊ'tʲɛɪktʲɪ krʲɛ'dʲɪta:] |
| guarantee | garántija (m) | [ga'rantʲɪjɛ] |

## 44. Telephone. Phone conversation

| telephone | telefònas (v) | [tʲɛlʲɛ'fonas] |
| cell phone | mobilùsis telefònas (v) | [mobʲɪ'lʊsʲɪs tʲɛlʲɛ'fonas] |

| | | |
|---|---|---|
| answering machine | autoatsakìklis (v) | [ɑutoatsa'kʲɪklʲɪs] |
| to call (by phone) | skaṁbinti | ['skambʲɪntʲɪ] |
| phone call | skambùtis (v) | [skam'butʲɪs] |

| | | |
|---|---|---|
| to dial a number | surìnkti nùmerį | [sʊ'rʲɪŋktʲɪ 'nʊmʲɛrʲɪ:] |
| Hello! | Aliò! | [a'lʲo!] |
| to ask (vt) | pakláusti | [pak'lʲɑustʲɪ] |
| to answer (vi, vt) | atsakýti | [atsa'kʲi:tʲɪ] |

| | | |
|---|---|---|
| to hear (vt) | girdéti | [gʲɪr'dʲe:tʲɪ] |
| well (adv) | geraĩ | [gʲɛ'rʌɪ] |
| not well (adv) | prastaĩ | [pras'tʌɪ] |
| noises (interference) | trukdžiaĩ (v dgs) | [trʊk'dʒʲɛɪ] |

| | | |
|---|---|---|
| receiver | ragẽlis (v) | [ra'gʲælʲɪs] |
| to pick up (~ the phone) | pakélti ragẽlį | [pa'kʲɛlʲtʲɪ ra'gʲælʲɪ:] |
| to hang up (~ the phone) | padéti ragẽlį | [pa'dʲe:tʲɪ ra'gʲælʲɪ:] |

| | | |
|---|---|---|
| busy (engaged) | ùžimtas | ['ʊʒʲɪmtas] |
| to ring (ab. phone) | skambéti | [skam'bʲe:tʲɪ] |
| telephone book | telefònų knygà (m) | [tʲɛlʲɛ'fonu: knʲi:'ga] |

| | | |
|---|---|---|
| local (adj) | viẽtinis | ['vʲiɛtʲɪnʲɪs] |
| local call | viẽtinis skambùtis (v) | ['vʲiɛtʲɪnʲɪs skam'butʲɪs] |
| long distance (~ call) | tarpmiestìnis | [tarpmʲiɛs'tʲɪnʲɪs] |
| long-distance call | tarpmiestìnis skambùtis (v) | [tarpmʲiɛs'tʲɪnʲɪs skam'butʲɪs] |
| international (adj) | tarptautìnis | [tarptɑu'tʲɪnʲɪs] |
| international call | tarptautìnis skambùtis (v) | [tarptɑu'tʲɪnʲɪs skam'butʲɪs] |

## 45. Cell phone

| | | |
|---|---|---|
| cell phone | mobilùsis telefònas (v) | [mobʲɪ'lʊsʲɪs tʲɛlʲɛ'fonas] |
| display | ekrãnas (v) | [ɛk'ra:nas] |
| button | mygtùkas (v) | [mʲi:k'tukas] |
| SIM card | SIM-kortẽlė (m) | [sʲɪm-kor'tʲælʲe:] |

| | | |
|---|---|---|
| battery | akumuliãtorius (v) | [akʊmu'lʲætorʲʊs] |
| to be dead (battery) | išsikráuti | [ɪʃsʲɪ'krɑutʲɪ] |
| charger | įkrovìklis (v) | [i:kro'vʲɪ:klʲɪs] |

| | | |
|---|---|---|
| menu | valgiãraštis (v) | [valʲ'gʲæraʃtʲɪs] |
| settings | nustãtymai (v dgs) | [nʊ'sta:tʲi:mʌɪ] |
| tune (melody) | melòdija (m) | [mʲɛ'lʲodʲɪjɛ] |
| to select (vt) | pasirìnkti | [pasʲɪ'rʲɪŋktʲɪ] |

| | | |
|---|---|---|
| calculator | skaičiuotùvas (v) | [skʌɪtʃʲʊo'tuvas] |
| voice mail | baĺso pãštas (v) | ['balʲsɔ 'pa:ʃtas] |
| alarm clock | žadintùvas (v) | [ʒadʲɪn'tuvas] |
| contacts | telefònų knygà (m) | [tʲɛlʲɛ'fonu: knʲi:'ga] |

| | | |
|---|---|---|
| SMS (text message) | **SMS žinutė** (m) | [εsε'mεs ʒɪnutʲeː] |
| subscriber | **abonentas** (v) | [abo'nʲεntas] |

## 46. Stationery

| | | |
|---|---|---|
| ballpoint pen | **automatinis šratinukas** (v) | [auto'maːtʲɪnʲɪs ʃratʲɪ'nukas] |
| fountain pen | **plunksnakotis** (v) | [plʲuŋk'snaːkotʲɪs] |
| pencil | **pieštukas** (v) | [pʲiεʃ'tukas] |
| highlighter | **žymėklis** (v) | [ʒʲiː'mʲæklʲɪs] |
| felt-tip pen | **flomasteris** (v) | [flʲo'maːstʲεrʲɪs] |
| notepad | **bloknotas** (v) | [blʲok'notas] |
| agenda (diary) | **dienoraštis** (v) | [dʲiε'noraʃtʲɪs] |
| ruler | **liniuotė** (m) | [lʲɪ'nʲuoːtʲeː] |
| calculator | **skaičiuotuvas** (v) | [skʌɪtʃʲuo'tuvas] |
| eraser | **trintukas** (v) | [trʲɪn'tukas] |
| thumbtack | **smeigtukas** (v) | [smʲεɪk'tukas] |
| paper clip | **sąvaržėlė** (m) | [saːvar'ʒʲeːlʲeː] |
| glue | **klijai** (v dgs) | [klʲɪ'jʌɪ] |
| stapler | **segiklis** (v) | [sʲε'gʲɪklʲɪs] |
| hole punch | **skylamušis** (v) | [skʲiː'lʲaːmuʃʲɪs] |
| pencil sharpener | **drožtukas** (v) | [droʒ'tukas] |

## 47. Foreign languages

| | | |
|---|---|---|
| language | **kalba** (m) | [kalʲ'ba] |
| foreign (adj) | **užsienio** | ['uʒsʲiεnʲɔ] |
| foreign language | **užsienio kalba** (m) | ['uʒsʲiεnʲɔ kalʲba] |
| to study (vt) | **studijuoti** | [studʲɪ'juatʲɪ] |
| to learn (language, etc.) | **mokytis** | ['mokʲɪ:tʲɪs] |
| to read (vi, vt) | **skaityti** | [skʌɪ'tʲiːtʲɪ] |
| to speak (vi, vt) | **kalbėti** | [kalʲ'bʲeːtʲɪ] |
| to understand (vt) | **suprasti** | [sup'rastʲɪ] |
| to write (vt) | **rašyti** | [ra'ʃɪːtʲɪ] |
| fast (adv) | **greitai** | ['grʲεɪtʌɪ] |
| slowly (adv) | **lėtai** | [lʲeː'tʌɪ] |
| fluently (adv) | **laisvai** | [lʲʌɪs'vʌɪ] |
| rules | **taisyklės** (m dgs) | [tʌɪ'sʲiː:klʲeːs] |
| grammar | **gramatika** (m) | [gra'maːtʲɪka] |
| vocabulary | **leksika** (m) | ['lʲεksʲɪka] |
| phonetics | **fonetika** (m) | [fo'nʲεtʲɪka] |

| | | |
|---|---|---|
| textbook | **vadovėlis** (v) | [vado'vʲeːlʲɪs] |
| dictionary | **žodýnas** (v) | [ʒo'dʲiːnas] |
| teach-yourself book | **savimokos vadovėlis** (v) | [sa'vʲɪmokos vado'vʲeːlʲɪs] |
| phrasebook | **pasikalbėjimų knygėlė** (m) | [pasʲɪkalʲʲbʲɛjɪmu: knʲiː'gʲælʲe:] |
| | | |
| cassette, tape | **kasetė** (m) | [ka'sʲɛtʲeː] |
| videotape | **vaizdajuostė** (m) | [vʌɪz'daːjuɑstʲeː] |
| CD, compact disc | **kompāktinis diskas** (v) | [kom'paːktʲɪnʲɪs 'dʲɪskas] |
| DVD | **DVD diskas** (v) | [dʲɪvʲɪ'dʲɪ dʲɪs'kas] |
| | | |
| alphabet | **abėcėlė** (m) | [abʲe:'tsʲeːlʲeː] |
| to spell (vt) | **sakýti paraidžiuî** | [sa'kʲiːtʲɪ parʌɪ'dʒʲuɪ] |
| pronunciation | **tarìmas** (v) | [ta'rʲɪmas] |
| | | |
| accent | **akceñtas** (v) | [ak'tsʲɛntas] |
| with an accent | **sù akcentù** | ['su aktsʲɛn'tu] |
| without an accent | **bè akceñto** | ['bʲɛ ak'tsʲɛnto] |
| | | |
| word | **žõdis** (v) | ['ʒoːdʲɪs] |
| meaning | **prasmė̃** (m) | [pras'mʲeː] |
| | | |
| course (e.g., a French ~) | **kùrsai** (v dgs) | ['kursʌɪ] |
| to sign up | **užsirašýti** | [uʒsʲɪra'ʃʲɪːtʲɪ] |
| teacher | **déstytojas** (v) | ['dʲeːstʲiːto:jɛs] |
| | | |
| translation (process) | **vertìmas** (v) | [vʲer'tʲɪmas] |
| translation (text, etc.) | **vertìmas** (v) | [vʲer'tʲɪmas] |
| translator | **vertéjas** (v) | [vʲɛr'tʲeːjas] |
| interpreter | **vertéjas** (v) | [vʲɛr'tʲeːjas] |
| | | |
| polyglot | **poliglòtas** (v) | [polʲɪ'glotas] |
| memory | **atmintìs** (m) | [atmʲɪn'tʲɪs] |

.

# MEALS. RESTAURANT

**T&P Books Publishing**

## 48. Table setting

| | | |
|---|---|---|
| spoon | **šáukštas** (v) | ['ʃɑʊkʃtas] |
| knife | **peĩlis** (v) | ['pʲɛɪˠɪs] |
| fork | **šakùtė** (m) | [ʃa'kʊtʲeː] |
| cup (e.g., coffee ~) | **puodùkas** (v) | [pʊɑ'dʊkas] |
| plate (dinner ~) | **lėkštė̃** (m) | [lʲeːkʃtʲeː] |
| saucer | **lėkštẽlė** (m) | [lʲeːkʃtʲælʲeː] |
| napkin (on table) | **servetẽlė** (m) | [sʲɛrveˈtʲeːlʲeː] |
| toothpick | **dantų̃ krapštùkas** (v) | [dan'tu: krapʃtʊkas] |

## 49. Restaurant

| | | |
|---|---|---|
| restaurant | **restorãnas** (v) | [rʲɛsto'ra:nas] |
| coffee house | **kavìnė** (m) | [ka'vʲɪnʲeː] |
| pub, bar | **bãras** (v) | ['ba:ras] |
| tearoom | **arbãtos salõnas** (v) | [ar'ba:tos sa'lʲonas] |
| | | |
| waiter | **padavė́jas** (v) | [pada'vʲeːjas] |
| waitress | **padavė́ja** (m) | [pada'vʲeːja] |
| bartender | **bármenas** (v) | ['barmʲɛnas] |
| | | |
| menu | **meniù** (v) | [mʲɛ'nʲʊ] |
| wine list | **vỹnų žemė́lapis** (v) | ['vʲi:nu: ʒe'mʲeːlˠapʲɪs] |
| to book a table | **rezervúoti staliùką** | [rʲɛzʲɛr'vʊatʲɪ sta'lʲʊka:] |
| | | |
| course, dish | **pãtiekalas** (v) | ['pa:tʲiɛkalˠas] |
| to order (meal) | **užsisakýti** | [ʊʒsʲɪsak'ˠi:tʲɪ] |
| to make an order | **padarýti užsãkymą** | [pada'rʲi:tʲɪ ʊʒ'sa:kʲi:ma:] |
| | | |
| aperitif | **aperitỹvas** (v) | [apʲɛrʲɪ'tʲi:vas] |
| appetizer | **ùžkandis** (v) | ['ʊʒkandʲɪs] |
| dessert | **desèrtas** (v) | [dʲɛ'sʲɛrtas] |
| | | |
| check | **są́skaita** (m) | ['sa:skʌɪta] |
| to pay the check | **apmokė́ti są́skaitą** | [apmo'kʲeːtʲɪ 'sa:skʌɪta:] |
| to give change | **dúoti grąžõs** | ['dʊatʲɪ gra:'ʒo:s] |
| tip | **arbãtpinigiai** (v dgs) | [ar'ba:tpʲɪnʲɪgʲɛɪ] |

## 50. Meals

| | | |
|---|---|---|
| food | **válgis** (v) | ['valˠgʲɪs] |
| to eat (vi, vt) | **válgyti** | ['valˠgʲi:tʲɪ] |

| breakfast | pusryčiai (v dgs) | ['pʊsrʲi:tʃʲɛɪ] |
| to have breakfast | pusryčiauti | ['pʊsrʲi:tʃʲɛʊtʲɪ] |
| lunch | piētūs (v) | ['pʲɛ'tu:s] |
| to have lunch | pietauti | [pʲiɛ'taʊtʲɪ] |
| dinner | vakarienė (m) | [vakaʲrʲɛnʲe:] |
| to have dinner | vakarieniauti | [vakarʲiɛ'nʲæʊtʲɪ] |

| appetite | apetitas (v) | [apʲɛ'tʲɪtas] |
| Enjoy your meal! | Gēro apetito! | ['gʲæro apʲɛ'tʲɪto!] |

| to open (~ a bottle) | atidaryti | [atʲɪda'rʲi:tʲɪ] |
| to spill (liquid) | išpilti | [ɪʃ'pʲɪlʲtʲɪ] |
| to spill out (vi) | iššipilti | [ɪʃsʲɪ'pʲɪlʲtʲɪ] |

| to boil (vi) | virti | ['vʲɪrtʲɪ] |
| to boil (vt) | virinti | ['vʲɪrʲɪntʲɪ] |
| boiled (~ water) | virintas | ['vʲɪrʲɪntas] |
| to chill, cool down (vt) | atvėsinti | [atvʲe:'sʲɪntʲɪ] |
| to chill (vi) | vėsinti | [vʲe:'sʲɪntʲɪ] |

| taste, flavor | skōnis (v) | ['sko:nʲɪs] |
| aftertaste | prieskonis (v) | ['prʲiɛskonʲɪs] |

| to slim down (lose weight) | laikyti diētos | [lʲʌɪ'kʲi:tʲɪ 'dʲɛtos] |
| diet | dieta (m) | [dʲiɛ'ta] |
| vitamin | vitaminas (v) | [vʲɪta'mʲɪnas] |
| calorie | kalorija (m) | [ka'lʲorʲɪjɛ] |
| vegetarian (n) | vegetaras (v) | [vʲɛgʲɛ'ta:ras] |
| vegetarian (adj) | vegetariškas | [vʲɛgʲɛ'ta:rʲɪʃkas] |

| fats (nutrient) | riebalai (v dgs) | [rʲiɛba'lʲʌɪ] |
| proteins | baltymai (v dgs) | [balʲtʲi:'mʌɪ] |
| carbohydrates | angliavandeniai (v dgs) | [an'glʲæevandʲɛnʲɛɪ] |
| slice (of lemon, ham) | griežinys (v) | [grʲiɛʒʲɪ'nʲi:s] |
| piece (of cake, pie) | gabalas (v) | ['ga:balʲas] |
| crumb (of bread, cake, etc.) | trupinys (v) | [trʊpʲɪ'nʲi:s] |

## 51. Cooked dishes

| course, dish | patiekalas (v) | ['pa:tʲiɛkalʲas] |
| cuisine | virtuvė (m) | [vʲɪr'tʊvʲe:] |
| recipe | receptas (v) | [rʲɛ'tsʲɛptas] |
| portion | porcija (m) | ['portsʲɪjɛ] |

| salad | salōtos (m) | [sa'lʲo:tos] |
| soup | sriuba (m) | [srʲʊ'ba] |

| clear soup (broth) | sultinys (v) | [sʊlʲtʲɪ'nʲi:s] |
| sandwich (bread) | sumuštinis (v) | [sʊmʊʃtʲɪnʲɪs] |

| | | |
|---|---|---|
| fried eggs | kiaušinienė (m) | [kʲɛʊʃɪ'nʲɛnʲeː] |
| hamburger (beefburger) | mėsainis (v) | [mʲeː'sʌɪnʲɪs] |
| beefsteak | bifšteksas (v) | [bʲɪfʃtʲɛksas] |

| | | |
|---|---|---|
| side dish | garnyras (v) | [gar'nʲiːras] |
| spaghetti | spagečiai (v dgs) | [spa'gʲɛtʂʲɛɪ] |
| mashed potatoes | bulvių košė (m) | ['buʎvʲuː 'koːʃeː] |
| pizza | pica (m) | [pʲɪ'tsa] |
| porridge (oatmeal, etc.) | košė (m) | ['koːʃeː] |
| omelet | omletas (v) | [om'lʲɛtas] |

| | | |
|---|---|---|
| boiled (e.g., ~ beef) | virtas | ['vʲɪrtas] |
| smoked (adj) | rūkytas | [ru:'kʲiːtas] |
| fried (adj) | keptas | ['kʲæptas] |
| dried (adj) | džiovintas | [dʒʲoˈvʲɪntas] |
| frozen (adj) | šaldytas | ['ʃalʲdʲiːtas] |
| pickled (adj) | marinuotas | [marʲɪ'nuɑtas] |

| | | |
|---|---|---|
| sweet (sugary) | saldus | [salʲ'dʊs] |
| salty (adj) | sūrus | [su:'rʊs] |
| cold (adj) | šaltas | ['ʃalʲtas] |
| hot (adj) | karštas | ['karʃtas] |
| bitter (adj) | kartus | [kar'tʊs] |
| tasty (adj) | skanus | [ska'nʊs] |

| | | |
|---|---|---|
| to cook in boiling water | virti | ['vʲɪrtʲɪ] |
| to cook (dinner) | gaminti | [ga'mʲɪntʲɪ] |
| to fry (vt) | kepti | ['kʲɛptʲɪ] |
| to heat up (food) | pašildyti | [pa'ʃɪlʲdʲiːtʲɪ] |

| | | |
|---|---|---|
| to salt (vt) | sūdyti | ['su:dʲiːtʲɪ] |
| to pepper (vt) | įberti pipirų | [i:'bʲɛrtʲɪ pʲɪ'pʲɪːru:] |
| to grate (vt) | tarkuoti | [tar'kuɑtʲɪ] |
| peel (n) | luoba (m) | ['lʲuɑba] |
| to peel (vt) | lupti bulves | ['lʊptʲɪ 'bulʲvʲɛs] |

## 52. Food

| | | |
|---|---|---|
| meat | mėsa (m) | [mʲe:'sa] |
| chicken | višta (m) | [vʲɪʃ'ta] |
| Rock Cornish hen (poussin) | viščiukas (v) | [vʲɪʃ'tʂʲʊkas] |
| duck | antis (m) | ['antʲɪs] |
| goose | žąsinas (v) | ['ʒa:sʲɪnas] |
| game | žvėriena (m) | [ʒvʲe:'rʲiɛna] |
| turkey | kalakutiena (m) | [kalʲaku'tʲiɛna] |
| pork | kiauliena (m) | [kʲɛʊ'lʲiɛna] |
| veal | veršiena (m) | [vʲɛrʃʲiɛna] |
| lamb | aviena (m) | [a'vʲiɛna] |

| | | |
|---|---|---|
| beef | **jáutiena** (m) | ['jɑʊtʲiɛna] |
| rabbit | **triùšis** (v) | ['trʲʊʃɪs] |
| | | |
| sausage (bologna, pepperoni, etc.) | **dešrà** (m) | [dʲɛʃra] |
| vienna sausage (frankfurter) | **dešrėlė** (m) | [dʲɛʃrʲælʲe:] |
| bacon | **bekònas** (v) | [bʲɛ'konas] |
| ham | **kumpis** (v) | ['kʊmpʲɪs] |
| gammon | **kumpis** (v) | ['kʊmpʲɪs] |
| | | |
| pâté | **paštètas** (v) | [paʃtʲɛtas] |
| liver | **kėpenys** (m dgs) | [kʲɛpe'nʲi:s] |
| hamburger (ground beef) | **fáršas** (v) | ['farʃas] |
| tongue | **liežùvis** (v) | [lʲiɛ'ʒʊvʲɪs] |
| | | |
| egg | **kiaušìnis** (v) | [kʲɛʊ'ʃɪnʲɪs] |
| eggs | **kiaušìniai** (v dgs) | [kʲɛʊ'ʃɪnʲɛɪ] |
| egg white | **báltymas** (v) | ['balʲtʲi:mas] |
| egg yolk | **trynỹs** (v) | [trʲi:'nʲi:s] |
| | | |
| fish | **žuvìs** (m) | [ʒʊ'vʲɪs] |
| seafood | **júros gėrýbės** (m dgs) | ['ju:ros gʲe:'rʲi:bʲe:s] |
| crustaceans | **vėžiãgyviai** (v dgs) | [vʲe:'ʒʲægʲi:vʲɛɪ] |
| caviar | **ìkrai** (v dgs) | ['ɪkrʌɪ] |
| | | |
| crab | **krãbas** (v) | ['kra:bas] |
| shrimp | **krevètė** (m) | [krʲɛ'vʲɛtʲe:] |
| oyster | **áustrė** (m) | ['ɑʊstrʲe:] |
| spiny lobster | **langùstas** (v) | [lʲan'gustas] |
| octopus | **aštuonkõjis** (v) | [aʃtʊɑŋ'ko:jis] |
| squid | **kalmãras** (v) | [kalʲma:ras] |
| | | |
| sturgeon | **eršketíena** (m) | [ɛrʃkʲɛ'tʲiɛna] |
| salmon | **lašišà** (m) | [lʲaʃɪʃa] |
| halibut | **õtas** (v) | ['o:tas] |
| | | |
| cod | **ménkė** (m) | ['mʲɛŋkʲe:] |
| mackerel | **skùmbrė** (m) | ['skʊmbrʲe:] |
| tuna | **tùnas** (v) | ['tʊnas] |
| eel | **ungurỹs** (v) | [ʊŋgʊ'rʲi:s] |
| | | |
| trout | **upétakis** (v) | [ʊ'pʲe:takʲɪs] |
| sardine | **sardìnė** (m) | [sar'dʲɪnʲe:] |
| pike | **lydekà** (m) | [lʲi:dʲɛ'ka] |
| herring | **sílkė** (m) | ['sʲɪlʲkʲe:] |
| | | |
| bread | **dúona** (m) | ['dʊɑna] |
| cheese | **sūris** (v) | ['su:rʲɪs] |
| sugar | **cùkrus** (v) | ['tsʊkrʊs] |
| salt | **druskà** (m) | [drʊs'ka] |
| rice | **rýžiai** (v) | ['rʲi:ʒʲɛɪ] |

| pasta (macaroni) | makarõnai (v dgs) | [makaˈroːnʌɪ] |
| noodles | lãkštiniai (v dgs) | [ˈlʲaːkʃtʲɪnʲɛɪ] |

| butter | svíestas (v) | [ˈsvʲiɛstas] |
| vegetable oil | augalìnis aliẽjus (v) | [ɑʊgalʲɪnʲɪs aˈlʲɛjʊs] |
| sunflower oil | saulégrąžų aliẽjus (v) | [sɑʊˈlʲeːgraːʒuː aˈlʲɛjʊs] |
| margarine | margarìnas (v) | [margaˈrʲɪnas] |

| olives | alývuogės (m dgs) | [aˈlʲiːvʊagʲeːs] |
| olive oil | alývuogių aliẽjus (v) | [aˈlʲiːvʊagʲu aˈlʲɛjʊs] |

| milk | píenas (v) | [ˈpʲiɛnas] |
| condensed milk | sutírštintas píenas (v) | [sʊˈtʲɪrʃtʲɪntas ˈpʲiɛnas] |
| yogurt | jogùrtas (v) | [joˈgʊrtas] |
| sour cream | grietìnė (m) | [grʲiɛˈtʲɪnʲeː] |
| cream (of milk) | grietinẽlė (m) | [grʲiɛtʲɪˈnʲeːlʲeː] |

| mayonnaise | majonẽzas (v) | [majoˈnʲɛzas] |
| buttercream | krẽmas (v) | [ˈkrʲɛmas] |

| cereal grains (wheat, etc.) | kruõpos (m dgs) | [ˈkrʊapos] |
| flour | mìltai (v dgs) | [ˈmʲɪlʲtʌɪ] |
| canned food | konsèrvai (v dgs) | [kɔnˈsʲɛrvʌɪ] |

| cornflakes | kukurū̃zų drìbsniai (v dgs) | [kʊkuˈruːzu ˈdrʲɪbsnʲɛɪ] |
| honey | medùs (v) | [mʲɛˈdʊs] |
| jam | džẽmas (v) | [ˈdʒʲɛmas] |
| chewing gum | kram̃tomoji gumà (m) | [kramtoˈmojɪ gʊˈma] |

## 53. Drinks

| water | vanduõ (v) | [vanˈdʊa] |
| drinking water | gẽriamas vanduõ (v) | [ˈgʲærʲæmas vanˈdʊa] |
| mineral water | minerãlinis vanduõ (v) | [mʲɪnʲɛˈraːlʲɪnʲɪs vanˈdʊa] |

| still (adj) | bè gãzo | [ˈbʲɛ ˈgaːzɔ] |
| carbonated (adj) | gazúotas | [gaˈzʊatas] |
| sparkling (adj) | gazúotas | [gaˈzʊatas] |
| ice | lẽdas (v) | [ˈlʲædas] |
| with ice | sù ledaìs | [ˈsʊ lʲɛˈdʌɪs] |

| non-alcoholic (adj) | nealkohòlonis | [nʲɛalʲkoˈɣolonʲɪs] |
| soft drink | nealkohòlonis gẽrimas (v) | [nʲɛalʲkoˈɣolonʲɪs ˈgʲɛrʲɪmas] |
| refreshing drink | gaivùsis gẽrimas (v) | [gʌɪˈvʊsʲɪs ˈgʲeːrʲɪmas] |
| lemonade | limonãdas (v) | [lʲɪmoˈnaːdas] |

| liquors | alkohòliniai gẽrimai (v dgs) | [alʲkoˈɣolʲɪnʲɛɪ ˈgʲeːrʲɪmʌɪ] |
| wine | vỹnas (v) | [ˈvʲiːnas] |
| white wine | báltas vỹnas (v) | [ˈbalʲtas ˈvʲiːnas] |

| red wine | raudónas vỹnas (v) | [rɑʊ'donas 'vʲi:nas] |
| liqueur | lìkeris (v) | ['lʲɪkʲɛrʲɪs] |
| champagne | šampãnas (v) | [ʃam'pa:nas] |
| vermouth | vèrmutas (v) | ['vʲɛrmʊtas] |

| whiskey | vìskis (v) | ['vʲɪskʲɪs] |
| vodka | degtìnė (m) | [dʲɛk'tʲɪnʲe:] |
| gin | džìnas (v) | ['dʒʲɪnas] |
| cognac | konjãkas (v) | [kɔn'ja:kas] |
| rum | ròmas (v) | ['romas] |

| coffee | kavà (m) | [ka'va] |
| black coffee | juodà kavà (m) | [jʊɑ'da ka'va] |
| coffee with milk | kavà sù píenu (m) | [ka'va 'sʊ 'pʲiɛnʊ] |
| cappuccino | kapučìno kavà (m) | [kapu'tʂɪno ka'va] |
| instant coffee | tirpì kavà (m) | [tʲɪr'pʲɪ ka'va] |

| milk | píenas (v) | ['pʲiɛnas] |
| cocktail | koktèilis (v) | [kɔk'tʲɛɪlʲɪs] |
| milkshake | píeniškas koktèilis (v) | ['pʲiɛnʲɪʃkas kɔk'tʲɛɪlʲɪs] |

| juice | sùltys (m dgs) | ['sʊlʲtʲi:s] |
| tomato juice | pomidòrų sùltys (m dgs) | [pomʲɪ'doru: 'sʊlʲtʲi:s] |
| orange juice | apelsìnų sùltys (m dgs) | [apʲɛlʲ'sʲɪnu: 'sʊlʲtʲi:s] |
| freshly squeezed juice | šviežiaĩ spáustos sùltys (m dgs) | [ʃvʲiɛ'ʒʲɛɪ 'spɑʊstos 'sʊlʲtʲi:s] |

| beer | alùs (v) | [a'lʲʊs] |
| light beer | šviesùs alùs (v) | [ʃvʲiɛ'sʊs a'lʲʊs] |
| dark beer | tamsùs alùs (v) | [tam'sʊs a'lʲʊs] |

| tea | arbatà (m) | [arba'ta] |
| black tea | juodà arbatà (m) | [jʊɑ'da arba'ta] |
| green tea | žalià arbatà (m) | [ʒa'lʲæ arba'ta] |

## 54. Vegetables

| vegetables | daržóvės (m dgs) | [dar'ʒovʲe:s] |
| greens | žalumýnai (v) | [ʒalʲʊ'mʲi:nʌɪ] |

| tomato | pomidòras (v) | [pomʲɪ'doras] |
| cucumber | agur̃kas (v) | [a'gʊrkas] |
| carrot | morkà (m) | [mor'ka] |
| potato | bùlvė (m) | ['bʊlʲvʲe:] |
| onion | svogū̃nas (v) | [svo'gu:nas] |
| garlic | česnãkas (v) | [tʂʲɛs'na:kas] |

| cabbage | kopū̃stas (v) | [kɔ'pu:stas] |
| cauliflower | kalafiòras (v) | [kalʲa'fʲoras] |
| Brussels sprouts | briùselio kopū̃stas (v) | ['brʲʊsʲɛlʲo ko'pu:stas] |

| | | |
|---|---|---|
| broccoli | brokolių kopūstas (v) | ['brokolʲu: ko'pu:stas] |
| beetroot | ruñkelis, burõkas (v) | ['ruŋkʲɛlʲɪs], [bu'ro:kas] |
| eggplant | baklažānas (v) | [baklʲa'ʒa:nas] |
| zucchini | agurõtis (v) | [agu'ro:tʲɪs] |
| pumpkin | rópė (m) | ['ropʲe:] |
| turnip | moliũgas (v) | [mo'lʲu:gas] |
| | | |
| parsley | petrãžolė (m) | [pʲɛ'tra:ʒolʲe:] |
| dill | krāpas (v) | ['kra:pas] |
| lettuce | salõta (m) | [sa'lʲo:ta] |
| celery | saliēras (v) | [sa'lʲɛras] |
| asparagus | smidras (v) | ['smʲɪdras] |
| spinach | špinātas (v) | [ʃpʲɪ'na:tas] |
| | | |
| pea | žirniai (v dgs) | ['ʒʲɪrnʲɛɪ] |
| beans | pùpos (m dgs) | ['pupos] |
| corn (maize) | kukurūzas (v) | [kuku'ru:zas] |
| kidney bean | pupēlės (m dgs) | [pu'pʲælʲe:s] |
| | | |
| bell pepper | pipiras (v) | [pʲɪ'pʲɪras] |
| radish | ridikas (v) | [rʲɪ'dʲɪkas] |
| artichoke | artišõkas (v) | [artʲɪ'ʃokas] |

## 55. Fruits. Nuts

| | | |
|---|---|---|
| fruit | vaìsius (v) | ['vʌɪsʲus] |
| apple | obuolỹs (v) | [obuɑ'lʲi:s] |
| pear | kriáušė (m) | ['krʲæuʃʲe:] |
| lemon | citrinà (m) | [tsʲɪtrʲɪ'na] |
| orange | apelsìnas (v) | [apʲɛlʲ'sʲɪnas] |
| strawberry (garden ~) | brãškė (m) | ['bra:ʃkʲe:] |
| | | |
| mandarin | mandarìnas (v) | [manda'rʲɪnas] |
| plum | slyvà (m) | [slʲi:'va] |
| peach | pèrsikas (v) | ['pʲɛrsʲɪkas] |
| apricot | abrikõsas (v) | [abrʲɪ'kosas] |
| raspberry | aviētė (m) | [a'vʲɛtʲe:] |
| pineapple | ananãsas (v) | [ana'na:sas] |
| | | |
| banana | banãnas (v) | [ba'na:nas] |
| watermelon | arbūzas (v) | [ar'bu:zas] |
| grape | vỹnuogės (m dgs) | ['vʲi:nuɑgʲe:s] |
| sour cherry | vyšnià (m) | [vʲi:ʃnʲæ] |
| sweet cherry | trēšnė (m) | ['tʲræʃnʲe:] |
| melon | meliõnas (v) | [mʲɛ'lʲonas] |
| | | |
| grapefruit | greìpfrutas (v) | ['grʲɛɪpfrutas] |
| avocado | avokādas (v) | [avo'kadas] |
| papaya | papája (m) | [pa'pa ja] |
| mango | mángo (v) | ['mango] |

| | | |
|---|---|---|
| pomegranate | granãtas (v) | [gra'na:tas] |
| redcurrant | raudoníeji serbeñtai (v dgs) | [rauˈdoˈnʲɛji sʲɛrˈbʲɛntʌɪ] |
| blackcurrant | juodíeji serbeñtai (v dgs) | [juɑˈdʲiɛjɪ sʲɛrˈbʲɛntʌɪ] |
| gooseberry | agrãstas (v) | [ag'ra:stas] |
| bilberry | mélynės (m dgs) | [mʲeːˈlʲiːnʲeːs] |
| blackberry | gérvuogės (m dgs) | [ˈgʲɛrvuɑgʲeːs] |

| | | |
|---|---|---|
| raisin | razìnos (m dgs) | [ra'zʲɪnos] |
| fig | figà (m) | [fʲɪˈga] |
| date | datùlė (m) | [da'tʊlʲeː] |

| | | |
|---|---|---|
| peanut | žémės riešutaì (v) | [ˈʒʲæmʲeːs rʲiɛʃʊ'tʌɪ] |
| almond | migdõlas (v) | [mʲɪg'do:lʲas] |
| walnut | graìkinis ríešutas (v) | [ˈgrʌɪkʲɪnʲɪs 'rʲiɛʃutas] |
| hazelnut | ríešutas (v) | [ˈrʲiɛʃutas] |
| coconut | kòkoso ríešutas (v) | [ˈkokosɔ 'rʲiɛʃutas] |
| pistachios | pistãcijos (m dgs) | [pʲɪs'ta:tsʲɪjɔs] |

## 56. Bread. Candy

| | | |
|---|---|---|
| bakers' confectionery (pastry) | konditėrijos gaminiaì (v) | [kɔndʲɪ'tʲɛrʲɪjɔs gamʲɪ'nʲɛɪ] |
| bread | dúona (m) | [ˈduɑna] |
| cookies | sausaìniai (v) | [sɑʊ'sʌɪnʲɛɪ] |

| | | |
|---|---|---|
| chocolate (n) | šokolãdas (v) | [ʃoko'lʲa:das] |
| chocolate (as adj) | šokolãdinis | [ʃoko'lʲa:dʲɪnʲɪs] |
| candy (wrapped) | saldaìnis (v) | [salʲ'dʌɪnʲɪs] |
| cake (e.g., cupcake) | pyragáitis (v) | [pʲiːra'gʌɪtʲɪs] |
| cake (e.g., birthday ~) | tòrtas (v) | [ˈtortas] |

| | | |
|---|---|---|
| pie (e.g., apple ~) | pyrãgas (v) | [pʲiːˈra:gas] |
| filling (for cake, pie) | ídaras (v) | [ˈiːdaras] |

| | | |
|---|---|---|
| jam (whole fruit jam) | uogiẽnė (m) | [uɑ'gʲɛnʲeː] |
| marmalade | marmelãdas (v) | [marmʲɛ'lʲa:das] |
| waffles | vãfliai (v dgs) | [ˈva:flʲɛɪ] |
| ice-cream | ledaì (v dgs) | [lʲɛˈdʌɪ] |
| pudding | pùdingas (v) | [ˈpʊdʲɪngas] |

## 57. Spices

| | | |
|---|---|---|
| salt | druskà (m) | [drʊs'ka] |
| salty (adj) | sūrùs | [su:'rʊs] |
| to salt (vt) | sū́dyti | [ˈsu:dʲi:tʲɪ] |

| | | |
|---|---|---|
| black pepper | juodíeji pipìrai (v) | [juɑˈdʲiɛjɪ pʲɪˈpʲɪrʌɪ] |
| red pepper (milled ~) | raudoníeji pipìrai (v) | [rɑʊˈdoˈnʲiɛjɪ pʲɪˈpʲɪrʌɪ] |

| mustard | garstyčios (v) | [gar'stʲiːtsʲos] |
| horseradish | krienaĩ (v dgs) | [krʲiɛ'nʌɪ] |

| condiment | príeskonis (v) | ['prʲiɛskonʲɪs] |
| spice | príeskonis (v) | ['prʲiɛskonʲɪs] |
| sauce | pãdažas (v) | ['paːdaʒas] |
| vinegar | ãctas (v) | ['aːtstas] |

| anise | anýžius (v) | [a'nʲiːʒʲʊs] |
| basil | bazìlikas (v) | [ba'zʲɪlʲɪkas] |
| cloves | gvazdìkas (v) | [gvaz'dʲɪkas] |
| ginger | im̃bieras (v) | ['ɪmbʲiɛras] |
| coriander | kaléndra (m) | [ka'lʲɛndra] |
| cinnamon | cinamònas (v) | [tsʲɪna'monas] |

| sesame | sezãmas (v) | [sʲɛ'zaːmas] |
| bay leaf | láuro lãpas (v) | ['lʲɑʊrɔ 'lʲaːpas] |
| paprika | pãprika (m) | ['pa:prʲɪka] |
| caraway | kmỹnai (v) | ['kmʲiːnʌɪ] |
| saffron | šafrãnas (v) | [ʃafʲra:nas] |

# PERSONAL
# INFORMATION. FAMILY

**T&P Books Publishing**

| name (first name) | vardas (v) | ['vardas] |
| surname (last name) | pavardė (m) | [pavar'dʲeː] |
| date of birth | gimìmo datà (m) | [gʲɪ'mʲɪmɔ da'ta] |
| place of birth | gimìmo vietà (m) | [gʲɪ'mʲɪmɔ vʲɪɛ'ta] |
| | | |
| nationality | tautýbė (m) | [tɑʊ'tʲiːbʲeː] |
| place of residence | gyvènamoji vietà (m) | [gʲiːvʲæna'mojɪ vʲɪɛ'ta] |
| country | šalìs (m) | [ʃa'lʲɪs] |
| profession (occupation) | profèsija (m) | [profʲɛsʲɪjɛ] |
| | | |
| gender, sex | lýtis (m) | ['lʲiːtʲɪs] |
| height | ū̃gis (v) | ['uːgʲɪs] |
| weight | svõris (v) | ['svoːrʲɪs] |

| mother | mótina (m) | ['motʲɪna] |
| father | tévas (v) | ['tʲeːvas] |
| son | sūnùs (v) | [su:'nʊs] |
| daughter | dukrà, duktė̃ (m) | [dʊk'ra], [dʊk'tʲeː] |
| | | |
| younger daughter | jaunesnióji duktė̃ (m) | [jɛʊnes'nʲo:jɪ dʊk'tʲeː] |
| younger son | jaunesnýsis sūnùs (v) | [jɛʊnʲɛs'nʲiːsʲɪs su:'nʊs] |
| eldest daughter | vyresnióji duktė̃ (m) | [vʲɪ'res'nʲo:jɪ dʊk'tʲeː] |
| eldest son | vyresnýsis sūnùs (v) | [vʲɪ:rʲɛs'nʲiːsʲɪs su:'nʊs] |
| | | |
| brother | brólis (v) | ['brolʲɪs] |
| elder brother | vyresnýsis brólis (v) | [vʲɪ:rʲɛs'nʲiːsʲɪs 'brolʲɪs] |
| younger brother | jaunesnýsis brólis (v) | [jɛʊnʲɛs'nʲiːsʲɪs 'brolʲɪs] |
| sister | sesuõ (m) | [sʲɛ'sʊɑ] |
| elder sister | vyresnióji sesuõ (m) | [vʲɪ:rʲɛs'nʲo:jɪ sʲɛ'sʊɑ] |
| younger sister | jaunesnióji sesuõ (m) | [jɛʊnʲɛs'nʲo:jɪ sʲɛ'sʊɑ] |
| | | |
| cousin (masc.) | pùsbrolis (v) | ['pʊsbrolʲɪs] |
| cousin (fem.) | pùsseserė (m) | ['pʊsseserʲeː] |
| mom, mommy | mamà (m) | [ma'ma] |
| dad, daddy | tė̃tis (v) | ['tʲeːtʲɪs] |
| parents | tėvaĩ (v) | [tʲeː'vʌɪ] |
| child | vaĩkas (v) | ['vʌɪkas] |
| children | vaikaĩ (v) | [vʌɪ'kʌɪ] |
| grandmother | senẽlė (m) | [sʲɛ'nʲælʲeː] |
| grandfather | senẽlis (v) | [sʲɛ'nʲælʲɪs] |

| grandson | anūkas (v) | [a'nu:kas] |
| granddaughter | anūkė (m) | [a'nu:kʲe:] |
| grandchildren | anūkai (v) | [a'nu:kʌɪ] |

| uncle | dėdė (v) | ['dʲe:dʲe:] |
| aunt | teta (m) | [tʲɛ'ta] |
| nephew | sūnėnas (v) | [su:'nʲe:nas] |
| niece | dukterėčia (m) | [dʊkte'rʲe:tʂʲæ] |

| mother-in-law (wife's mother) | uošvė (m) | ['ʊaʃvʲe:] |
| father-in-law (husband's father) | uošvis (v) | ['ʊaʃvʲɪs] |
| son-in-law (daughter's husband) | žéntas (v) | ['ʒʲɛntas] |
| stepmother | pāmotė (m) | ['pa:motʲe:] |
| stepfather | patėvis (v) | [pa'tʲe:vʲɪs] |

| infant | kūdikis (v) | ['ku:dʲɪkʲɪs] |
| baby (infant) | naujāgimis (v) | [nɑʊ'ja:gʲɪmʲɪs] |
| little boy, kid | vaikas (v) | ['vʌɪkas] |

| wife | žmona (m) | [ʒmo'na] |
| husband | výras (v) | ['vʲi:ras] |
| spouse (husband) | sutuoktinis (v) | [sʊtʊak'tʲɪnʲɪs] |
| spouse (wife) | sutuoktinė (m) | [sʊtʊak'tʲɪnʲe:] |

| married (masc.) | vėdęs | ['vʲædʲɛ:s] |
| married (fem.) | ištekėjusi | [ɪʃtʲɛ'kʲe:jusʲɪ] |
| single (unmarried) | vienguñgis | [vʲɪɛŋ'gʊŋgʲɪs] |
| bachelor | vienguñgis (v) | [vʲɪɛŋ'gʊŋgʲɪs] |
| divorced (masc.) | išsiskýręs | [ɪʃsʲɪ'skʲi:rʲɛ:s] |
| widow | našlė (m) | [naʃ'lʲe:] |
| widower | našlỹs (v) | [naʃ'lʲi:s] |

| relative | giminaitis (v) | [gʲɪmʲɪ'nʌɪtʲɪs] |
| close relative | artimas giminaitis (v) | ['artʲɪmas gʲɪmʲɪ'nʌɪtʲɪs] |
| distant relative | tolimas giminaitis (v) | ['tolʲɪmas gʲɪmʲɪ'nʌɪtʲɪs] |
| relatives | giminės (m dgs) | ['gʲɪmʲɪnʲe:s] |

| orphan (boy or girl) | našlaitis (v) | [naʃ'lʲʌɪtʲɪs] |
| guardian (of a minor) | globėjas (v) | [glʲo'bʲe:jas] |
| to adopt (a boy) | įsūnyti | [i:'su:nʲɪ:tʲɪ] |
| to adopt (a girl) | įdukrinti | [i:'dʊkrʲɪntʲɪ] |

## 60. Friends. Coworkers

| friend (masc.) | draūgas (v) | ['drɑʊgas] |
| friend (fem.) | draugė (m) | [drɑʊ'gʲe:] |
| friendship | draugỹstė (m) | [drɑʊ'gʲi:stʲe:] |

| to be friends | draugáuti | [drɑʊˈgɑʊtⁱɪ] |
| buddy (masc.) | pažįstamas (v) | [paˈʒⁱɪːstamas] |
| buddy (fem.) | pažįstamà (m) | [paʒⁱɪːstaˈma] |
| partner | pártneris (v) | [ˈpartnⁱɛrⁱɪs] |

| chief (boss) | šèfas (v) | [ˈʃɛfas] |
| superior (n) | vìršininkas (v) | [ˈvⁱɪrʃɪnⁱɪŋkas] |
| owner, proprietor | savininkas (v) | [savⁱɪˈnⁱɪŋkas] |
| subordinate (n) | pavaldinỹs (v) | [pavalⁱdⁱɪˈnⁱiːs] |
| colleague | kolegà (v) | [kɔlⁱɛˈga] |

| acquaintance (person) | pažįstamas (v) | [paˈʒⁱɪːstamas] |
| fellow traveler | pakeleìvis (v) | [pakⁱɛˈlⁱɛɪvⁱɪs] |
| classmate | klasiókas (v) | [klⁱaˈsⁱoːkas] |

| neighbor (masc.) | kaimýnas (v) | [kʌɪˈmⁱiːnas] |
| neighbor (fem.) | kaimýnė (m) | [kʌɪˈmⁱiːnⁱeː] |
| neighbors | kaimýnai (v) | [kʌɪˈmⁱiːnʌɪ] |

# HUMAN BODY. MEDICINE

**T&P Books Publishing**

| | | |
|---|---|---|
| head | galvà (m) | [galʲˈva] |
| face | véidas (v) | [ˈvʲɛɪdas] |
| nose | nósis (m) | [ˈnosʲɪs] |
| mouth | burnà (m) | [bʊrˈna] |
| | | |
| eye | akìs (m) | [aˈkʲɪs] |
| eyes | ākys (m dgs) | [ˈaːkʲiːs] |
| pupil | vyzdỹs (v) | [vʲiːzˈdʲiːs] |
| eyebrow | añtakis (v) | [ˈantakʲɪs] |
| eyelash | blakstíena (m) | [blʲakˈstʲiɛna] |
| eyelid | vókas (v) | [ˈvoːkas] |
| | | |
| tongue | liežùvis (v) | [lʲiɛˈʒʊvʲɪs] |
| tooth | dantìs (v) | [danˈtʲɪs] |
| lips | lū̃pos (m dgs) | [ˈlʲuːpos] |
| cheekbones | skruostìkauliai (v dgs) | [skrʊɑˈstʲɪkɑʊlʲɛɪ] |
| gum | dantenõs (m dgs) | [dantʲɛˈnoːs] |
| palate | gomurỹs (v) | [gomʊˈrʲiːs] |
| | | |
| nostrils | šnérvės (m dgs) | [ˈʃnʲærvʲeːs] |
| chin | smākras (v) | [ˈsmaːkras] |
| jaw | žandìkaulis (v) | [ʒanˈdʲɪkɑʊlʲɪs] |
| cheek | skrúostas (v) | [ˈskrʊɑstas] |
| | | |
| forehead | kaktà (m) | [kakˈta] |
| temple | smilkinỹs (v) | [smʲɪlʲkʲɪˈnʲiːs] |
| ear | ausìs (m) | [ɑʊˈsʲɪs] |
| back of the head | pakáušis, sprándas (v) | [paˈkɑʊʃɪs], [ˈsprandas] |
| neck | kāklas (v) | [ˈkaːklʲas] |
| throat | gerklė̃ (m) | [gʲɛrkˈlʲeː] |
| | | |
| hair | plaukaì (v dgs) | [plʲɑʊˈkʌɪ] |
| hairstyle | šukúosena (m) | [ʃʊˈkʊɑsʲɛna] |
| haircut | kirpìmas (v) | [kʲɪrˈpʲɪmas] |
| wig | perùkas (v) | [pʲɛˈrʊkas] |
| | | |
| mustache | ū̃sai (v dgs) | [ˈuːsʌɪ] |
| beard | barzdà (m) | [barzˈda] |
| to have (a beard, etc.) | nešióti | [nʲɛˈʃʲotʲɪ] |
| braid | kasà (m) | [kaˈsa] |
| sideburns | žándenos (m dgs) | [ˈʒandʲɛnos] |
| | | |
| red-haired (adj) | rùdis | [ˈrʊdʲɪs] |
| gray (hair) | žìlas | [ˈʒʲɪlʲas] |

| bald (adj) | plìkas | ['plʲɪkas] |
| bald patch | plìkė (m) | ['plʲɪkʲe:] |

| ponytail | uodegà (m) | [ʊadʲɛ'ga] |
| bangs | kĩrpčiai (v dgs) | ['kʲɪrptʂʲɛɪ] |

## 62. Human body

| hand | plãštaka (m) | ['plʲa:ʃtaka] |
| arm | rankà (m) | [raŋ'ka] |

| finger | pĩrštas (v) | ['pʲɪrʃtas] |
| thumb | nykštỹs (v) | [nʲi:kʃʲtʲi:s] |
| little finger | mažàsis pĩrštas (v) | [ma'ʒasʲɪs 'pʲɪrʃtas] |
| nail | nãgas (v) | ['na:gas] |

| fist | kùmštis (v) | ['kʊmʃtʲɪs] |
| palm | délnas (v) | ['dʲɛlʲnas] |
| wrist | ríešas (v) | ['rʲiɛʃas] |
| forearm | dìlbis (v) | ['dʲɪlʲbʲɪs] |
| elbow | alkū́nė (m) | [alʲˈku:nʲe:] |
| shoulder | petìs (v) | [pʲɛˈtʲɪs] |

| leg | kója (m) | ['koja] |
| foot | pėdà (m) | [pʲe:'da] |
| knee | kẽlias (v) | ['kʲælʲæs] |
| calf (part of leg) | blauzdà (m) | [blʲaʊz'da] |

| hip | šlaunìs (m) | [ʃlʲaʊ'nʲɪs] |
| heel | kulnas (v) | ['kʊlʲnas] |

| body | kū́nas (v) | ['ku:nas] |
| stomach | pìlvas (v) | ['pʲɪlʲvas] |
| chest | krūtìnė (m) | [kru:'tʲɪnʲe:] |
| breast | krūtìs (m) | [kru:'tʲɪs] |
| flank | šónas (v) | ['ʃonas] |
| back | nùgara (m) | ['nʊgara] |

| lower back | juosmuõ (v) | [jʊas'mʊa] |
| waist | liemuõ (v) | [lʲiɛ'mʊa] |

| navel (belly button) | bámba (m) | ['bamba] |
| buttocks | sédmenys (v dgs) | ['sʲe:dmenʲi:s] |
| bottom | pastùrgalis, ùžpakalis (v) | [pas'tʊrgalʲɪs], ['ʊʒpakalʲɪs] |

| beauty mark | ãpgamas (v) | ['a:pgamas] |
| birthmark (café au lait spot) | ãpgamas (v) | ['a:pgamas] |
| tattoo | tatuiruõtė (m) | [tatʊi'rʊatʲe:] |
| scar | rándas (v) | ['randas] |

## 63. Diseases

| | | |
|---|---|---|
| sickness | ligà (m) | [lʲɪ'ga] |
| to be sick | sĩrgti | ['sʲɪrktʲɪ] |
| health | sveikatà (m) | [svʲɛɪka'ta] |
| | | |
| runny nose (coryza) | slogà (m) | [slʲo'ga] |
| tonsillitis | anginà (m) | [angʲɪ'na] |
| cold (illness) | péršalimas (v) | ['pʲɛrʃalʲɪmas] |
| to catch a cold | péršalti | ['pʲɛrʃalʲtʲɪ] |
| | | |
| bronchitis | bronchìtas (v) | [bron'xʲɪtas] |
| pneumonia | plaũčių uždegìmas (v) | ['plʲɑutʂʲu: uʒdʲɛ'gʲɪmas] |
| flu, influenza | grìpas (v) | ['grʲɪpas] |
| | | |
| nearsighted (adj) | trumparēgis | [trumpa'rʲægʲɪs] |
| farsighted (adj) | toliarēgis | [tolʲæ'rʲægʲɪs] |
| strabismus (crossed eyes) | žvairùmas (v) | [ʒvʌɪ'rumas] |
| cross-eyed (adj) | žvaĩras | ['ʒvʌɪras] |
| cataract | kataraktà (m) | [katarak'ta] |
| glaucoma | glaukomà (m) | [glʲɑuko'ma] |
| | | |
| stroke | insùltas (v) | [ɪn'sulʲtas] |
| heart attack | infárktas (v) | [ɪn'farktas] |
| myocardial infarction | miokárda infárktas (v) | [mʲɪjo'karda in'farktas] |
| paralysis | paralỹžius (v) | [para'lʲi:ʒʲus] |
| to paralyze (vt) | paraližúoti | [paralʲɪ'ʒuatʲɪ] |
| | | |
| allergy | alèrgija (m) | [a'lʲɛrgʲɪjɛ] |
| asthma | astmà (m) | [ast'ma] |
| diabetes | diabètas (v) | [dʲɪja'bʲɛtas] |
| | | |
| toothache | dantų̃ skaũsmas (v) | [dan'tu: 'skɑusmas] |
| caries | kãriesas (v) | ['ka:rʲɛsas] |
| | | |
| diarrhea | diaréja (m) | [dʲɪjarʲe:ja] |
| constipation | vidurių̃ užkietéjimas (v) | [vʲɪdu'rʲu: uʒkʲɪɛ'tʲɛjɪmas] |
| stomach upset | skrañdžio sutrikìmas (v) | ['skrandʒʲɔ sutrʲɪ'kʲɪmas] |
| food poisoning | apsinuōdijimas (v) | [apsʲɪ'nuadʲɪjimas] |
| to get food poisoning | apsinuōdyti | [apsʲɪ'nuadʲi:tʲɪ] |
| | | |
| arthritis | artrìtas (v) | [art'rʲɪtas] |
| rickets | rachìtas (v) | [ra'xʲɪtas] |
| rheumatism | reumatìzmas (v) | [rʲɛuma'tʲɪzmas] |
| atherosclerosis | ateroskleròzė (m) | [aterosklʲɛ'rozʲe:] |
| | | |
| gastritis | gastrìtas (v) | [gas'trʲɪtas] |
| appendicitis | apendicìtas (v) | [apʲɛndʲɪ'tsʲɪtas] |
| cholecystitis | cholecistìtas (v) | [xolʲɛtsʲɪs'tʲɪtas] |
| ulcer | opà (m) | [o'pa] |
| measles | tymaĩ (v) | [tʲi:'mʌɪ] |

| rubella (German measles) | raudoniùkė (m) | [rɑʊdo'nʲʊkʲe:] |
| jaundice | geltà (m) | [gʲɛlʲ'ta] |
| hepatitis | hepatìtas (v) | [ɣʲɛpa'tʲɪtas] |

| schizophrenia | šizofrènija (m) | [ʃɪzo'frʲɛnʲɪjɛ] |
| rabies (hydrophobia) | pasiùtligė (m) | [pa'sʲʊtlʲɪgʲe:] |
| neurosis | neuròzė (m) | [nʲɛʊ'rozʲe:] |
| concussion | smegenų̃ sutrenkìmas (v) | [smʲɛgʲɛ'nu: sʊtrʲɛŋ'kʲɪmas] |

| cancer | vėžỹs (v) | [vʲe:'ʒʲi:s] |
| sclerosis | skleròzė (m) | [sklʲɛ'rozʲe:] |
| multiple sclerosis | išsėtìnė skleròzė (m) | [ɪʃsʲe:'tʲɪnʲe: sklʲɛ'rozʲe:] |

| alcoholism | alkoholìzmas (v) | [alʲkoɣo'lʲɪzmas] |
| alcoholic (n) | alokoholikas (v) | [aloko'ɣolʲɪkas] |
| syphilis | sìfilis (v) | ['sʲɪfʲɪlʲɪs] |
| AIDS | ŽIV (v) | ['ʒʲɪv] |

| tumor | auglỹs (v) | [ɑʊg'lʲi:s] |
| fever | kar̃štligė (m) | ['karʃtlʲɪgʲe:] |
| malaria | maliãrija (m) | [ma'lʲær̃ʲɪjɛ] |
| gangrene | gangrenà (m) | [gangrʲɛ'na] |
| seasickness | jū́ros ligà (m) | ['ju:ros lʲɪ'ga] |
| epilepsy | epilèpsija (m) | [ɛpʲɪ'lʲɛpsʲɪjɛ] |

| epidemic | epidèmija (m) | [ɛpʲɪ'dʲɛmʲɪjɛ] |
| typhus | šíltinė (m) | ['ʃɪlʲtʲɪnʲe:] |
| tuberculosis | tuberkuliòzė (m) | [tʊberkʊ'lʲɔzʲe:] |
| cholera | chòlera (m) | ['xolʲɛra] |
| plague (bubonic ~) | mãras (v) | ['ma:ras] |

## 64. Symptoms. Treatments. Part 1

| symptom | simptòmas (v) | [sʲɪmp'tomas] |
| temperature | temperatūrà (m) | [tʲɛmpʲɛratu:'ra] |
| high temperature (fever) | aukštà temperatūrà (m) | [ɑʊkʃʲ'ta tʲɛmpʲɛratu:'ra] |
| pulse | pùlsas (v) | ['pʊlʲsas] |

| dizziness (vertigo) | galvõs svaigìmas (v) | [galʲ'vo:s svʌɪ'gʲɪmas] |
| hot (adj) | kár̃štas | ['karʃtas] |
| shivering | drebulỹs (v) | [drʲɛbʊ'lʲi:s] |
| pale (e.g., ~ face) | išbãlęs | [ɪʃ'ba:lʲɛ:s] |

| cough | kosulỹs (v) | [kɔsʊ'lʲi:s] |
| to cough (vi) | kósėti | ['kosʲe:tʲɪ] |
| to sneeze (vi) | čiáudėti | ['tʂʲæʊdʲe:tʲɪ] |
| faint | nualpimas (v) | [nʊ'alʲpʲɪmas] |
| to faint (vi) | nualpti | [nʊ'alʲptʲɪ] |
| bruise (hématome) | mėlỹnė (m) | [mʲe:'lʲi:nʲe:] |

| | | |
|---|---|---|
| bump (lump) | gùzas (v) | ['gʊzas] |
| to bang (bump) | atsitreñkti | [atsʲɪ'trʲɛŋktʲɪ] |
| contusion (bruise) | sumušĭmas (v) | [sʊmʊ'ʃɪmas] |
| to get a bruise | susimùšti | [sʊsʲɪ'mʊʃtʲɪ] |
| | | |
| to limp (vi) | šlubúoti | [ʃlʲʊ'bʊatʲɪ] |
| dislocation | išnirĭmas (v) | [ɪʃnʲɪ'rʲɪmas] |
| to dislocate (vt) | išnarĭnti | [ɪʃna'rʲɪntʲɪ] |
| fracture | lūžis (v) | ['lʲuːʒʲɪs] |
| to have a fracture | susilaúžyti | [sʊsʲɪ'lʲaʊʒʲiːtʲɪ] |
| | | |
| cut (e.g., paper ~) | įpjovĭmas (v) | [iːpjɔ'vʲiːmas] |
| to cut oneself | įsipjáuti | [iːsʲɪ'pjaʊtʲɪ] |
| bleeding | kraujãvimas (v) | [kraʊ'ja:vʲɪmas] |
| | | |
| burn (injury) | nudegĭmas (v) | [nʊdʲɛ'gʲɪmas] |
| to get burned | nusidĕginti | [nʊsʲɪ'dʲægʲɪntʲɪ] |
| | | |
| to prick (vt) | įdùrti | [iː'dʊrtʲɪ] |
| to prick oneself | įsidùrti | [iːsʲɪ'dʊrtʲɪ] |
| to injure (vt) | susižalóti | [sʊsʲɪʒa'lʲotʲɪ] |
| injury | sužalójimas (v) | [sʊʒa'lʲoːjɪmas] |
| wound | žaizdà (m) | [ʒʌɪz'da] |
| trauma | tráuma (m) | ['traʊma] |
| | | |
| to be delirious | sapalióti | [sapa'lʲotʲɪ] |
| to stutter (vi) | mikčióti | [mʲɪk'tʂʲotʲɪ] |
| sunstroke | sáulės smūgis (v) | ['saʊlʲeːs 'smuːgʲɪs] |

## 65. Symptoms. Treatments. Part 2

| | | |
|---|---|---|
| pain, ache | skaũsmas (v) | ['skaʊsmas] |
| splinter (in foot, etc.) | rakštĭs (m) | [rakʃtʲɪs] |
| | | |
| sweat (perspiration) | prãkaitas (v) | ['pra:kʌɪtas] |
| to sweat (perspire) | prakaitúoti | [prakʌɪ'tʊatʲɪ] |
| vomiting | pỹkinimas (v) | ['pʲiːkʲɪnʲɪmas] |
| convulsions | traukùliai (v) | [traʊ'kʊlʲɛɪ] |
| | | |
| pregnant (adj) | nėščia | [nʲe'ʃtʂʲæ] |
| to be born | gìmti | ['gʲɪmtʲɪ] |
| delivery, labor | gim̃dymas (v) | ['gʲɪmdʲiːmas] |
| to deliver (~ a baby) | gimdýti | [gʲɪm'dʲiːtʲɪ] |
| abortion | abòrtas (v) | [a'bortas] |
| | | |
| breathing, respiration | kvėpãvimas (v) | [kvʲe'pa:vʲɪmas] |
| in-breath (inhalation) | įkvėpis (v) | ['iːkvʲe'pʲɪs] |
| out-breath (exhalation) | iškvėpĭmas (v) | [ɪʃkvʲe'pʲɪmas] |
| to exhale (breathe out) | iškvėpti | [ɪʃkvʲe'ptʲɪ] |
| to inhale (vi) | įkvėpti | [iː'kvʲe'ptʲɪ] |

| | | |
|---|---|---|
| disabled person | **invalìdas** (v) | [ɪnva'lʲɪdas] |
| cripple | **luošỹs** (v) | [lʲʊɑ'ʃɪːs] |
| drug addict | **narkomãnas** (v) | [narko'maːnas] |
| | | |
| deaf (adj) | **kurčias** | ['kʊrtʃʲæs] |
| mute (adj) | **nebylỹs** | [nʲɛbʲiː'lʲiːs] |
| deaf mute (adj) | **kurčnebylis** | ['kʊrtʃnʲɛbʲiːlʲɪs] |
| | | |
| mad, insane (adj) | **pamìšęs** | [pa'mʲɪʃɛːs] |
| madman (demented person) | **pamìšęs** (v) | [pa'mʲɪʃɛːs] |
| madwoman | **pamìšusi** (m) | [pa'mʲɪʃʊsʲɪ] |
| to go insane | **išprotéti** | [ɪʃpro'tʲeːtʲɪ] |
| | | |
| gene | **gènas** (v) | ['gʲɛnas] |
| immunity | **imunitètas** (v) | [ɪmʊnʲɪ'tʲɛtas] |
| hereditary (adj) | **pavéldimas** | [pa'vʲɛlʲdʲɪmas] |
| congenital (adj) | **įgimtas** | ['iːgʲɪmtas] |
| | | |
| virus | **vìrusas** (v) | ['vʲɪrʊsas] |
| microbe | **mikròbas** (v) | [mʲɪk'robas] |
| bacterium | **baktèrija** (m) | [bak'tʲɛrʲɪjɛ] |
| infection | **infèkcija** (m) | [ɪn'fʲɛktsʲɪjɛ] |

## 66. Symptoms. Treatments. Part 3

| | | |
|---|---|---|
| hospital | **ligóninė** (m) | [lʲɪ'gonʲɪnʲeː] |
| patient | **pacieñtas** (v) | [pa'tsʲiɛntas] |
| | | |
| diagnosis | **diagnòzė** (m) | [dʲɪjag'nozʲeː] |
| cure | **gýdymas** (v) | ['gʲiːdʲiːmas] |
| medical treatment | **gýdymas** (v) | ['gʲiːdʲiːmas] |
| to get treatment | **gýdytis** | ['gʲiːdʲiːtʲɪs] |
| to treat (~ a patient) | **gýdyti** | ['gʲiːdʲiːtʲɪ] |
| to nurse (look after) | **slaugýti** | [slʲɑʊ'gʲiːtʲɪ] |
| care (nursing ~) | **slaugà** (m) | [slʲɑʊ'ga] |
| | | |
| operation, surgery | **operãcija** (m) | [opʲɛ'raːtsʲɪjɛ] |
| to bandage (head, limb) | **pérrišti** | ['pʲɛrrʲɪʃtʲɪ] |
| bandaging | **pérrišimas** (v) | ['pʲɛrrʲɪʃɪmas] |
| | | |
| vaccination | **skiẽpas** (v) | ['skʲɛpas] |
| to vaccinate (vt) | **skiẽpyti** | ['skʲɛpʲiːtʲɪ] |
| injection, shot | **įdūrimas** (v) | [iːdu:'rʲɪːmas] |
| to give an injection | **suléisti váistus** | [sʊ'lʲɛɪstʲɪ 'vʌɪstʊs] |
| | | |
| attack | **príepuolis** (v) | ['prʲɪɛpʊɑlʲɪs] |
| amputation | **amputãcija** (m) | [ampʊ'ta:tsʲɪjɛ] |
| to amputate (vt) | **amputúoti** | [ampʊ'tʊɑtʲɪ] |
| coma | **komà** (m) | [kɔ'ma] |

| | | |
|---|---|---|
| to be in a coma | būti kõmoje | ['buːtʲɪ 'kõmojɛ] |
| intensive care | reanimãcija (m) | [rʲɛanʲɪ'maːtsʲɪjɛ] |
| | | |
| to recover (~ from flu) | sveĩkti ... | ['svʲɛɪktʲɪ ...] |
| condition (patient's ~) | būklė (m) | ['buːklʲeː] |
| consciousness | sąmonė (m) | ['saːmonʲeː] |
| memory (faculty) | atmintìs (m) | [atmʲɪn'tʲɪs] |
| | | |
| to pull out (tooth) | šãlinti | ['ʃaːlʲɪntʲɪ] |
| filling | plomba (m) | ['plʲomba] |
| to fill (a tooth) | plombúoti | [plʲom'buatʲɪ] |
| | | |
| hypnosis | hipnõzė (m) | [ɣʲɪp'nozʲeː] |
| to hypnotize (vt) | hipnotizúoti | [ɣʲɪpnotʲɪ'zuatʲɪ] |

## 67. Medicine. Drugs. Accessories

| | | |
|---|---|---|
| medicine, drug | vaĩstas (v) | ['vʌɪstas] |
| remedy | príemonė (m) | ['prʲiɛmonʲeː] |
| to prescribe (vt) | išrašýti | [ɪʃra'ʃɪːtʲɪ] |
| prescription | recèptas (v) | [rʲɛ'tsʲɛptas] |
| | | |
| tablet, pill | tabletė (m) | [tab'lʲɛtʲeː] |
| ointment | tēpalas (v) | ['tʲæpalʲas] |
| ampule | ámpulė (m) | ['ampulʲeː] |
| mixture | mikstūrà (m) | [mʲɪkstuː'ra] |
| syrup | sìrupas (v) | ['sʲɪrupas] |
| pill | piliùlė (m) | [pʲɪ'lʲiulʲeː] |
| powder | miltēliai (v dgs) | [mʲɪlʲ'tʲælʲɛɪ] |
| | | |
| gauze bandage | bìntas (v) | ['bʲɪntas] |
| cotton wool | vatà (m) | [va'ta] |
| iodine | jòdas (v) | [jɔ das] |
| | | |
| Band-Aid | pleĩstras (v) | ['plʲɛɪstras] |
| eyedropper | pipetė (m) | [pʲɪ'pʲɛtʲeː] |
| thermometer | termomètras (v) | [tʲɛrmo'mʲɛtras] |
| syringe | švìrkštas (v) | ['ʃvʲɪrkʃtas] |
| | | |
| wheelchair | neĩgaliojo vežimēlis (v) | [nʲɛɪ:ga'lʲiojo vʲɛ'ʒʲɪmʲeːlʲɪs] |
| crutches | rameñtai (v dgs) | [ra'mʲɛntʌɪ] |
| | | |
| painkiller | skaũsmą malšìnantys vaĩstai (v dgs) | ['skausmaː malʲ'ʃɪnantʲiːs 'vʌɪstʌɪ] |
| | | |
| laxative | láisvinantys vaĩstai (v dgs) | ['lʲʌɪsvʲɪnantʲiːs 'vʌɪstʌɪ] |
| spirits (ethanol) | spìritas (v) | ['spʲɪrʲɪtas] |
| medicinal herbs | žolė (m) | [ʒo'lʲeː] |
| herbal (~ tea) | žolìnis | [ʒo'lʲɪnʲɪs] |

# APARTMENT

**T&P Books Publishing**

## 68. Apartment

| | | |
|---|---|---|
| apartment | bùtas (v) | ['butas] |
| room | kambarỹs (v) | [kamba'rʲiːs] |
| bedroom | miegamàsis (v) | [mʲiɛga'masʲɪs] |
| dining room | valgomàsis (v) | [valʲgo'masʲɪs] |
| living room | svečių̃ kambarỹs (v) | [svʲɛ'tsʲu: kamba'rʲiːs] |
| study (home office) | kabinètas (v) | [kabʲɪ'nʲɛtas] |
| | | |
| entry room | príeškambaris (v) | ['prʲiɛʃkambarʲɪs] |
| bathroom (room with a bath or shower) | voniõs kambarỹs (v) | [vo'nʲoːs kamba'rʲiːs] |
| half bath | tualètas (v) | [tʊa'lʲɛtas] |
| | | |
| ceiling | lùbos (m dgs) | ['lʲʊbos] |
| floor | grindys (m dgs) | ['grʲɪndʲiːs] |
| corner | kam̃pas (v) | ['kampas] |

## 69. Furniture. Interior

| | | |
|---|---|---|
| furniture | baldai (v) | ['balʲdʌɪ] |
| table | stãlas (v) | ['sta:lʲas] |
| chair | kėdė̃ (m) | [kʲe:'dʲe:] |
| bed | lóva (m) | ['lʲova] |
| couch, sofa | sofà (m) | [so'fa] |
| armchair | fotelis (v) | ['fotʲɛlʲɪs] |
| | | |
| bookcase | spìnta (m) | ['spʲɪnta] |
| shelf | lentýna (m) | [lʲɛn'tʲiːna] |
| | | |
| wardrobe | drabùžių spìnta (m) | [dra'buʒʲu: 'spʲɪnta] |
| coat rack (wall-mounted ~) | pakabà (m) | [paka'ba] |
| coat stand | kabyklà (m) | [kabʲiːkʲlʲa] |
| | | |
| bureau, dresser | komodà (m) | [komo'da] |
| coffee table | žurnãlinis staliùkas (v) | [ʒʊr'na:lʲɪnʲɪs sta'lʲʊkas] |
| | | |
| mirror | véidrodis (v) | ['vʲɛɪdrodʲɪs] |
| carpet | kìlimas (v) | ['kʲɪlʲɪmas] |
| rug, small carpet | kilimėlis (v) | [kʲɪlʲɪ'mʲe:lʲɪs] |
| | | |
| fireplace | židinỹs (v) | [ʒʲɪdʲɪ'nʲiːs] |
| candle | žvãkė (m) | ['ʒva:kʲe:] |
| candlestick | žvakidė (m) | [ʒva'kʲɪdʲe:] |

| | | |
|---|---|---|
| drapes | **užúolaidos** (m dgs) | [ʊ'ʒʊɑlⁱʌɪdos] |
| wallpaper | **tapètai** (v) | [ta'pⁱɛtʌɪ] |
| blinds (jalousie) | **žáliuzès** (m dgs) | ['ʒaːlⁱʊzⁱeːs] |

| | | |
|---|---|---|
| table lamp | **stalìnè lémpa** (m) | [sta'lⁱɪnⁱeː 'lⁱɛmpa] |
| wall lamp (sconce) | **šviestùvas** (v) | [ʃvⁱɛ'stʊvas] |
| floor lamp | **toršèras** (v) | [tor'ʃɛras] |
| chandelier | **sietýnas** (v) | [sⁱɛ'tⁱiːnas] |

| | | |
|---|---|---|
| leg (of chair, table) | **kojýtè** (m) | [kɔ'jiːtⁱeː] |
| armrest | **raňktūris** (v) | ['raŋktuːrⁱɪs] |
| back (backrest) | **átlošas** (v) | ['aːtlⁱoʃas] |
| drawer | **stálčius** (v) | ['stalⁱtʂⁱʊs] |

## 70. Bedding

| | | |
|---|---|---|
| bedclothes | **pãtalynè** (m) | ['paːtalⁱiːnⁱeː] |
| pillow | **pagálvè** (m) | [pa'galⁱvⁱeː] |
| pillowcase | **ùžvalkalas** (v) | ['ʊʒvalⁱkalas] |
| duvet, comforter | **užklótas** (v) | [ʊʒ'klⁱotas] |
| sheet | **paklõdè** (m) | [pak'lⁱoːdⁱeː] |
| bedspread | **lovãtiesè** (m) | [lⁱo'vaːtⁱɛsⁱeː] |

## 71. Kitchen

| | | |
|---|---|---|
| kitchen | **virtùvè** (m) | [vⁱɪr'tʊvⁱeː] |
| gas | **dùjos** (m dgs) | ['dʊjos] |
| gas stove (range) | **dùjinè** (m) | ['dʊjinⁱeː] |
| electric stove | **elektrìnè** (m) | [ɛlⁱɛk'trⁱɪnⁱeː] |
| oven | **órkaitè** (m) | ['orkʌɪtⁱeː] |
| microwave oven | **mikrobangų krosnëlè** (m) | [mⁱɪkroban'gu: kros'nⁱælⁱeː] |

| | | |
|---|---|---|
| refrigerator | **šaldytùvas** (v) | [ʃalⁱdⁱiː'tʊvas] |
| freezer | **šáldymo kãmera** (m) | ['ʃalⁱdⁱiːmɔ 'kaːmɛra] |
| dishwasher | **iňdų plovìmo mašinà** (m) | ['ɪndu: plⁱo'vⁱɪmɔ maʃɪ'na] |

| | | |
|---|---|---|
| meat grinder | **mésmalè** (m) | ['mⁱeːsmalⁱeː] |
| juicer | **sulčiãspaudè** (m) | [sʊlⁱ'tʂⁱæspɑʊdⁱeː] |
| toaster | **tòsteris** (v) | ['tostⁱɛrⁱɪs] |
| mixer | **mìkseris** (v) | ['mⁱɪksⁱɛrⁱɪs] |

| | | |
|---|---|---|
| coffee machine | **kavõs aparãtas** (v) | [ka'vo:s apa'ra:tas] |
| coffee pot | **kavinùkas** (v) | [kavⁱɪ'nʊkas] |
| coffee grinder | **kavãmalè** (m) | [ka'va:malⁱeː] |

| | | |
|---|---|---|
| kettle | **arbatinùkas** (v) | [arbatⁱɪ'nʊkas] |
| teapot | **arbãtinis** (v) | [arba:'tⁱɪnⁱɪs] |
| lid | **dangtèlis** (v) | [daŋk'tⁱælⁱɪs] |

| | | |
|---|---|---|
| tea strainer | sietelis (v) | [s<sup>j</sup>iɛ't<sup>j</sup>ælʲɪs] |
| spoon | šáukštas (v) | ['ʃaukʃtas] |
| teaspoon | arbãtinis šaukštelis (v) | [ar'ba:t<sup>j</sup>ɪn<sup>j</sup>ɪs ʃaukʃ't<sup>j</sup>ælʲɪs] |
| soup spoon | válgomasis šáukštas (v) | ['valʲgomas<sup>j</sup>ɪs 'ʃaukʃtas] |
| fork | šakùtė (m) | [ʃa'kut<sup>j</sup>e:] |
| knife | peĩlis (v) | ['p<sup>j</sup>ɛɪlʲɪs] |

| | | |
|---|---|---|
| tableware (dishes) | iñdai (v) | ['ɪndʌɪ] |
| plate (dinner ~) | lėkštė̃ (m) | [lʲe:kʃt<sup>j</sup>e:] |
| saucer | lėkštelė̃ (m) | [lʲe:kʃt<sup>j</sup>ælʲe:] |

| | | |
|---|---|---|
| shot glass | taurẽlė (m) | [tau'rʲælʲe:] |
| glass (tumbler) | stiklìnė (m) | [st<sup>j</sup>ɪk'lʲɪn<sup>j</sup>e:] |
| cup | puodùkas (v) | [puɑ'dukas] |

| | | |
|---|---|---|
| sugar bowl | cùkrinė (m) | ['tsukr<sup>j</sup>ɪn<sup>j</sup>e:] |
| salt shaker | drùskinė (m) | ['drusk<sup>j</sup>ɪn<sup>j</sup>e:] |
| pepper shaker | pipìrinė (m) | [p<sup>j</sup>ɪ'p<sup>j</sup>ɪr<sup>j</sup>ɪn<sup>j</sup>e:] |
| butter dish | svíestinė (m) | ['sv<sup>j</sup>iɛst<sup>j</sup>ɪn<sup>j</sup>e:] |

| | | |
|---|---|---|
| stock pot (soup pot) | púodas (v) | ['puɑdas] |
| frying pan (skillet) | keptùvė (m) | [k<sup>j</sup>ɛp'tuv<sup>j</sup>e:] |
| ladle | sámtis (v) | ['samt<sup>j</sup>ɪs] |
| colander | kiaurãsamtis (v) | [k<sup>j</sup>ɛu'ra:samt<sup>j</sup>ɪs] |
| tray (serving ~) | padė̃klas (v) | [pa'd<sup>j</sup>e:klʲas] |

| | | |
|---|---|---|
| bottle | bùtelis (v) | ['but<sup>j</sup>ɛlʲɪs] |
| jar (glass) | stiklaĩnis (v) | [st<sup>j</sup>ɪk'lʲʌɪn<sup>j</sup>ɪs] |
| can | skardìnė (m) | [skar'd<sup>j</sup>ɪn<sup>j</sup>e:] |

| | | |
|---|---|---|
| bottle opener | atidarytùvas (v) | [at<sup>j</sup>ɪdar<sup>j</sup>i:'tuvas] |
| can opener | konsérvų atidarytùvas (v) | [kɔn's<sup>j</sup>ɛrvu: at<sup>j</sup>ɪdar<sup>j</sup>i:'tuvas] |
| corkscrew | kamščiãtraukis (v) | [kamʃ'tʂ<sup>j</sup>ætrɑuk<sup>j</sup>ɪs] |
| filter | fìltras (v) | ['f<sup>j</sup>ɪlʲtras] |
| to filter (vt) | filtrúoti | [f<sup>j</sup>ɪlʲ'truɑt<sup>j</sup>ɪ] |

| | | |
|---|---|---|
| trash, garbage (food waste, etc.) | šiùkšlės (m dgs) | ['ʃukʃlʲe:s] |
| trash can (kitchen ~) | šiùkšlių kìbiras (v) | ['ʃukʃlʲu: 'k<sup>j</sup>ɪb<sup>j</sup>ɪras] |

## 72. Bathroom

| | | |
|---|---|---|
| bathroom | voniõs kambarỹs (v) | [vo'n<sup>j</sup>o:s kamba'r<sup>j</sup>i:s] |
| water | vanduõ (v) | [van'duɑ] |
| faucet | čiáupas (v) | ['tʂ<sup>j</sup>æupas] |
| hot water | kárštas vanduõ (v) | ['karʃtas van'duɑ] |
| cold water | šáltas vanduõ (v) | ['ʃalʲtas van'duɑ] |

| | | |
|---|---|---|
| toothpaste | dantų̃ pastà (m) | [dan'tu: pas'ta] |
| to brush one's teeth | valýti dantìs | [va'lʲi:t<sup>j</sup>ɪ dan't<sup>j</sup>ɪs] |

| | | |
|---|---|---|
| toothbrush | dantų šepetėlis (v) | [dan'tu: ʃepe'tʲe:lʲɪs] |
| to shave (vi) | skustis | ['skʊstʲɪs] |
| shaving foam | skutìmosi putos (m dgs) | [skʊ'tʲɪmosʲɪ 'pʊtos] |
| razor | skutìmosi peiliukas (v) | [skʊ'tʲɪmosʲɪ pʲɛɪ'lʲʊkas] |
| | | |
| to wash (one's hands, etc.) | plauti | ['plʲaʊtʲɪ] |
| to take a bath | maudytis, praustis | ['maʊdʲi:tʲɪs], ['praʊstʲɪs] |
| shower | dušas (v) | ['dʊʃas] |
| to take a shower | praustis dušè | ['praʊstʲɪs dʊ'ʃɛ] |
| | | |
| bathtub | vonià (m) | [vo'nʲæ] |
| toilet (toilet bowl) | unitàzas (v) | [ʊnʲɪ'ta:zas] |
| sink (washbasin) | kriauklė (m) | [krʲɛʊk'lʲe:] |
| | | |
| soap | muilas (v) | ['mʊɪlʲas] |
| soap dish | muilinė (m) | ['mʊɪlʲɪnʲe:] |
| | | |
| sponge | kempìnė (m) | [kʲɛm'pʲɪnʲe:] |
| shampoo | šampūnas (v) | [ʃam'pu:nas] |
| towel | rankšluostis (v) | ['raŋkʃlʲʊɑstʲɪs] |
| bathrobe | chalatas (v) | [xa'lʲa:tas] |
| | | |
| laundry (process) | skalbìmas (v) | [skalʲ'bʲɪmas] |
| washing machine | skalbìmo mašinà (m) | [skalʲ'bʲɪmɔ maʃɪ'na] |
| to do the laundry | skalbti baltinius | ['skʌlʲptʲɪ 'ba lʲtʲɪnʲʊs] |
| laundry detergent | skalbìmo miltėliai (v dgs) | [skalʲ'bʲɪmɔ mʲɪlʲ'tʲælʲɛɪ] |

## 73. Household appliances

| | | |
|---|---|---|
| TV set | televìzorius (v) | [tʲɛlʲɛ'vʲɪzorʲʊs] |
| tape recorder | magnetofònas (v) | [magnʲɛto'fonas] |
| VCR (video recorder) | video magnetofònas (v) | [vʲɪdʲɛɔ magnʲɛto'fonas] |
| radio | imtuvas (v) | [ɪm'tʊvas] |
| player (CD, MP3, etc.) | grotuvas (v) | [gro'tʊvas] |
| | | |
| video projector | video projèktorius (v) | ['vʲɪdʲɛɔ pro'jæktorʲʊs] |
| home movie theater | namų kìno teàtras (v) | [na'mu: 'kʲɪnɔ tʲɛ'a:tras] |
| DVD player | DVD grotuvas (v) | [dʲɪvʲɪ'dʲɪ gro'tʊvas] |
| amplifier | stiprintuvas (v) | [stʲɪprʲɪn'tʊvas] |
| video game console | žaidìmų príedėlis (v) | [ʒʌɪ'dʲɪmu: 'prʲɪɛdʲe:lʲɪs] |
| | | |
| video camera | videokamera (m) | [vʲɪdʲɛo'ka:mʲɛra] |
| camera (photo) | fotoaparatas (v) | [fotoapa'ra:tas] |
| digital camera | skaitmenìnis fotoaparatas (v) | [skʌɪtmʲɛ'nʲɪnʲɪs fotoapa'ra:tas] |
| | | |
| vacuum cleaner | dulkių siurblys (v) | ['dʊlʲkʲu: sʲʊr'blʲi:s] |
| iron (e.g., steam ~) | lygintuvas (v) | [lʲi:gʲɪn'tʊvas] |
| ironing board | lýginimo lentà (m) | ['lʲi:gʲɪnʲɪmɔ lʲɛn'ta] |
| telephone | telefònas (v) | [tʲɛlʲɛ'fonas] |

| cell phone | **mobilùs telefònas** (v) | [mobʲɪ'lʊsʲɪs tʲɛlʲɛ'fonas] |
| typewriter | **rãšymo mašinẽlė** (m) | ['raːʃɪːmɔ maʃɪ'nʲeːlʲeː] |
| sewing machine | **siuvìmo mašinà** (m) | [sʲʊ'vʲɪmɔ maʃɪ'na] |

| microphone | **mikrofònas** (v) | [mʲɪkro'fonas] |
| headphones | **ausìnės** (m dgs) | [ɑʊ'sʲɪnʲeːs] |
| remote control (TV) | **pùltas** (v) | ['pʊlʲtas] |

| CD, compact disc | **kompãktinis dìskas** (v) | [kɔm'paːktʲɪnʲɪs 'dʲɪskas] |
| cassette, tape | **kasètė** (m) | [ka'sʲɛtʲeː] |
| vinyl record | **plokštẽlė** (m) | [plokʃ'tʲælʲeː] |

# THE EARTH. WEATHER

**T&P Books Publishing**

| | | |
|---|---|---|
| space | kòsmosas (v) | ['kosmosas] |
| space (as adj) | kòsminis | ['kosmʲɪnʲɪs] |
| outer space | kòsminė erdvě (m) | ['kosmʲɪnʲe: ɛrd'vʲe:] |
| world | visatà (m) | [vʲɪsa'ta] |
| universe | pasáulis (v) | [pa'sɑʊlʲɪs] |
| galaxy | galāktika (m) | [ga'lʲa:ktʲɪka] |
| star | žvaigždě (m) | [ʒvʌɪg'ʒdʲe:] |
| constellation | žvaigždýnas (v) | [ʒvʌɪgʒ'dʲi:nas] |
| planet | planetà (m) | [plʲanʲɛ'ta] |
| satellite | palydõvas (v) | [palʲi:'do:vas] |
| meteorite | meteorìtas (v) | [mʲɛtʲɛo'rʲɪtas] |
| comet | kometà (m) | [komʲɛ'ta] |
| asteroid | asteròidas (v) | [astʲɛ'rɔɪdas] |
| orbit | orbità (m) | [orbʲɪ'ta] |
| to revolve | sùktis | ['sʊktʲɪs] |
| (~ around the Earth) | | |
| atmosphere | atmosferà (m) | [atmosfʲɛ'ra] |
| the Sun | Sáulė (m) | ['sɑʊlʲe:] |
| solar system | Sáulės sistemà (m) | ['sɑʊlʲe:s sʲɪste'ma] |
| solar eclipse | Sáulės užtemìmas (v) | ['sɑʊlʲe:s ʊʒtʲɛ'mʲɪmas] |
| the Earth | Žēmė (m) | ['ʒʲæmʲe:] |
| the Moon | Mėnùlis (v) | [mʲe:'nʊlʲɪs] |
| Mars | Mársas (v) | ['marsas] |
| Venus | Venerà (m) | [vʲɛnʲɛ'ra] |
| Jupiter | Jupìteris (v) | [jʊ'pʲɪtʲɛrʲɪs] |
| Saturn | Satùrnas (v) | [sa'tʊrnas] |
| Mercury | Merkùrijus (v) | [mʲɛr'kʊrʲɪjʊs] |
| Uranus | Urānas (v) | [ʊ'ra:nas] |
| Neptune | Neptũnas (v) | [nʲɛp'tu:nas] |
| Pluto | Plutònas (v) | [plʲʊ'tonas] |
| Milky Way | Paũkščių Tākas (v) | ['pɑʊkʃʦʲu: 'ta:kas] |
| Great Bear (Ursa Major) | Didíeji Grĵžulo Rātai (v dgs) | [dʲɪ'dʲiejɪ 'grʲɪ:ʒʊlʲɔ 'ra:tʌɪ] |
| North Star | Šiaurìnė žvaigždě (m) | [ʃɛʊ'rʲɪnʲe: ʒvʌɪg'ʒdʲe:] |
| Martian | marsiẽtis (v) | [mar'sʲɛtʲɪs] |
| extraterrestrial (n) | ateĩvis (v) | [a'tʲɛɪvʲɪs] |

| alien | ateĩvis (v) | [aˈtʲɛɪvʲɪs] |
| flying saucer | skraĩdanti lėkštė̃ (m) | [ˈskrʌɪdantʲɪ lʲeːkʃˈtʲeː] |

| spaceship | kòsminis laĩvas (v) | [ˈkosmʲɪnʲɪs ˈlʲʌɪvas] |
| space station | orbìtos stotìs (m) | [orˈbʲɪtos stoˈtʲɪs] |
| blast-off | stártas (v) | [ˈstartas] |

| engine | varìklis (v) | [vaˈrʲɪklʲɪs] |
| nozzle | tū̃tà (m) | [tuːˈta] |
| fuel | kùras (v) | [ˈkʊras] |

| cockpit, flight deck | kabinà (m) | [kabʲɪˈna] |
| antenna | antenà (m) | [antʲɛˈna] |
| porthole | iliuminãtorius (v) | [ɪlʲʊmʲɪˈnaːtorʲʊs] |
| solar panel | sáulės batèrija (m) | [ˈsɑʊlʲeːs baˈtʲɛrʲɪjɛ] |
| spacesuit | skafándras (v) | [skaˈfandras] |

| weightlessness | nesvarùmas (v) | [nʲɛsvaˈrumas] |
| oxygen | deguõnis (v) | [dʲɛˈgʊɑnʲɪs] |

| docking (in space) | susijungìmas (v) | [sʊsʲɪjʊnˈgʲɪmas] |
| to dock (vi, vt) | susijùngti | [sʊsʲɪˈjʊŋktʲɪ] |

| observatory | observatòrija (m) | [obsʲɛrvaˈtorʲɪjɛ] |
| telescope | teleskòpas (v) | [tʲɛlʲɛˈskopas] |
| to observe (vt) | stebéti | [stʲeˈbʲeːtʲɪ] |
| to explore (vt) | tyrinéti | [tʲiːrʲɪˈnʲeːtʲɪ] |

## 75. The Earth

| the Earth | Žẽmė (m) | [ˈʒʲæmʲeː] |
| the globe (the Earth) | žẽmės rutulỹs (v) | [ˈʒʲæmʲeːs rʊtʊˈlʲiːs] |
| planet | planetà (m) | [plʲanʲɛˈta] |

| atmosphere | atmosferà (m) | [atmosfʲɛˈra] |
| geography | geogrãfija (m) | [gʲɛoˈgraːfʲɪjɛ] |
| nature | gamtà (m) | [gamˈta] |

| globe (table ~) | gaublỹs (v) | [gɑʊbˈlʲiːs] |
| map | žemė́lapis (v) | [ʒeˈmʲeːlʲapʲɪs] |
| atlas | ãtlasas (v) | [ˈaːtlʲasas] |

| Europe | Europà (m) | [ɛʊroˈpa] |
| Asia | ã̇zija (m) | [ˈaːzʲɪjɛ] |
| Africa | ãfrika (m) | [ˈaːfrʲɪka] |
| Australia | Austrãlija (m) | [ɑʊsˈtraːlʲɪjɛ] |

| America | Amèrika (m) | [aˈmʲɛrʲɪka] |
| North America | Šiáurės Amèrika (m) | [ˈʃæʊrʲeːs aˈmʲɛrʲɪka] |
| South America | Pietũ Amèrika (m) | [pʲɪɛˈtu: aˈmʲɛrʲɪka] |

| Antarctica | Antarktida (m) | [antarkt'ı'da] |
| the Arctic | Árktika (m) | ['arkt'ıka] |

## 76. Cardinal directions

| north | šiáurė (m) | ['ʃæur'e:] |
| to the north | į šiáurę | [i: 'ʃæur'ɛ:] |
| in the north | šiáurėje | ['ʃæur'e:je] |
| northern (adj) | šiaurìnis | [ʃɛu'r'ın'ıs] |

| south | pietùs (v) | [p'iɛ'tʊs] |
| to the south | į pietùs | [i: p'iɛ'tʊs] |
| in the south | pietuosè | [p'iɛtʊa's'ɛ] |
| southern (adj) | pietìnis | [p'iɛ't'ın'ıs] |

| west | vakaraì (v dgs) | [vaka'rʌı] |
| to the west | į vãkarus | [i: 'va:karʊs] |
| in the west | vakaruosè | [vakarʊa's'ɛ] |
| western (adj) | vakariẽtiškas | [vaka'r'ɛt'ıʃkas] |

| east | rytaì (v dgs) | [r'i:'tʌı] |
| to the east | į rýtus | [i: 'r'ı:tʊs] |
| in the east | rytuosè | [r'i:tʊa's'ɛ] |
| eastern (adj) | rytiẽtiškas | [r'i:'t'ɛt'ıʃkas] |

## 77. Sea. Ocean

| sea | jū́ra (m) | ['ju:ra] |
| ocean | vandenýnas (v) | [vand'ɛ'n'i:nas] |
| gulf (bay) | į́lanka (m) | ['i:l'aŋka] |
| straits | są́siauris (v) | ['sa:s'ɛur'ıs] |

| continent (mainland) | žemýnas (v) | [ʒ'ɛ'm'i:nas] |
| island | salà (m) | [sa'l'a] |
| peninsula | pusiãsalis (v) | [pʊ's'æsal'ıs] |
| archipelago | archipelãgas (v) | [arx'ıp'ɛ'l'a:gas] |

| bay, cove | užùtekis (v) | [ʊʒʊt'ɛk'ıs] |
| harbor | úostas (v) | ['ʊastas] |
| lagoon | lagūnà (m) | [l'agu:'na] |
| cape | iškyšulỹs (v) | [ıʃk'i:ʃʊ'l'i:s] |

| atoll | atólas (v) | [a'tol'as] |
| reef | rìfas (v) | ['r'ıfas] |
| coral | korãlas (v) | [kɔ'ra:l'as] |
| coral reef | korãlų rìfas (v) | [kɔ'ra:l'u: 'r'ıfas] |
| deep (adj) | gilùs | [g'ı'l'ʊs] |
| depth (deep water) | gỹlis (v) | ['g'i:l'ıs] |

| | | |
|---|---|---|
| abyss | bedùgnė (m) | [bʲɛ'dʊgnʲeː] |
| trench (e.g., Mariana ~) | ĭduba (m) | ['iːdʊba] |
| | | |
| current (Ocean ~) | srově (m) | [sro'vʲeː] |
| to surround (bathe) | skaláuti | [ska'lʲɑʊtʲɪ] |
| | | |
| shore | pajūris (v) | ['pajūris] |
| coast | pakrántė (m) | [pak'rantʲeː] |
| | | |
| flow (flood tide) | antplūdis (v) | ['antplʲuːdʲɪs] |
| ebb (ebb tide) | atoslūgis (v) | [a'toslʲuːgʲɪs] |
| shoal | atābradas (v) | [a'taːbradas] |
| bottom (~ of the sea) | dùgnas (v) | ['dʊgnas] |
| | | |
| wave | bangà (m) | [ban'ga] |
| crest (~ of a wave) | bangōs keterà (m) | [ban'goːs kʲɛtʲɛ'ra] |
| spume (sea foam) | pùtos (m dgs) | ['pʊtos] |
| | | |
| storm (sea storm) | audrà (m) | [ɑʊd'ra] |
| hurricane | uragānas (v) | [ʊra'gaːnas] |
| tsunami | cunāmis (v) | [tsʊ'naːmʲɪs] |
| calm (dead ~) | štiliùs (v) | [ʃtʲɪ'lʲʊs] |
| quiet, calm (adj) | ramùs | [ra'mʊs] |
| | | |
| pole | ašĭgalis (v) | [a'ʃɪgalʲɪs] |
| polar (adj) | poliārinis | [po'lʲærʲɪnʲɪs] |
| | | |
| latitude | platumà (m) | [plʲatʊ'ma] |
| longitude | ilgumà (m) | [ɪlʲgʊ'ma] |
| parallel | paralèlė (m) | [para'lʲɛlʲeː] |
| equator | ekvātorius (v) | [ɛk'va:torʲʊs] |
| | | |
| sky | dangùs (v) | [dan'gʊs] |
| horizon | horizòntas (v) | [ɣorʲɪ'zontas] |
| air | óras (v) | ['oras] |
| | | |
| lighthouse | švytury̆s (v) | [ʃvʲi:tʊ'rʲiːs] |
| to dive (vi) | nárdyti | ['nardʲiːtʲɪ] |
| to sink (ab. boat) | nuskęsti | [nʊ'skʲɛːstʲɪ] |
| treasures | lōbis (v) | ['lʲo:bʲɪs] |

## 78. Seas' and Oceans' names

| | | |
|---|---|---|
| Atlantic Ocean | Atlánto vandeny̆nas (v) | [at'lʲanto vandʲɛ'nʲiːnas] |
| Indian Ocean | Ĭndijos vandeny̆nas (v) | ['ɪndʲɪjos vandʲɛ'nʲiːnas] |
| Pacific Ocean | Ramùsis vandeny̆nas (v) | [ra'mʊsʲɪs vandʲɛ'nʲiːnas] |
| Arctic Ocean | Árkties vandeny̆nas (v) | ['arktʲiɛs vandʲɛ'nʲiːnas] |
| | | |
| Black Sea | Juodóji jŭra (m) | [jʊɑ'do:jɪ 'ju:ra] |
| Red Sea | Raudonóji jŭra (m) | [rɑʊdo'no:jɪ 'ju:ra] |

| Yellow Sea | Geltonóji júra (m) | [gʲɛlʲto'noːjɪ 'juːra] |
| White Sea | Baltóji júra (m) | [balʲ'toːjɪ 'juːra] |
| | | |
| Caspian Sea | Káspijos júra (m) | ['kaːspʲɪjɔs 'juːra] |
| Dead Sea | Negyvóji júra (m) | [nʲɛgʲiː'voːjɪ 'juːra] |
| Mediterranean Sea | Vidúržemio júra (m) | [vʲɪ'durʒʲɛmʲɔ 'juːra] |
| | | |
| Aegean Sea | Egéjo júra (m) | [ɛ'gʲæjɔ 'juːra] |
| Adriatic Sea | ádrijos júra (m) | ['aːdrʲɪjɔs 'juːra] |
| | | |
| Arabian Sea | Arábijos júra (m) | [a'rabʲɪjɔs 'juːra] |
| Sea of Japan | Japònijos júra (m) | [ja'ponʲɪjɔs juːra] |
| Bering Sea | Bèringo júra (m) | ['bʲɛrʲɪngɔ 'juːra] |
| South China Sea | Pietų Kìnijos júra (m) | [pʲiɛ'tuː 'kʲɪnʲɪjɔs 'juːra] |
| | | |
| Coral Sea | Korálų júra (m) | [kɔ'raːlʲuː 'juːra] |
| Tasman Sea | Tasmánų júra (m) | [tas'manu 'juːra] |
| Caribbean Sea | Karìbų júra (m) | [ka'rʲɪbu 'juːra] |
| | | |
| Barents Sea | Bárenco júra (m) | [barʲɛntsɔ 'juːra] |
| Kara Sea | Kársko júra (m) | ['karskɔ 'juːra] |
| | | |
| North Sea | Šiáurės júra (m) | ['ʃæurʲeːs 'juːra] |
| Baltic Sea | Báltijos júra (m) | ['balʲtʲɪjɔs 'juːra] |
| Norwegian Sea | Norvègijos júra (m) | [nor'vʲɛgʲɪjɔs 'juːra] |

## 79. Mountains

| mountain | kálnas (v) | ['kalʲnas] |
| mountain range | kalnų vìrtinė (m) | [kalʲ'nu: vʲɪrtʲɪnʲeː] |
| mountain ridge | kalnagūbris (v) | [kalʲ'na:gu:brʲɪs] |
| | | |
| summit, top | viršúnė (m) | [vʲɪr'ʃuːnʲeː] |
| peak | pìkas (v) | ['pʲɪkas] |
| foot (~ of the mountain) | papédė (m) | [pa'pʲeːdʲeː] |
| slope (mountainside) | núokalnė (m) | ['nuɑkalʲnʲeː] |
| | | |
| volcano | ugnìkalnis (v) | [ʊg'nʲɪkalʲnʲɪs] |
| active volcano | veìkiantis ugnìkalnis (v) | ['vʲɛɪkʲænʲtʲɪs ʊg'nʲɪkalʲnʲɪs] |
| dormant volcano | užgésęs ugnìkalnis (v) | [ʊʒ'gʲæsʲɛːs ʊg'nʲɪkalʲnʲɪs] |
| | | |
| eruption | išsivéržimas (v) | [ɪʃsʲɪvʲɛrʲʒʲɪmas] |
| crater | kráteris (v) | ['kra:tʲɛrʲɪs] |
| magma | magmà (m) | [mag'ma] |
| lava | lavà (m) | [lʲa'va] |
| molten (~ lava) | įkaìtęs | [iː'kʌɪtʲɛːs] |
| | | |
| canyon | kanjònas (v) | [ka'njɔ nas] |
| gorge | tarpùkalnė (m) | [tar'pukalʲnʲeː] |
| crevice | tarpéklis (m) | [tar'pʲæklʲɪs] |

| pass, col | kalnākelis (m) | [kalʲˈnakʲɛlʲɪs] |
| plateau | gulstė (m) | [gʊlʲˈstʲeː] |
| cliff | uola (m) | [ʊɑˈlʲa] |
| hill | kalva (m) | [kalʲˈva] |

| glacier | ledýnas (v) | [lʲɛˈdʲiːnas] |
| waterfall | krioklỹs (v) | [krʲokˈlʲiːs] |
| geyser | geìzeris (v) | [ˈgʲɛɪzʲɛrʲɪs] |
| lake | ẽžeras (v) | [ˈɛʒʲɛras] |

| plain | lygumà (m) | [lʲiːgʊˈma] |
| landscape | peizāžas (v) | [pʲɛɪˈzaːʒas] |
| echo | aìdas (v) | [ˈʌɪdas] |

| alpinist | alpinìstas (v) | [alʲpʲɪˈnʲɪstas] |
| rock climber | uolakopỹs (v) | [ʊɑlʲakoˈpʲiːs] |
| to conquer (in climbing) | pavérgti | [paˈvʲɛrktʲɪ] |
| climb (an easy ~) | kopìmas (v) | [kɔˈpʲɪmas] |

## 80. Mountains names

| The Alps | Álpės (m dgs) | [ˈalʲpʲeːs] |
| Mont Blanc | Monblãnas (v) | [monˈblʲaːnas] |
| The Pyrenees | Pirénai (v) | [pʲɪˈrʲeːnʌɪ] |

| The Carpathians | Karpãtai (v dgs) | [karˈpaːtʌɪ] |
| The Ural Mountains | Urãlo kalnaĩ (v dgs) | [ʊˈraːlo kalʲˈnʌɪ] |
| The Caucasus Mountains | Kaukãzas (v) | [kɑʊˈkaːzas] |
| Mount Elbrus | Elbrùsas (v) | [ɛlʲˈbrʊsas] |

| The Altai Mountains | Altãjus (v) | [alʲˈtaːjʊs] |
| The Tian Shan | Tian Šãnis (v) | [tʲæn ˈʃaːnʲɪs] |
| The Pamir Mountains | Pamỹras (v) | [paˈmʲiːras] |
| The Himalayas | Himalãjai (v dgs) | [ɣʲɪmaˈlʲaːjʌɪ] |
| Mount Everest | Everèstas (v) | [ɛvʲɛˈrʲɛstas] |

| The Andes | Añdai (v) | [ˈandʌɪ] |
| Mount Kilimanjaro | Kilimandžãras (v) | [kʲɪlʲɪmanˈdʒaːras] |

## 81. Rivers

| river | ùpė (m) | [ˈʊpʲeː] |
| spring (natural source) | šaltìnis (v) | [ʃalʲˈtʲɪnʲɪs] |
| riverbed (river channel) | vagà (v) | [vaˈga] |
| basin (river valley) | baseìnas (v) | [baˈsʲɛɪnas] |
| to flow into ... | įtekéti į̃ ... | [iːtʲɛˈkʲeːtʲɪ iː ..] |
| tributary | añtplūdis (v) | [ˈantplʲuːdʲɪs] |
| bank (of river) | krañtas (v) | [ˈkrantas] |

| | | |
|---|---|---|
| current (stream) | srovė (m) | [sro'vʲe:] |
| downstream (adv) | pasroviuì | [pasro'vʲʊɪ] |
| upstream (adv) | priẽš srõvę | ['prʲeʃ 'sro:vʲɛ:] |
| | | |
| inundation | põtvynis (v) | ['potvʲi:nʲɪs] |
| flooding | põplūdis (v) | ['poplʲu:dʲɪs] |
| to overflow (vi) | išsilíeti | [ɪʃsɪ'lʲietʲɪ] |
| to flood (vt) | tvìndyti | ['tvɪndʲi:tʲɪ] |
| | | |
| shallow (shoal) | seklumà (m) | [sʲɛklʲʊ'ma] |
| rapids | sleñkstis (v) | ['slʲɛŋkstʲɪs] |
| | | |
| dam | ùžtvanka (m) | ['ʊʒtvaŋka] |
| canal | kanãlas (v) | [ka'na:lʲas] |
| reservoir (artificial lake) | vandeñs saugyklà (m) | [van'dʲɛns saʊɡʲi:k'lʲa] |
| sluice, lock | šliùzas (v) | ['ʃlʲʊzas] |
| | | |
| water body (pond, etc.) | vandeñs telkinỹs (v) | [van'dʲɛns tʲɛlʲkʲɪ'nʲi:s] |
| swamp (marshland) | pélkė (m) | ['pʲɛlʲkʲe:] |
| bog, marsh | liūnas (v) | ['lʲu:nas] |
| whirlpool | verpẽtas (v) | [vʲɛr'pʲætas] |
| | | |
| stream (brook) | upẽlis (v) | [ʊ'pʲælʲɪs] |
| drinking (ab. water) | gėriamas | ['ɡʲærʲæmas] |
| fresh (~ water) | gėlas | ['ɡʲe:lʲas] |
| | | |
| ice | lẽdas (v) | ['lʲædas] |
| to freeze over (ab. river, etc.) | užšálti | [ʊʒ'ʃalʲtʲɪ] |

## 82. Rivers' names

| | | |
|---|---|---|
| Seine | Senà (m) | [sʲɛ'na] |
| Loire | Luarà (m) | [lʲʊa'ra] |
| | | |
| Thames | Temžė (m) | ['tʲɛmzʲe:] |
| Rhine | Reìnas (v) | ['rʲɛɪnas] |
| Danube | Dunõjus (v) | [dʊ'no:jʊs] |
| | | |
| Volga | Võlga (m) | ['volʲga] |
| Don | Dònas (v) | ['donas] |
| Lena | Lenà (m) | [lʲɛ'na] |
| | | |
| Yellow River | Geltonóji ùpė (m) | [ɡʲɛlʲto'no:jɪ 'ʊpʲe:] |
| Yangtze | Jangdzė̃ (m) | [jang'dzʲe:] |
| Mekong | Mekòngas (v) | [mʲɛ'koŋgas] |
| Ganges | Gángas (v) | ['gangas] |
| | | |
| Nile River | Nìlas (v) | ['nʲɪlʲas] |
| Congo River | Kòngas (v) | ['koŋgas] |

| Okavango River | Okavángas (v) | [oka'va ngas] |
| Zambezi River | Zambèzé (m) | [zam'bʲɛzʲe:] |
| Limpopo River | Limpopò (v) | [lʲɪmpo'po] |
| Mississippi River | Misisìpé (m) | [mʲɪsʲɪ'sʲɪpʲe:] |

## 83. Forest

| forest, wood | mìškas (v) | ['mʲɪʃkas] |
| forest (as adj) | miškìnis | [mʲɪʃkʲɪnʲɪs] |
| | | |
| thick forest | tankumýnas (v) | [taŋkʊ'mʲi:nas] |
| grove | giraìté (m) | [gʲɪ'rʌɪtʲe:] |
| forest clearing | laũkas (v) | ['lʲɑʊkas] |
| | | |
| thicket | žolýnas, beržýnas (v) | [ʒo'lʲi:nas], [bʲɛr'ʒʲi:nas] |
| scrubland | krūmýnas (v) | [kru:'mʲi:nas] |
| | | |
| footpath (troddenpath) | takélis (v) | [ta'kʲælʲɪs] |
| gully | griovỹs (v) | [grʲo'vʲi:s] |
| | | |
| tree | mẽdis (v) | ['mʲædʲɪs] |
| leaf | lãpas (v) | ['lʲa:pas] |
| leaves (foliage) | lapijà (m) | [lʲapʲɪ'ja] |
| | | |
| fall of leaves | lãpų kritìmas (v) | ['lʲa:pu: krʲɪ'tʲɪmas] |
| to fall (ab. leaves) | krìsti | ['krʲɪstʲɪ] |
| top (of the tree) | viršūné (m) | [vʲɪr'ʃu:nʲe:] |
| | | |
| branch | šakà (m) | [ʃa'ka] |
| bough | šakà (m) | [ʃa'ka] |
| bud (on shrub, tree) | pum̃puras (v) | ['pʊmpʊras] |
| needle (of pine tree) | spyglỹs (v) | [spʲi:g'lʲi:s] |
| pine cone | kankorėžis (v) | [kaŋ'korʲe:ʒʲɪs] |
| | | |
| hollow (in a tree) | úoksas (v) | ['ʊɑksas] |
| nest | lìzdas (v) | ['lʲɪzdas] |
| burrow (animal hole) | olà (m) | [o'lʲa] |
| | | |
| trunk | kamíenas (v) | [ka'mʲiɛnas] |
| root | šaknìs (m) | [ʃak'nʲɪs] |
| bark | žievé (m) | [ʒʲiɛ'vʲe:] |
| moss | sãmana (m) | ['sa:mana] |
| | | |
| to uproot (remove trees or tree stumps) | ráuti | ['rɑʊtʲɪ] |
| to chop down | kìrsti | ['kʲɪrstʲɪ] |
| to deforest (vt) | iškìrsti | [ɪʃ'kʲɪrstʲɪ] |
| tree stump | kélmas (v) | ['kʲɛlʲmas] |
| campfire | láužas (v) | ['lʲɑʊʒas] |
| forest fire | gaìsras (v) | ['gʌɪsras] |

| to extinguish (vt) | gesìnti | [gʲɛ'sʲɪntʲɪ] |
| forest ranger | mìškininkas (v) | ['mʲɪʃkʲɪnʲɪŋkas] |
| protection | apsaugà (m) | [apsɑu'ga] |
| to protect (~ nature) | sáugoti | ['sɑugotʲɪ] |
| poacher | brakoniẽrius (v) | [brako'nʲɛrʲʊs] |
| steel trap | spą́stai (v dgs) | ['spaːstʌɪ] |

| to pick (mushrooms) | grybáuti | [grʲiː'bɑutʲɪ] |
| to pick (berries) | uogáuti | [ʊɑ'gɑutʲɪ] |
| to lose one's way | pasiklýsti | [pasʲɪ'klʲiːstʲɪ] |

## 84. Natural resources

| natural resources | gamtìniai ištekliai (v dgs) | [gam'tʲɪnʲɛɪ 'ɪʃtʲɛklʲɛɪ] |
| minerals | naudìngos iškasenos (m dgs) | [nɑu'dʲɪngos 'ɪʃkasʲɛnos] |
| deposits | telkiniaì (v dgs) | [tʲɛlʲkʲɪ'nʲɛɪ] |
| field (e.g., oilfield) | telkinỹs (v) | [tʲɛlʲkʲɪ'nʲiːs] |

| to mine (extract) | iškàsti | [ɪʃ'kastʲɪ] |
| mining (extraction) | laimìkis (v) | [lʲʌɪ'mʲɪkʲɪs] |
| ore | rūdà (m) | [ruː'da] |
| mine (e.g., for coal) | rūdýnas (v) | [ruː'dʲiːnas] |
| shaft (mine ~) | šachtà (m) | [ʃax'ta] |
| miner | šáchtininkas (v) | ['ʃaːxtʲɪnʲɪŋkas] |

| gas (natural ~) | dùjos (m dgs) | ['dujos] |
| gas pipeline | dujótiekis (v) | [du'jotʲiɛkʲɪs] |

| oil (petroleum) | naftà (m) | [naf'ta] |
| oil pipeline | naftótiekis (v) | [naf'totʲiɛkʲɪs] |
| oil well | náftos bókštas (v) | ['naːftos 'bokʃtas] |
| derrick (tower) | grę̃žimo bókštas (v) | ['grʲɛːʒʲɪmɔ 'bokʃtas] |
| tanker | tánklaivis (v) | ['taŋklʲʌɪvʲɪs] |

| sand | smė̃lis (v) | ['smʲeːlʲɪs] |
| limestone | kálkinis akmuõ (v) | ['kalʲkʲɪnʲɪs ak'mʊɑ] |
| gravel | žvýras (v) | ['ʒvʲiːras] |
| peat | dùrpės (m dgs) | ['durpʲeːs] |
| clay | mólis (v) | ['molʲɪs] |
| coal | anglìs (m) | [ang'lʲɪs] |

| iron (ore) | geležìs (v) | [gʲɛlʲɛ'ʒʲɪs] |
| gold | áuksas (v) | ['ɑuksas] |
| silver | sidãbras (v) | [sʲɪ'daːbras] |
| nickel | nìkelis (v) | ['nʲɪkʲɛlʲɪs] |
| copper | vãris (v) | ['vaːrʲɪs] |

| zinc | cìnkas (v) | ['tsʲɪŋkas] |
| manganese | mangãnas (v) | [man'gaːnas] |

| | | |
|---|---|---|
| mercury | gývsidabris (v) | ['gʲiːvsʲɪdabrʲɪs] |
| lead | švìnas (v) | ['ʃvʲɪnas] |
| | | |
| mineral | minerãlas (v) | [mʲɪnʲɛ'raːlʲas] |
| crystal | kristãlas (v) | [krʲɪs'taːlʲas] |
| marble | mármuras (v) | ['marmʊras] |
| uranium | urãnas (v) | [ʊ'raːnas] |

## 85. Weather

| | | |
|---|---|---|
| weather | óras (v) | ['oras] |
| weather forecast | óro prognòzė (m) | ['orɔ prog'nozʲeː] |
| temperature | temperatūrà (m) | [tʲɛmpʲɛratuː'ra] |
| thermometer | termomètras (v) | [tʲɛrmo'mʲɛtras] |
| barometer | baromètras (v) | [baro'mʲɛtras] |
| | | |
| humid (adj) | drégnas | ['drʲeːgnas] |
| humidity | drėgmė̃ (m) | [drʲeːg'mʲeː] |
| heat (extreme ~) | kar̃štis (v) | ['karʃtʲɪs] |
| hot (torrid) | kár̃štas | ['karʃtas] |
| it's hot | kar̃šta | ['karʃta] |
| | | |
| it's warm | šìlta | ['ʃɪlʲta] |
| warm (moderately hot) | šìltas | ['ʃɪlʲtas] |
| | | |
| it's cold | šálta | ['ʃalʲta] |
| cold (adj) | šáltas | ['ʃalʲtas] |
| | | |
| sun | sáulė (m) | ['saʊlʲeː] |
| to shine (vi) | šviẽsti | ['ʃvʲɛstʲɪ] |
| sunny (day) | sauléta | [saʊ'lʲeːta] |
| to come up (vi) | pakìlti | [pa'kʲɪlʲtʲɪ] |
| to set (vi) | léistis | ['lʲɛɪstʲɪs] |
| | | |
| cloud | debesìs (v) | [dʲɛbʲɛ'sʲɪs] |
| cloudy (adj) | debesúota | [dʲɛbʲɛ'sʊata] |
| rain cloud | debesìs (v) | [dʲɛbʲɛ'sʲɪs] |
| somber (gloomy) | apsiniáukę | [apsʲɪ'nʲæʊkʲɛː] |
| | | |
| rain | lietùs (v) | [lʲiɛ'tʊs] |
| it's raining | lỹja | ['lʲiːja] |
| rainy (~ day, weather) | lietìngas | [lʲiɛ'tʲɪngas] |
| to drizzle (vi) | lynóti | [lʲiː'notʲɪ] |
| | | |
| pouring rain | liū́tis (m) | ['lʲuːtʲɪs] |
| downpour | liū́tis (m) | ['lʲuːtʲɪs] |
| heavy (e.g., ~ rain) | stiprùs | [stʲɪp'rʊs] |
| puddle | balà (m) | [ba'lʲa] |
| to get wet (in rain) | šlàpti | ['ʃlʲaptʲɪ] |
| fog (mist) | rū̃kas (v) | ['ruːkas] |

| foggy | miglótas | [mʲɪgˈlʲotas] |
| snow | sniẽgas (v) | [ˈsnʲɛgas] |
| it's snowing | sniñga | [ˈsnʲɪŋga] |

## 86. Severe weather. Natural disasters

| thunderstorm | perkū́nija (m) | [pʲɛrˈkuːnʲɪjɛ] |
| lightning (~ strike) | žaĩbas (v) | [ˈʒʌɪbas] |
| to flash (vi) | žaibúoti | [ʒʌɪˈbuɑtʲɪ] |

| thunder | griaustìnis (v) | [grʲɛusˈtʲɪnʲɪs] |
| to thunder (vi) | griáudėti | [ˈgrʲæudʲeːtʲɪ] |
| it's thundering | griáudėja griaustìnis | [ˈgrʲæudʲeːja grʲɛusˈtʲɪnʲɪs] |

| hail | krušà (m) | [kruˈʃa] |
| it's hailing | kriñta krušà | [ˈkrʲɪnta kruˈʃa] |

| to flood (vt) | užlíeti | [uʒˈlʲiɛtʲɪ] |
| flood, inundation | pótvynis (v) | [ˈpotvʲiːnʲɪs] |

| earthquake | žẽmės drebė́jimas (v) | [ˈʒʲæmʲeːs dreˈbʲɛjɪmas] |
| tremor, quake | smū́gis (m) | [ˈsmuːgʲɪs] |
| epicenter | epiceñtras (v) | [ɛpʲɪˈtsʲɛntras] |

| eruption | išsiveržìmas (v) | [ɪʃʲɪvʲɛrˈʒʲɪmas] |
| lava | lavà (m) | [lʲaˈva] |

| twister | víesulas (v) | [ˈvʲiɛsulʲas] |
| tornado | tornãdo (v) | [torˈnaːdɔ] |
| typhoon | taifū̃nas (v) | [tʌɪˈfuːnas] |

| hurricane | uragãnas (v) | [uraˈgaːnas] |
| storm | audrà (m) | [ɑuˈdra] |
| tsunami | cunãmis (v) | [tsuˈnaːmʲɪs] |

| cyclone | ciklònas (v) | [tsʲɪkˈlʲonas] |
| bad weather | dárgana (m) | [ˈdargana] |
| fire (accident) | gaĩsras (v) | [ˈgʌɪsras] |
| disaster | katastrofà (m) | [katastroˈfa] |
| meteorite | meteorìtas (v) | [mʲɛtʲɛoˈrʲɪtas] |

| avalanche | lavinà (m) | [lʲavʲɪˈna] |
| snowslide | griūtìs (m) | [grʲuːˈtʲɪs] |
| blizzard | pūgà (m) | [puːˈga] |
| snowstorm | pūgà (m) | [puːˈga] |

# FAUNA

**T&P Books Publishing**

## 87. Mammals. Predators

| | | |
|---|---|---|
| predator | plėšrū́nas (v) | [plʲeːʃruːnas] |
| tiger | tìgras (v) | ['tʲɪgras] |
| lion | liū́tas (v) | ['lʲuːtas] |
| wolf | vìlkas (v) | ['vʲɪlʲkas] |
| fox | lãpė (m) | ['lʲaːpʲeː] |
| | | |
| jaguar | jaguãras (v) | [jaguˈaːras] |
| leopard | leopárdas (v) | [lʲeoˈpardas] |
| cheetah | gepárdas (v) | [gʲɛˈpardas] |
| | | |
| black panther | panterà (m) | [pantʲɛˈra] |
| puma | pumà (m) | [puˈma] |
| snow leopard | snieginis leopárdas (v) | [snʲiɛˈgʲɪnʲɪs lʲeoˈpardas] |
| lynx | lū́šis (m) | ['lʲuːʃɪs] |
| | | |
| coyote | kojòtas (v) | [kɔˈjɔ tas] |
| jackal | šakãlas (v) | [ʃaˈkaːlʲas] |
| hyena | hienà (m) | [ɣʲiɛˈna] |

## 88. Wild animals

| | | |
|---|---|---|
| animal | gyvū́nas (v) | [gʲiːˈvuːnas] |
| beast (animal) | žvėrìs (v) | [ʒvʲeːˈrʲɪs] |
| | | |
| squirrel | voverė̃ (m) | [voveˈrʲeː] |
| hedgehog | ežỹs (v) | [ɛʒʲiːs] |
| hare | kìškis, zuĩkis (v) | ['kʲɪʃkʲɪs], ['zuɪkʲɪs] |
| rabbit | triùšis (v) | ['trʲuʃɪs] |
| | | |
| badger | barsùkas (v) | [barˈsukas] |
| raccoon | meškénas (v) | [mʲɛʃˈkʲeːnas] |
| hamster | žiurkénas (v) | [ʒʲurˈkʲeːnas] |
| marmot | švilpìkas (v) | [ʃvʲɪlʲpʲɪkas] |
| | | |
| mole | kùrmis (v) | ['kurmʲɪs] |
| mouse | pelė̃ (m) | [pʲɛˈlʲeː] |
| rat | žiùrkė (m) | ['ʒʲurkʲeː] |
| bat | šikšnósparnis (v) | [ʃɪkʃˈnosparnʲɪs] |
| | | |
| ermine | šermuonė̃lis (v) | [ʃermuɑˈnʲeːlʲɪs] |
| sable | sãbalas (v) | ['sa:balʲas] |
| marten | kiáunė (m) | ['kʲæunʲeː] |

| weasel | žebenkštis (m) | [ʒʲɛbʲɛŋkʃtʲɪs] |
| mink | audìnė (m) | [ɑuˈdʲɪnʲeː] |
| | | |
| beaver | bẽbras (v) | [ˈbʲæbras] |
| otter | ū́dra (m) | [ˈuːdra] |
| | | |
| horse | arklỹs (v) | [arkˈlʲiːs] |
| moose | bríedis (v) | [ˈbrʲiɛdʲɪs] |
| deer | élnias (v) | [ˈɛlʲnʲæs] |
| camel | kupranugā́ris (v) | [kupranʊˈgaːrʲɪs] |
| | | |
| bison | bizònas (v) | [bʲɪˈzonas] |
| aurochs | stum̃bras (v) | [ˈstumbras] |
| buffalo | bùivolas (v) | [ˈbuivolʲas] |
| | | |
| zebra | zèbras (v) | [ˈzʲɛbras] |
| antelope | antilòpė (m) | [antʲɪˈlʲopʲeː] |
| roe deer | stìrna (m) | [ˈstʲɪrna] |
| fallow deer | daniẽlius (v) | [daˈnʲɛlʲʊs] |
| chamois | gemžė̃ (m) | [ˈgʲɛmzʲeː] |
| wild boar | šérnas (v) | [ˈʃɛrnas] |
| | | |
| whale | bangìnis (v) | [banˈgʲɪnʲɪs] |
| seal | rúonis (v) | [ˈrʊɑnʲɪs] |
| walrus | vėplỹs (v) | [vʲeːpˈlʲiːs] |
| fur seal | kòtikas (v) | [ˈkotʲɪkas] |
| dolphin | delfìnas (v) | [dʲɛlʲˈfʲɪnas] |
| | | |
| bear | lokỹs (v), meška (m) | [lʲoˈkʲiːs], [mʲɛʃka] |
| polar bear | baltàsis lokỹs (v) | [balʲˈtasʲɪs lʲoˈkʲiːs] |
| panda | pánda (m) | [ˈpanda] |
| | | |
| monkey | beždžiõnė (m) | [bʲɛʒˈdʑʲoːnʲeː] |
| chimpanzee | šimpánzė (m) | [ʃɪmˈpanzʲeː] |
| orangutan | orangutángas (v) | [orangʊˈtangas] |
| gorilla | gorilà (m) | [gorʲɪˈlʲʲa] |
| macaque | makakà (m) | [makaˈka] |
| gibbon | gibònas (v) | [gʲɪˈbonas] |
| | | |
| elephant | dramblỹs (v) | [dramˈblʲiːs] |
| rhinoceros | raganòsis (v) | [ragaˈnoːsʲɪs] |
| | | |
| giraffe | žirafà (m) | [ʒʲɪraˈfa] |
| hippopotamus | begemòtas (v) | [bʲɛgʲɛˈmotas] |
| | | |
| kangaroo | kengūrà (m) | [kʲɛnguːˈra] |
| koala (bear) | koalà (m) | [kɔaˈlʲa] |
| | | |
| mongoose | mangustà (m) | [mangʊsˈta] |
| chinchilla | šinšilà (m) | [ʃɪnʃɪˈlʲʲa] |
| skunk | skùnkas (v) | [ˈskuŋkas] |
| porcupine | dygliuotis (v) | [dʲiːgˈlʲʊotʲɪs] |

## 89. Domestic animals

| | | |
|---|---|---|
| cat | katė (m) | [ka'tʲeː] |
| tomcat | kātinas (v) | ['kaːtʲɪnas] |
| dog | šuõ (v) | ['ʃʊɑ] |
| | | |
| horse | arklỹs (v) | [ark'lʲiːs] |
| stallion (male horse) | er̃žilas (v) | ['ɛrʒʲɪlʲas] |
| mare | kumēlė (m) | [kʊ'mʲælʲeː] |
| | | |
| cow | kárvė (m) | ['karvʲeː] |
| bull | bùlius (v) | ['bʊlʲʊs] |
| ox | jáutis (v) | ['jɑʊtʲɪs] |
| | | |
| sheep (ewe) | avìs (m) | [a'vʲɪs] |
| ram | ãvinas (v) | ['aːvʲɪnas] |
| goat | ožkà (m) | [oʒ'ka] |
| billy goat, he-goat | ožỹs (v) | [o'ʒʲiːs] |
| | | |
| donkey | ãsilas (v) | ['aːsʲɪlʲas] |
| mule | mùlas (v) | ['mʊlʲas] |
| | | |
| pig, hog | kiaũlė (m) | ['kʲɛʊlʲeː] |
| piglet | paršėlis (v) | [par'ʃælʲɪs] |
| rabbit | triùšis (v) | ['trʲʊʃɪs] |
| | | |
| hen (chicken) | vištà (m) | [vʲɪʃ'ta] |
| rooster | gaidỹs (v) | [gʌɪ'dʲiːs] |
| | | |
| duck | ántis (m) | ['antʲɪs] |
| drake | añtinas (v) | ['antʲɪnas] |
| goose | žąsinas (v) | ['ʒaːsʲɪnas] |
| | | |
| tom turkey, gobbler | kalakùtas (v) | [kalʲa'kʊtas] |
| turkey (hen) | kalakùtė (m) | [kalʲa'kʊtʲeː] |
| | | |
| domestic animals | namìniai gyvū̃nai (v dgs) | [na'mʲɪnʲɛɪ gʲiː'vuːnʌɪ] |
| tame (e.g., ~ hamster) | prijaukìntas | [prʲɪ'jɛʊ'kʲɪntas] |
| to tame (vt) | prijaukìnti | [prʲɪ'jɛʊ'kʲɪntʲɪ] |
| to breed (vt) | augìnti | [ɑʊ'gʲɪntʲɪ] |
| | | |
| farm | fèrma (m) | ['fʲɛrma] |
| poultry | namìnis paũkštis (v) | [na'mʲɪnʲɪs 'pɑʊkʃtʲɪs] |
| cattle | galvìjas (v) | [galʲ'vʲɪjɛs] |
| herd (cattle) | bandà (m) | [ban'da] |
| | | |
| stable | arklìdė (m) | [ark'lʲɪdʲeː] |
| pigpen | kiaulìdė (m) | [kʲɛʊ'lʲɪdʲeː] |
| cowshed | karvìdė (m) | [kar'vʲɪdʲeː] |
| rabbit hutch | triušìdė (m) | [trʲʊ'ʃɪdʲeː] |
| hen house | vištìdė (m) | [vʲɪʃ'tʲɪdʲeː] |

## 90. Birds

| | | |
|---|---|---|
| bird | **paũkštis** (v) | ['pɑʊkʃtʲɪs] |
| pigeon | **balañdis** (v) | [ba'lʲandʲɪs] |
| sparrow | **žvìrblis** (v) | ['ʒvʲɪrblʲɪs] |
| tit (great tit) | **zýlė** (m) | ['zʲiːlʲeː] |
| magpie | **šárka** (m) | ['ʃarka] |
| | | |
| raven | **var̃nas** (v) | ['varnas] |
| crow | **várna** (m) | ['varna] |
| jackdaw | **kúosa** (m) | ['kʊɑsa] |
| rook | **kovàs** (v) | [kɔ'vas] |
| | | |
| duck | **ántis** (m) | ['antʲɪs] |
| goose | **žą̃sinas** (v) | ['ʒaːsʲɪnas] |
| pheasant | **fazãnas** (v) | [fa'zaːnas] |
| | | |
| eagle | **erẽlis** (v) | [ɛ'rʲælʲɪs] |
| hawk | **vãnagas** (v) | ['vaːnagas] |
| falcon | **sãkalas** (v) | ['saːkalʲas] |
| vulture | **grìfas** (v) | ['grʲɪfas] |
| condor (Andean ~) | **kondòras** (v) | [kɔn'dɔras] |
| | | |
| swan | **gul̃bė** (m) | ['gʊlʲbʲeː] |
| crane | **gérvė** (m) | ['gʲɛrvʲeː] |
| stork | **gañdras** (v) | ['gandras] |
| | | |
| parrot | **papūgà** (m) | [papuː'ga] |
| hummingbird | **kolìbris** (v) | [kɔ'lʲɪbrʲɪs] |
| peacock | **póvas** (v) | ['povas] |
| | | |
| ostrich | **strùtis** (v) | ['strʊtʲɪs] |
| heron | **garnỹs** (v) | [gar'nʲiːs] |
| flamingo | **flamìngas** (v) | [flʲa'mʲɪngas] |
| pelican | **pelikãnas** (v) | [pʲɛlʲɪ'kaːnas] |
| | | |
| nightingale | **lakštiñgala** (m) | [lʲakʃtʲɪŋgalʲa] |
| swallow | **kregždė̃** (m) | [krʲɛgʒ'dʲeː] |
| | | |
| thrush | **strãzdas** (v) | ['straːzdas] |
| song thrush | **strãzdas giesminiñkas** (v) | ['straːzdas gʲiɛsmʲɪ'nʲɪŋkas] |
| blackbird | **juodàsis strãzdas** (v) | [jʊɑ'dasʲɪs s'traːzdas] |
| | | |
| swift | **čiurlỹs** (v) | [tʃʊr'lʲiːs] |
| lark | **vyturỹs, vieversỹs** (v) | [vʲiːtʊ'rʲiːs], [vʲiɛvɛr'sʲiːs] |
| quail | **pùtpelė** (m) | ['pʊtpelʲeː] |
| | | |
| woodpecker | **genỹs** (v) | [gʲɛ'nʲiːs] |
| cuckoo | **gegùtė** (m) | [gʲɛ'gʊtʲeː] |
| owl | **peléda** (m) | [pʲɛ'lʲeːda] |

| | | |
|---|---|---|
| eagle owl | apuokas (v) | [a'puɑkas] |
| wood grouse | kurtinỹs (v) | [kʊrtʲɪ'nʲiːs] |
| black grouse | tẽtervinas (v) | ['tʲætʲɛrvʲɪnas] |
| partridge | kurapkà (m) | [kʊrap'ka] |

| | | |
|---|---|---|
| starling | varnénas (v) | [var'nʲeːnas] |
| canary | kanarėlė (m) | [kana'rʲeːlʲeː] |
| hazel grouse | jerubė̃ (m) | [jerʊ'bʲeː] |
| chaffinch | kikìlis (v) | [kʲɪ'kʲɪlʲɪs] |
| bullfinch | sniẽgena (m) | ['snʲɛgʲena] |

| | | |
|---|---|---|
| seagull | žuvédra (m) | [ʒʊ'vʲeːdra] |
| albatross | albatròsas (v) | [alʲba't'rosas] |
| penguin | pingvìnas (v) | [pʲɪng'vʲɪnas] |

## 91. Fish. Marine animals

| | | |
|---|---|---|
| bream | karšis (v) | ['karʃɪs] |
| carp | kárpis (v) | ['karpʲɪs] |
| perch | ešerỹs (v) | [ɛʃɛ'rʲiːs] |
| catfish | šãmas (v) | ['ʃaːmas] |
| pike | lydekà (m) | [lʲiːdʲɛ'ka] |

| | | |
|---|---|---|
| salmon | lašišà (m) | [lʲaʃɪ'ʃa] |
| sturgeon | eršketas (v) | [erʃ'kʲeːtas] |

| | | |
|---|---|---|
| herring | sìlkė (m) | ['sʲɪlʲkʲeː] |
| Atlantic salmon | lašišà (m) | [lʲaʃɪ'ʃa] |
| mackerel | skùmbrė (m) | ['skʊmbrʲeː] |
| flatfish | plẽkšnė (m) | ['plʲækʃnʲeː] |

| | | |
|---|---|---|
| zander, pike perch | starkis (v) | ['starkʲɪs] |
| cod | ménkė (m) | ['mʲɛŋkʲeː] |
| tuna | tùnas (v) | ['tʊnas] |
| trout | upétakis (v) | [ʊ'pʲeːtakʲɪs] |

| | | |
|---|---|---|
| eel | ungurỹs (v) | [ʊngʊ'rʲiːs] |
| electric ray | elektrìnė rajà (m) | [ɛlʲɛk'trʲɪnʲeː ra'ja] |
| moray eel | murėnà (m) | [mʊrʲɛ'na] |
| piranha | pirãnija (m) | [pʲɪ'raːnʲɪjɛ] |

| | | |
|---|---|---|
| shark | ryklỹs (v) | [rʲɪk'lʲiːs] |
| dolphin | delfìnas (v) | [dʲɛlʲ'fʲɪnas] |
| whale | bangìnis (v) | [ban'gʲɪnʲɪs] |

| | | |
|---|---|---|
| crab | krãbas (v) | ['kraːbas] |
| jellyfish | medūzà (m) | [mʲɛduː'za] |
| octopus | aštuonkõjis (v) | [aʃtʊɑŋ'koːjis] |
| starfish | júros žvaigždė̃ (m) | ['juːros ʒvʌɪgʒ'dʲeː] |
| sea urchin | júros ežỹs (v) | ['juːros ɛ'ʒʲiːs] |

| seahorse | júros arkliùkas (v) | ['ju:ros ark'lʲʊkas] |
| oyster | áustrė (m) | ['ɑustrʲe:] |
| shrimp | krevètė (m) | [krʲɛ'vʲɛtʲe:] |
| lobster | omãras (v) | [o'ma:ras] |
| spiny lobster | langùstas (v) | [lʲan'gʊstas] |

## 92. Amphibians. Reptiles

| snake | gyvãtė (m) | [gʲi:'va:tʲe:] |
| venomous (snake) | nuodìngas | [nʊɑ'dʲɪngas] |
| | | |
| viper | angìs (v) | [an'gʲɪs] |
| cobra | kobrà (m) | [kob'ra] |
| python | pitònas (v) | [pʲɪ'tonas] |
| boa | smauglỹs (v) | [smɑʊg'lʲi:s] |
| | | |
| grass snake | žaltỹs (v) | [ʒalʲ'tʲi:s] |
| rattle snake | barškuõlė (m) | [barʃ'kʊalʲe:] |
| anaconda | anakònda (m) | [ana'konda] |
| | | |
| lizard | dríežas (v) | ['drʲiɛʒas] |
| iguana | iguanà (m) | [ɪgʊa'na] |
| monitor lizard | varãnas (v) | [va'ra:nas] |
| salamander | salamándra (m) | [salʲa'mandra] |
| chameleon | chameleònas (v) | [xamʲɛlʲɛ'onas] |
| scorpion | skorpiònas (v) | [skorpʲɪ'ɔnas] |
| | | |
| turtle | vėžlỹs (v) | [vʲe:ʒ'lʲi:s] |
| frog | varlė̃ (m) | [var'lʲe:] |
| toad | rùpūžė (m) | ['rʊpu:ʒʲe:] |
| crocodile | krokodìlas (v) | [kroko'dʲɪlʲas] |

## 93. Insects

| insect, bug | vabzdỹs (v) | [vabz'dʲi:s] |
| butterfly | drugèlis (v) | [drʊ'gʲælʲɪs] |
| ant | skruzdė̃lė (m) | [skrʊz'dʲælʲe:] |
| fly | mùsė (m) | ['mʊsʲe:] |
| mosquito | úodas (v) | ['ʊadas] |
| beetle | vãbalas (v) | ['va:balʲas] |
| | | |
| wasp | vapsvà (m) | [vaps'va] |
| bee | bìtė (m) | ['bʲɪtʲe:] |
| bumblebee | kamã́nė (m) | [ka'ma:nʲe:] |
| gadfly (botfly) | gylỹs (v) | [gʲi:'lʲi:s] |
| | | |
| spider | vóras (v) | ['voras] |
| spiderweb | vorãtinklis (v) | [vo'ra:tʲɪŋklʲɪs] |

| dragonfly | laũmžirgis (v) | [ˈlʲaʊmʒʲɪrgʲɪs] |
| grasshopper | žiógas (v) | [ˈʒʲogas] |
| moth (night butterfly) | petelìškė (m) | [pʲɛtʲɛˈlʲɪʃkʲeː] |

| cockroach | tarakõnas (v) | [taraˈkoːnas] |
| tick | érkė (m) | [ˈærkʲeː] |
| flea | blusà (m) | [blʲʊˈsa] |
| midge | mãšalas (v) | [ˈmaːʃalʲas] |

| locust | skėrỹs (v) | [skʲeːˈrʲiːs] |
| snail | sráigė (m) | [ˈsrʌɪgʲeː] |
| cricket | svirplỹs (v) | [svʲɪrpˈlʲiːs] |
| lightning bug | jõnvabalis (v) | [ˈjɔːnvabalʲɪs] |
| ladybug | borùžė (m) | [boˈrʊʒʲeː] |
| cockchafer | grambuolỹs (v) | [grambʊɑˈlʲiːs] |

| leech | dėlẽ (m) | [dʲeːˈlʲeː] |
| caterpillar | vìkšras (v) | [ˈvʲɪkʃras] |
| earthworm | slíekas (v) | [ˈslʲiɛkas] |
| larva | kirmelė̃ (m) | [kʲɪrmeˈlʲeː] |

# FLORA

**T&P Books Publishing**

## 94. Trees

| | | |
|---|---|---|
| tree | **mēdis** (v) | ['mʲædʲɪs] |
| deciduous (adj) | **lapuōtis** | [lʲapu'atʲɪs] |
| coniferous (adj) | **spygliuōtis** | [spʲi:g'lʲuo:tʲɪs] |
| evergreen (adj) | **vìsžalis** | ['vʲɪsʒalʲɪs] |
| | | |
| apple tree | **obelìs** (m) | [obʲɛ'lʲɪs] |
| pear tree | **kriáušė** (m) | ['krʲæuʃʲe:] |
| sweet cherry tree | **trēšnė** (m) | ['trʲæʃnʲe:] |
| sour cherry tree | **vyšnià** (m) | [vʲi:ʃnʲæ] |
| plum tree | **slyvà** (m) | [slʲi:'va] |
| | | |
| birch | **béržas** (v) | ['bʲɛrʒas] |
| oak | **ąžuolas** (v) | ['a:ʒualʲas] |
| linden tree | **líepa** (m) | ['lʲiɛpa] |
| aspen | **drebulė** (m) | [drebʊ'lʲe:] |
| maple | **klēvas** (v) | ['klʲævas] |
| | | |
| spruce | **ēglė** (m) | ['ʲæglʲe:] |
| pine | **pušìs** (m) | [pʊ'ʃɪs] |
| larch | **maūmedis** (v) | ['maʊmʲɛdʲɪs] |
| | | |
| fir tree | **kēnis** (v) | ['kʲe:nʲɪs] |
| cedar | **kèdras** (v) | ['kʲɛdras] |
| | | |
| poplar | **túopa** (m) | ['tuapa] |
| rowan | **šermùkšnis** (v) | [ʃʲɛr'mʊkʃnʲɪs] |
| | | |
| willow | **glúosnis** (v) | ['glʲuasnʲɪs] |
| alder | **ãlksnis** (v) | ['alʲksnʲɪs] |
| | | |
| beech | **bùkas** (v) | ['bʊkas] |
| elm | **gúoba** (m) | ['guaba] |
| | | |
| ash (tree) | **úosis** (v) | ['uasʲɪs] |
| chestnut | **kaštõnas** (v) | [kaʃ'to:nas] |
| | | |
| magnolia | **magnòlija** (m) | [mag'nolʲɪjɛ] |
| palm tree | **pálmė** (m) | ['palʲmʲe:] |
| cypress | **kiparìsas** (v) | [kʲɪpa'rʲɪsas] |
| | | |
| mangrove | **mañgro mēdis** (v) | ['mañgrɔ 'mʲædʲɪs] |
| baobab | **baobãbas** (v) | [bao'ba:bas] |
| eucalyptus | **eukaliptas** (v) | [ɛʊka'lʲɪptas] |
| sequoia | **sekvojà** (m) | [sʲɛkvo:'jɛ ] |

## 95. Shrubs

| | | |
|---|---|---|
| bush | krū́mas (v) | ['kru:mas] |
| shrub | krūmýnas (v) | [kru:'mʲi:nas] |
| | | |
| grapevine | vynuogýnas (v) | [vʲi:nʊa'gʲi:nas] |
| vineyard | vynuogýnas (v) | [vʲi:nʊa'gʲi:nas] |
| | | |
| raspberry bush | aviẽtė (m) | [a'vʲɛtʲe:] |
| redcurrant bush | raudonàsis serbeñtas (v) | [raʊdo'nasʲɪs sʲɛr'bʲɛntas] |
| gooseberry bush | agrãstas (v) | [ag'ra:stas] |
| | | |
| acacia | akãcija (m) | [a'ka:tsʲɪjɛ] |
| barberry | raugeřškis (m) | [raʊ'gʲɛrʃkʲɪs] |
| jasmine | jazmìnas (v) | [jaz'mʲɪnas] |
| | | |
| juniper | kadagýs (v) | [kada'gʲi:s] |
| rosebush | rõžių krū́mas (v) | ['ro:ʒʲu: 'kru:mas] |
| dog rose | erškė́tis (v) | [erʃ'kʲe:tʲɪs] |

## 96. Fruits. Berries

| | | |
|---|---|---|
| fruit | vaĩsius (v) | ['vʌɪsʲʊs] |
| fruits | vaĩsiai (v dgs) | ['vʌɪsʲɛɪ] |
| apple | obuolỹs (v) | [obʊa'lʲi:s] |
| pear | kriáušė (m) | ['krʲæʊʃe:] |
| plum | slyvà (m) | [slʲi:'va] |
| | | |
| strawberry (garden ~) | brã̃škė (m) | ['bra:ʃkʲe:] |
| sour cherry | vyšnià (m) | [vʲi:ʃnʲæ] |
| sweet cherry | trẽšnė (m) | ['trʲæʃnʲe:] |
| grape | vỹnuogės (m dgs) | ['vʲi:nʊagʲe:s] |
| | | |
| raspberry | aviẽtė (m) | [a'vʲɛtʲe:] |
| blackcurrant | juodíeji serbeñtai (v dgs) | [jʊa'dʲiɛjɪ sʲɛr'bʲɛntʌɪ] |
| redcurrant | raudoníeji serbeñtai (v dgs) | [raʊdo'nʲɛjɪ sʲɛr'bʲɛntʌɪ] |
| gooseberry | agrãstas (v) | [ag'ra:stas] |
| cranberry | spañguolė (m) | ['spaŋgʊalʲe:] |
| | | |
| orange | apelsìnas (v) | [apʲɛlʲ'sʲɪnas] |
| mandarin | mandarìnas (v) | [manda'rʲɪnas] |
| pineapple | ananãsas (v) | [ana'na:sas] |
| banana | banãnas (v) | [ba'na:nas] |
| date | datùlė (m) | [da'tʊlʲe:] |
| | | |
| lemon | citrinà (m) | [tsʲɪtrʲɪ'na] |
| apricot | abrikòsas (v) | [abrʲɪ'kosas] |
| peach | pèrsikas (v) | ['pʲɛrsʲɪkas] |
| kiwi | kìvis (v) | ['kʲɪvʲɪs] |

| | | |
|---|---|---|
| grapefruit | greĩpfrutas (v) | ['grˢɛɪpfrutas] |
| berry | úoga (m) | ['ʊaga] |
| berries | úogos (m dgs) | ['ʊagos] |
| cowberry | brùknės (m dgs) | ['brʊknˢe:s] |
| wild strawberry | žémuogės (m dgs) | ['ʒˢæmʊagˢe:s] |
| bilberry | mėlỹnės (m dgs) | [mˢe:'lˢi:nˢe:s] |

## 97. Flowers. Plants

| | | |
|---|---|---|
| flower | gėlễ (m) | [gˢe:'lˢe:] |
| bouquet (of flowers) | púokštė (m) | ['pʊakʃtˢe:] |
| | | |
| rose (flower) | rõžė (m) | ['ro:ʒˢe:] |
| tulip | tùlpė (m) | ['tʊlˢpˢe:] |
| carnation | gvazdìkas (v) | [gvaz'dˢɪkas] |
| gladiolus | kardēlis (v) | [kar'dˢælˢɪs] |
| | | |
| cornflower | rùgiagėlė (m) | ['rʊgˢægˢe:lˢe:] |
| harebell | varpễlis (v) | [var'pˢælˢɪs] |
| dandelion | pìēnė (m) | ['pˢɛnˢe:] |
| camomile | ramùnė (m) | [ra'mʊnˢe:] |
| | | |
| aloe | alijõšius (v) | [alˢɪ'jo:ʃʊs] |
| cactus | kāktusas (v) | ['ka:ktʊsas] |
| rubber plant, ficus | fìkusas (v) | ['fˢɪkʊsas] |
| | | |
| lily | lelijà (m) | [lˢɛlˢɪ'ja] |
| geranium | pelargònija (m) | [pˢɛlˢar'gonˢɪjɛ] |
| hyacinth | hiacìntas (v) | [ɣˢɪja'tsˢɪntas] |
| | | |
| mimosa | mimozà (m) | [mˢɪmo'za] |
| narcissus | narcìzas (v) | [nar'tsˢɪzas] |
| nasturtium | nastùrta (m) | [nas'turta] |
| | | |
| orchid | orchidéja (m) | [orxˢɪ'dˢe:ja] |
| peony | bijūnas (v) | [bˢɪ'ju:nas] |
| violet | našlaitė (m) | [naʃˈlˢʌɪtˢe:] |
| | | |
| pansy | darželinė našláitė (m) | [darˈʒˢælˢɪnˢe: naʃˈlʌɪtˢe:] |
| forget-me-not | neužmirštuõlė (m) | [nˢɛʊʒmˢɪrʃˈtʊalˢe:] |
| daisy | saulùtė (m) | [sɑʊ'lˢutˢe:] |
| | | |
| poppy | aguonà (m) | [agʊɑ'na] |
| hemp | kanāpė (m) | [ka'na:pˢe:] |
| mint | mėtà (m) | [mˢe:'ta] |
| | | |
| lily of the valley | pakalnùtė (m) | [pakalˢˈnʊtˢe:] |
| snowdrop | sniẽgena (m) | ['snˢɛgˢɛna] |
| nettle | dilgễlė (m) | [dˢɪlˢˈgˢælˢe:] |
| sorrel | rūgštỹnė (m) | [ru:gʃˈtˢi:nˢe:] |

| water lily | vandeñs lelijà (m) | [van'dʲɛns lʲɛlʲɪ'ja] |
| fern | papártis (v) | [pa'partʲɪs] |
| lichen | kérpė (m) | ['kʲɛrpʲeː] |

| greenhouse (tropical ~) | oranžérija (m) | [oran'ʒʲɛrʲɪjɛ] |
| lawn | gazònas (v) | [ga'zonas] |
| flowerbed | klòmba (m) | ['klʲomba] |

| plant | áugalas (v) | ['ɑʊgalʲas] |
| grass | žolė̃ (m) | [ʒo'lʲeː] |
| blade of grass | žolelė̃ (m) | [ʒo'lʲælʲeː] |

| leaf | lãpas (v) | ['lʲaːpas] |
| petal | žíedlapis (v) | ['ʒʲiɛdlʲapʲɪs] |
| stem | stíebas (v) | ['stʲiɛbas] |
| tuber | gumbas (v) | ['gumbas] |

| young plant (shoot) | želmuõ (v) | [ʒʲɛlʲ'muɑ] |
| thorn | spyglỹs (v) | [spʲiːg'lʲiːs] |

| to blossom (vi) | žydéti | [ʒʲiː'dʲeːtʲɪ] |
| to fade, to wither | výsti | ['vʲiːstʲɪ] |
| smell (odor) | kvãpas (v) | ['kvaːpas] |
| to cut (flowers) | nupjáuti | [nʊ'pjɑʊtʲɪ] |
| to pick (a flower) | nuskìnti | [nʊ'skʲɪntʲɪ] |

## 98. Cereals, grains

| grain | grū́das (v) | ['gruːdas] |
| cereal crops | grūdìnės kultū́ros (m dgs) | [gruː'dʲɪnʲeːs kʊlʲ'tuːros] |
| ear (of barley, etc.) | várpa (m) | ['varpa] |

| wheat | kviečiaĩ (v dgs) | [kvʲiɛ'tʂʲɛɪ] |
| rye | rugiaĩ (v dgs) | [rʊ'gʲɛɪ] |
| oats | ãvižos (m dgs) | ['aːvʲɪʒos] |
| millet | sóra (m) | ['sora] |
| barley | miẽžiai (v dgs) | ['mʲɛʒʲɛɪ] |

| corn | kukurū́zas (v) | [kʊkʊ'ruːzas] |
| rice | rýžiai (v) | ['rʲiːʒʲɛɪ] |
| buckwheat | grìkiai (v dgs) | ['grʲɪkʲɛɪ] |

| pea plant | žìrniai (v dgs) | ['ʒʲɪrnʲɛɪ] |
| kidney bean | pupẽlės (m dgs) | [pʊ'pʲælʲeːs] |
| soy | sojà (m) | [so:'jɛ ] |
| lentil | lę̃šiai (v dgs) | ['lʲɛːʃɛɪ] |
| beans (pulse crops) | pùpos (m dgs) | ['pʊpos] |

# COUNTRIES OF
# THE WORLD

**T&P Books Publishing**

| Afghanistan | Afganistãnas (v) | [afganⁱɪ'sta:nas] |
|---|---|---|
| Albania | Albãnija (m) | [alⁱʲ'ba:nʲɪjɛ] |
| Argentina | Argentinà (m) | [argⁱɛntⁱɪ'na] |
| Armenia | Arménija (m) | [ar'mʲe:nʲɪjɛ] |
| Australia | Austrãlija (m) | [ɑʊs'tra:lʲɪjɛ] |
| Austria | Áustrija (m) | ['ɑʊstrʲɪjɛ] |
| Azerbaijan | Azerbaidžãnas (v) | [azⁱɛrbʌɪ'dʒa:nas] |
| | | |
| The Bahamas | Bahãmų salõs (m dgs) | [ba'ɣamu: 'salʲo:s] |
| Bangladesh | Bangladèšas (v) | [banglʲa'dⁱɛʃas] |
| Belarus | Baltarùsija (m) | [balⁱta'rʊsʲɪjɛ] |
| Belgium | Belgija (m) | ['bⁱɛlʲgʲɪjɛ] |
| Bolivia | Bolìvija (m) | [bo'lʲɪvʲɪjɛ] |
| Bosnia and Herzegovina | Bòsnija ìr Hercegovinà (m) | ['bosnʲɪja ir ɣⁱɛrtsⁱɛgovⁱɪ'na] |
| Brazil | Brazìlija (m) | [bra'zʲɪlʲɪjɛ] |
| Bulgaria | Bulgãrija (m) | [bʊlʲ'ga:rʲɪjɛ] |
| | | |
| Cambodia | Kambodžà (m) | [kambo'dʒa] |
| Canada | Kanadà (m) | [kana'da] |
| Chile | Čìlė (m) | ['tʂⁱɪlʲe:] |
| China | Kìnija (m) | ['kⁱɪnʲɪjɛ] |
| Colombia | Kolùmbija (m) | [kɔ'lʲʊmbⁱɪjɛ] |
| Croatia | Kroãtija (m) | [kro'a:tⁱɪjɛ] |
| Cuba | Kubà (m) | [kʊ'ba] |
| Cyprus | Kìpras (v) | ['kⁱɪpras] |
| Czech Republic | Čèkija (m) | ['tʂⁱɛkⁱɪjɛ] |
| | | |
| Denmark | Dãnija (m) | ['da:nⁱɪjɛ] |
| Dominican Republic | Dominìkos Respùblika (m) | [domⁱɪ'nⁱɪkos rⁱɛs'pʊblⁱɪka] |
| Ecuador | Ekvadòras (v) | [ɛkva'doras] |
| Egypt | Egìptas (v) | [ɛ'gⁱɪptas] |
| England | Ánglija (m) | ['anglⁱɪjɛ] |
| Estonia | Èstija (m) | ['ɛstⁱɪjɛ] |
| Finland | Súomija (m) | ['sʊɑmⁱɪjɛ] |
| France | Prancūzijà (m) | [prantsu:zʲɪ'ja] |
| French Polynesia | Prancūzìjos Polinèzija (m) | [prantsu:'zʲɪjɔs polⁱɪ'nⁱɛzⁱɪjɛ] |
| | | |
| Georgia | Grùzija (m) | ['grʊzⁱɪjɛ] |
| Germany | Vokietìja (m) | [vokⁱiɛ'tⁱɪja] |
| Ghana | Ganà (m) | [ga'na] |
| Great Britain | Didžiòji Britãnija (m) | [dⁱɪ'dʒⁱo:jɪ brⁱɪ'ta:nⁱɪjɛ] |
| Greece | Graìkija (m) | ['grʌɪkⁱɪjɛ] |

| Haiti | **Haìtis** (v) | [ɣʌˈɪtʲɪs] |
| Hungary | **Veñgrija** (m) | [ˈvʲɛŋgrʲɪjɛ] |

## 100. Countries. Part 2

| Iceland | **Islándija** (m) | [ɪsˈlʲandʲɪjɛ] |
| India | **Ìndija** (m) | [ˈɪndʲɪjɛ] |
| Indonesia | **Indonezijà** (m) | [ɪndonʲɛzʲɪˈja] |
| Iran | **Irãnas** (v) | [ɪˈraːnas] |
| Iraq | **Irãkas** (v) | [ɪˈraːkas] |
| Ireland | **Aìrija** (m) | [ˈʌɪrʲɪjɛ] |
| Israel | **Izraèlis** (v) | [ɪzraʲˈɛlʲɪs] |
| Italy | **Itãlija** (m) | [ɪˈtaːlʲɪjɛ] |

| Jamaica | **Jamáika** (m) | [jaˈmʌɪka] |
| Japan | **Japònija** (m) | [jaˈponʲɪjɛ] |
| Jordan | **Jordãnija** (m) | [jorˈdaːnʲɪjɛ] |
| Kazakhstan | **Kazãchija** (m) | [kaˈzaːxʲɪjɛ] |
| Kenya | **Kènija** (m) | [ˈkʲɛnʲɪjɛ] |
| Kirghizia | **Kirgìzija** (m) | [kʲɪrˈgʲɪzʲɪjɛ] |
| Kuwait | **Kuveìtas** (v) | [kʊˈvʲɛɪtas] |

| Laos | **Laòsas** (v) | [lʲaˈosas] |
| Latvia | **Lãtvija** (m) | [ˈlʲaːtvʲɪjɛ] |
| Lebanon | **Libãnas** (v) | [lʲɪˈbanas] |
| Libya | **Lìbija** (m) | [ˈlʲɪbʲɪjɛ] |
| Liechtenstein | **Lìchtenšteinas** (v) | [ˈlʲɪxtʲɛnʃtʲɛɪnas] |
| Lithuania | **Lietuvà** (m) | [lʲiɛtʊˈva] |
| Luxembourg | **Liùksemburgas** (v) | [ˈlʲʊksʲɛmbʊrgas] |

| Macedonia (Republic of ~) | **Makedònija** (m) | [makʲɛˈdonʲɪjɛ] |
| Madagascar | **Madagaskãras** (v) | [madagasˈkaːras] |
| Malaysia | **Malaìzija** (m) | [maˈlʲʌɪzʲɪjɛ] |
| Malta | **Maĺta** (m) | [ˈmalʲta] |
| Mexico | **Mèksika** (m) | [ˈmʲɛksʲɪka] |
| Moldova, Moldavia | **Moldãvija** (m) | [molʲˈdaːvʲɪjɛ] |

| Monaco | **Mònakas** (v) | [ˈmonakas] |
| Mongolia | **Mongòlija** (m) | [monˈgolʲɪjɛ] |
| Montenegro | **Juodkalnijà** (m) | [jʊɑdkalʲnʲɪˈja] |

| Morocco | **Maròkas** (v) | [maˈrokas] |
| Myanmar | **Mianmãras** (v) | [mʲænˈmaːras] |

| Namibia | **Namìbija** (m) | [naˈmʲɪbʲɪjɛ] |
| Nepal | **Nepãlas** (v) | [nʲɛˈpaːlʲas] |
| Netherlands | **Nýderlandai** (v dgs) | [ˈnʲiːdʲɛrlʲandʌɪ] |
| New Zealand | **Naujòji Zelándija** (m) | [nɑʊʲjoːjɪ zʲɛˈlʲandʲɪjɛ] |
| North Korea | **Šiáurės Koréja** (m) | [ˈʃæʊrʲeːs koˈrʲeːja] |
| Norway | **Norvègija** (m) | [norˈvʲɛgʲɪjɛ] |

## 101. Countries. Part 3

| English | Lithuanian | Pronunciation |
|---|---|---|
| Pakistan | **Pakistānas** (v) | [pakʲɪ'sta:nas] |
| Palestine | **Palestìna** (m) | [palʲɛs'tʲɪna] |
| Panama | **Panamà** (m) | [pana'ma] |
| Paraguay | **Paragvājus** (v) | [parag'va:jʊs] |
| Peru | **Perù** (v) | [pʲɛ'rʊ] |
| Poland | **Lénkija** (m) | ['lʲɛŋkʲɪjɛ] |
| Portugal | **Portugālija** (m) | [portʊ'ga:lʲɪjɛ] |
| Romania | **Rumùnija** (m) | [rʊ'mʊnʲɪjɛ] |
| Russia | **Rùsija** (m) | ['rʊsʲɪjɛ] |
| Saudi Arabia | **Saúdɔ Arābija** (m) | [sa'ʊdɔ a'ra:bʲɪjɛ] |
| Scotland | **Škòtija** (m) | ['ʃkotʲɪjɛ] |
| Senegal | **Senegālas** (v) | [sʲɛnʲɛ'ga:lʲas] |
| Serbia | **Sèrbija** (m) | ['sʲɛrbʲɪjɛ] |
| Slovakia | **Slovākija** (m) | [slʲo'va:kʲɪjɛ] |
| Slovenia | **Slovénija** (m) | [slʲo'vʲe:nʲɪjɛ] |
| South Africa | **Pietų̃ ā́frikos respùblika** (m) | [pʲiɛ'tu: 'a:frʲɪkos rʲɛs'pʊblʲɪka] |
| South Korea | **Pietų̃ Koréja** (m) | [pʲiɛ'tu: ko'rʲe:ja] |
| Spain | **Ispānija** (m) | [ɪs'pa:nʲɪjɛ] |
| Suriname | **Surināmis** (v) | [sʊrʲɪ'namʲɪs] |
| Sweden | **Švèdija** (m) | ['ʃvʲɛdʲɪjɛ] |
| Switzerland | **Šveicārija** (m) | [ʃvʲɛɪ'tsa:rʲɪjɛ] |
| Syria | **Sìrija** (m) | ['sʲɪrʲɪjɛ] |
| Taiwan | **Taivānis** (v) | [tʌɪ'vanʲɪs] |
| Tajikistan | **Tadžìkija** (m) | [tad'ʒʲɪkʲɪjɛ] |
| Tanzania | **Tanzānija** (m) | [tan'za:nʲɪjɛ] |
| Tasmania | **Tasmānija** (m) | [tas'ma:nʲɪjɛ] |
| Thailand | **Tailándas** (v) | [tʌɪ'lʲandas] |
| Tunisia | **Tunìsas** (v) | [tʊ'nʲɪsas] |
| Turkey | **Tùrkija** (m) | ['tʊrkʲɪjɛ] |
| Turkmenistan | **Turkménija** (m) | [tʊrk'mʲe:nʲɪjɛ] |
| Ukraine | **Ukrainà** (m) | [ʊkrʌɪ'na] |
| United Arab Emirates | **Jungtìniai Arābų Emiratai** (v dgs) | [jʊŋk'tʲɪnʲɛɪ a'ra:bu: ɛmʲɪratʌɪ] |
| United States of America | **Jungtìnės Amèrikos Valstìjos** (m dgs) | [jʊŋk'tʲɪnʲe:s a'mʲɛrʲɪkos valʲs'tʲɪjɔs] |
| Uruguay | **Urugvājus** (v) | [ʊrʊg'va:jʊs] |
| Uzbekistan | **Uzbèkija** (m) | [ʊz'bʲɛkʲɪjɛ] |
| Vatican | **Vatikānas** (v) | [vatʲɪka:nas] |
| Venezuela | **Venesuelà** (m) | [vʲɛnʲɛsʊ'ɛ'lʲa] |
| Vietnam | **Vietnāmas** (v) | [vʲɛt'na:mas] |
| Zanzibar | **Zanzibāras** (v) | [zanzʲɪ'ba:ras] |

# GASTRONOMIC GLOSSARY

This section contains a lot of
words and terms associated
with food. This dictionary will
make it easier for you to
understand the menu at a
restaurant and choose
the right dish

**T&P Books Publishing**

| | | |
|---|---|---|
| aftertaste | príeskonis (v) | ['prʲɪɛskonʲɪs] |
| almond | migdólas (v) | [mʲɪg'do:lʲas] |
| anise | anýžius (v) | [a'nʲiːʒʲʊs] |
| aperitif | aperitývas (v) | [apʲɛrʲɪ'tʲiːvas] |
| appetite | apetìtas (v) | [apʲɛ'tʲɪtas] |
| appetizer | ùžkandis (v) | ['ʊʒkandʲɪs] |
| apple | obuolỹs (v) | [obʊa'lʲiːs] |
| apricot | abrikòsas (v) | [abrʲɪ'kosas] |
| artichoke | artišòkas (v) | [artʲɪ'ʃokas] |
| asparagus | smìdras (v) | ['smʲɪdras] |
| Atlantic salmon | lašišà (m) | [lʲaʃʲɪ'ʃa] |
| avocado | avokàdas (v) | [avo'kadas] |
| bacon | bekònas (v) | [bʲɛ'konas] |
| banana | banãnas (v) | [ba'naːnas] |
| barley | miẽžiai (v dgs) | ['mʲɛʒʲɛɪ] |
| bartender | bármenas (v) | ['barmʲɛnas] |
| basil | bazìlikas (v) | [ba'zʲɪlʲɪkas] |
| bay leaf | láuro lãpas (v) | ['lʲaʊrɔ 'lʲaːpas] |
| beans | pùpos (m dgs) | ['pʊpos] |
| beef | jáutiena (m) | ['jaʊtʲɪɛna] |
| beer | alùs (v) | [a'lʲʊs] |
| beetroot | rùnkelis, burõkas (v) | ['rʊŋkʲɛlʲɪs], [bʊ'roːkas] |
| bell pepper | pipìras (v) | [pʲɪ'pʲɪras] |
| berries | úogos (m dgs) | ['ʊagos] |
| berry | úoga (m) | ['ʊaga] |
| bilberry | mélynės (m dgs) | [mʲɛ:'lʲiːnʲeːs] |
| birch bolete | lẽpšis (v) | ['lʲæpʃʲɪs] |
| bitter | kartùs | [kar'tʊs] |
| black coffee | juodà kavà (m) | [jʊa'da ka'va] |
| black pepper | juodíeji pipìrai (v) | [jʊa'dʲɪɛjɪ pʲɪ'pʲɪrʌɪ] |
| black tea | juodà arbatà (m) | [jʊa'da arba'ta] |
| blackberry | gérvuogės (m dgs) | ['gʲɛrvʊagʲeːs] |
| blackcurrant | juodíeji serbeñtai (v dgs) | [jʊa'dʲɪɛjɪ sʲɛr'bʲɛntʌɪ] |
| boiled | vìrtas | ['vʲɪrtas] |
| bottle opener | atidarytùvas (v) | [atʲɪdarʲiː'tʊvas] |
| bread | dúona (m) | ['dʊana] |
| breakfast | pùsryčiai (v dgs) | ['pʊsrʲiːtʃʲɛɪ] |
| bream | karšis (v) | ['karʃʲɪs] |
| broccoli | brokolių kopūstas (v) | ['brokolʲu: ko'puːstas] |
| Brussels sprouts | briùselio kopūstas (v) | ['brʲʊsʲɛlʲɔ ko'puːstas] |
| buckwheat | grìkiai (v dgs) | ['grʲɪkʲɛɪ] |
| butter | svíestas (v) | ['svʲɪɛstas] |
| buttercream | krèmas (v) | ['krʲɛmas] |
| cabbage | kopūstas (v) | [kɔ'puːstas] |

| | | |
|---|---|---|
| cake | pyragaitis (v) | [pʲiːraˈgʌɪtʲɪs] |
| cake | tortas (v) | [ˈtortas] |
| calorie | kalorija (m) | [kaˈlʲorʲɪjɛ] |
| can opener | konservų atidarytuvas (v) | [kɔnˈsʲɛrvuː atʲɪdarʲiːˈtʊvas] |
| candy | saldainis (v) | [salʲˈdʌɪnʲɪs] |
| canned food | konservai (v dgs) | [kɔnˈsʲɛrvʌɪ] |
| cappuccino | kapučino kava (m) | [kapuˈt̞sɪnɔ kaˈva] |
| caraway | kmynai (v) | [ˈkmʲiːnʌɪ] |
| carbohydrates | angliavandeniai (v dgs) | [anˈglʲævandʲɛnʲɛɪ] |
| carbonated | gazuotas | [gaˈzʊɑtas] |
| carp | karpis (v) | [ˈkarpʲɪs] |
| carrot | morka (m) | [morˈka] |
| catfish | šamas (v) | [ˈʃaːmas] |
| cauliflower | kalafioras (v) | [kalʲaˈfʲoras] |
| caviar | ikrai (v dgs) | [ˈɪkrʌɪ] |
| celery | salieras (v) | [saˈlʲɛras] |
| cep | baravykas (v) | [baraˈvʲiːkas] |
| cereal crops | grūdinės kultūros (m dgs) | [gruːˈdʲɪnʲeːs kʊlʲˈtuːros] |
| cereal grains | kruopos (m dgs) | [ˈkrʊɑpos] |
| champagne | šampanas (v) | [ʃamˈpaːnas] |
| chanterelle | voveraitė (m) | [voveˈrʌɪtʲeː] |
| check | sąskaita (m) | [ˈsaːskʌɪta] |
| cheese | sūris (v) | [ˈsuːrʲɪs] |
| chewing gum | kramtomoji guma (m) | [kramtoˈmojɪ gʊˈma] |
| chicken | višta (m) | [vʲɪʃˈta] |
| chocolate | šokoladas (v) | [ʃokoˈlʲaːdas] |
| chocolate | šokoladinis | [ʃokoˈlʲaːdʲɪnʲɪs] |
| cinnamon | cinamonas (v) | [tsʲɪnaˈmonas] |
| clear soup | sultinys (v) | [sʊlʲtʲɪˈnʲiːs] |
| cloves | gvazdikas (v) | [gvazˈdʲɪkas] |
| cocktail | kokteilis (v) | [kɔkˈtʲɛɪlʲɪs] |
| coconut | kokoso riešutas (v) | [ˈkokosɔ ˈrʲɪɛʃutas] |
| cod | menkė (m) | [ˈmʲɛŋkʲeː] |
| coffee | kava (m) | [kaˈva] |
| coffee with milk | kava su pienu (m) | [kaˈva ˈsʊ ˈpʲɪɛnʊ] |
| cognac | konjakas (v) | [kɔnʲˈjaːkas] |
| cold | šaltas | [ˈʃalʲtas] |
| condensed milk | sutirštintas pienas (v) | [sʊˈtʲɪrʃtʲɪntas ˈpʲɪɛnas] |
| condiment | prieskonis (v) | [ˈprʲɪɛskonʲɪs] |
| confectionery | konditerijos gaminiai (v) | [kɔndʲɪˈtʲɛrʲɪjos gamʲɪˈnʲɪɛɪ] |
| cookies | sausainiai (v) | [sɑʊˈsʌɪnʲɛɪ] |
| coriander | kalendra (v) | [kaˈlʲɛndra] |
| corkscrew | kamščiatraukis (v) | [kamʃˈtsʲætrɑʊkʲɪs] |
| corn | kukurūzas (v) | [kʊkʊˈruːzas] |
| corn | kukurūzas (v) | [kʊkʊˈruːzas] |
| cornflakes | kukurūzų dribsniai (v dgs) | [kʊkʊˈruːzu ˈdrʲɪbsnʲɛɪ] |
| course, dish | patiekalas (v) | [ˈpaːtʲɪɛkalʲas] |
| cowberry | bruknės (m dgs) | [ˈbrʊknʲeːs] |
| crab | krabas (v) | [ˈkraːbas] |
| cranberry | spanguolė (m) | [ˈspaŋgʊɑlʲeː] |
| cream | grietinėlė (m) | [grʲɪɛtʲɪˈnʲeːlʲeː] |
| crumb | trupinys (v) | [trʊpʲɪˈnʲiːs] |

| English | Lithuanian | Pronunciation |
|---|---|---|
| crustaceans | vėžiagyviai (v dgs) | [vʲeː'ʒʲægʲi:vʲɛɪ] |
| cucumber | agurkas (v) | [a'gurkas] |
| cuisine | virtuvė (m) | [vʲɪr'tuvʲeː] |
| cup | puodukas (v) | [puɑ'dukas] |
| dark beer | tamsùs alùs (v) | [tam'sus a'lʲus] |
| date | datulė (m) | [da'tulʲeː] |
| death cap | šungrybis (v) | ['ʃungrʲi:bʲɪs] |
| dessert | desertas (v) | [dʲɛ'sʲɛrtas] |
| diet | dieta (m) | [dʲiɛ'ta] |
| dill | krapas (v) | ['kra:pas] |
| dinner | vakarienė (m) | [vaka'rʲɛnʲe:] |
| dried | džiovintas | [dʒʲoˈvʲɪntas] |
| drinking water | geriamas vanduo (v) | ['gʲærʲæmas van'duɑ] |
| duck | antis (m) | ['antʲɪs] |
| ear | varpa (m) | ['varpa] |
| edible mushroom | valgomas grybas (v) | ['valʲgomas 'grʲi:bas] |
| eel | ungurys (v) | [ungu'rʲi:s] |
| egg | kiaušinis (v) | [kʲɛu'ʃɪnʲɪs] |
| egg white | baltymas (v) | ['balʲtʲi:mas] |
| egg yolk | trynys (v) | [trʲi:'nʲi:s] |
| eggplant | baklažanas (v) | [baklʲa'ʒa:nas] |
| eggs | kiaušiniai (v dgs) | [kʲɛu'ʃɪnʲɛɪ] |
| Enjoy your meal! | Gero apetito! | ['gʲæro apʲɛ'tʲɪto!] |
| fats | riebalai (v dgs) | [rʲiɛba'lʲʌɪ] |
| fig | figa (m) | [fʲɪ'ga] |
| filling | įdaras (v) | ['i:daras] |
| fish | žuvis (m) | [ʒu'vʲɪs] |
| flatfish | plekšnė (m) | ['plʲækʃnʲe:] |
| flour | miltai (v dgs) | ['mʲɪlʲtʌɪ] |
| fly agaric | musmirė (m) | ['musmʲɪrʲe:] |
| food | valgis (v) | ['valʲgʲɪs] |
| fork | šakutė (m) | [ʃa'kutʲe:] |
| freshly squeezed juice | šviežiai spaustos sultys (m dgs) | [ʃvʲiɛ'ʒʲɛɪ 'spɑustos 'sulʲtʲi:s] |
| fried | keptas | ['kʲæptas] |
| fried eggs | kiaušinienė (m) | [kʲɛuʃɪ'nʲɛnʲe:] |
| frozen | šaldytas | ['ʃalʲdʲi:tas] |
| fruit | vaisius (v) | ['vʌɪsʲus] |
| fruits | vaisiai (v dgs) | ['vʌɪsʲɛɪ] |
| game | žvėriena (m) | [ʒvʲe:'rʲiɛna] |
| gammon | kumpis (v) | ['kumpʲɪs] |
| garlic | česnakas (v) | [tʃɛs'na:kas] |
| gin | džinas (v) | ['dʒɪnas] |
| ginger | imbieras (v) | ['ɪmbʲiɛras] |
| glass | stiklas (v) | ['stʲɪklʲas] |
| glass | taurė (m) | [tɑu'rʲe:] |
| goose | žąsinas (v) | ['ʒa:sʲɪnas] |
| gooseberry | agrastas (v) | [ag'ra:stas] |
| grain | grūdas (v) | ['gru:das] |
| grape | vynuogės (m dgs) | ['vʲi:nuɑgʲe:s] |
| grapefruit | greipfrutas (v) | ['grʲɛɪpfrutas] |
| green tea | žalia arbata (m) | [ʒa'lʲæ arba'ta] |

| greens | žalumýnai (v) | [ʒalʲuˈmʲiːnʌɪ] |
| halibut | ōtas (v) | [ˈoːtas] |
| ham | kuṁpis (v) | [ˈkumpʲɪs] |
| hamburger | fáršas (v) | [ˈfarʃas] |
| hamburger | mėsaìnis (v) | [mʲeːˈsʌɪnʲɪs] |
| hazelnut | ríešutas (v) | [ˈrʲiɛʃutas] |
| herring | sílkė (m) | [ˈsʲɪlʲkʲeː] |
| honey | medùs (v) | [mʲɛˈdus] |
| horseradish | krienaĩ (v dgs) | [krʲɛˈnʌɪ] |
| hot | kárštas | [ˈkarʃtas] |
| ice | lẽdas (v) | [ˈlʲædas] |
| ice-cream | ledaĩ (v dgs) | [lʲɛˈdʌɪ] |
| instant coffee | tirpì kavà (m) | [tʲɪrˈpʲɪ kaˈva] |
| jam | džèmas (v) | [ˈdʒʲɛmas] |
| jam | uogiẽnė (m) | [uɑˈgʲɛnʲeː] |
| juice | sùltys (m dgs) | [ˈsulʲtʲiːs] |
| kidney bean | pupẽlės (m dgs) | [puˈpʲælʲeːs] |
| kiwi | kìvis (v) | [ˈkʲɪvʲɪs] |
| knife | peĩlis (v) | [ˈpʲɛɪlʲɪs] |
| lamb | avíena (m) | [aˈvʲɛna] |
| lemon | citrinà (m) | [tsʲɪtrʲɪˈna] |
| lemonade | limonãdas (v) | [lʲɪmoˈnaːdas] |
| lentil | lęšiai (v dgs) | [ˈlʲɛːʃɛɪ] |
| lettuce | salõta (m) | [saˈlʲoːta] |
| light beer | šviesùs alùs (v) | [ʃvʲɛˈsus aˈlʲus] |
| liqueur | lìkeris (v) | [ˈlʲɪkʲɛrʲɪs] |
| liquors | alkohòliniai gérimai (v dgs) | [alʲkoˈɣolʲɪnʲɛɪ ˈgʲeːrʲɪmʌɪ] |
| liver | kẽpenys (m dgs) | [ˈkʲeːpeˈnʲiːs] |
| lunch | piẽtūs (v) | [ˈpʲɛˈtuːs] |
| mackerel | skùmbrė (m) | [ˈskumbrʲeː] |
| mandarin | mandarìnas (v) | [mandaˈrʲɪnas] |
| mango | mángo (v) | [ˈmangɔ] |
| margarine | margarìnas (v) | [margaˈrʲɪnas] |
| marmalade | marmelãdas (v) | [marmʲɛˈlʲaːdas] |
| mashed potatoes | bùlvių kõšė (m) | [ˈbuʎvʲu ˈkoːʃʲeː] |
| mayonnaise | majonèzas (v) | [majɔˈnʲɛzas] |
| meat | mėsà (m) | [mʲeːˈsa] |
| melon | meliònas (v) | [mʲɛˈlʲonas] |
| menu | meniù (v) | [mʲɛˈnʲu] |
| milk | píenas (v) | [ˈpʲiɛnas] |
| milkshake | píeniškas koktèlis (v) | [ˈpʲiɛnʲɪʃkas kokˈtʲɛɪlʲɪs] |
| millet | sóra (m) | [ˈsora] |
| mineral water | minerãlinis vanduõ (v) | [mʲɪnʲɛˈraːlʲɪnʲɪs vanˈduɑ] |
| morel | briedžiùkas (v) | [brʲiɛˈdʒʲukas] |
| mushroom | grýbas (v) | [ˈgrʲiːbas] |
| mustard | garstýčios (v) | [garˈstʲiːtsʲos] |
| non-alcoholic | nealkohòlonis | [nʲɛalʲkoˈɣolonʲɪs] |
| noodles | lãkštiniai (v dgs) | [ˈlʲaːkʃtʲɪnʲɛɪ] |
| oats | ãvižos (m dgs) | [ˈaːvʲɪʒos] |
| olive oil | alývuogių alíejus (v) | [aˈlʲiːvuɑgʲu aˈlʲɛjus] |
| olives | alývuogės (m dgs) | [aˈlʲiːvuɑgʲeːs] |
| omelet | omlètas (v) | [omˈlʲɛtas] |

| onion | svogūnas (v) | [svo'gu:nas] |
|---|---|---|
| orange | apelsìnas (v) | [apʲɛlʲ'sʲɪnas] |
| orange juice | apelsìnų sùltys (m dgs) | [apʲɛlʲ'sʲɪnu: 'sulʲtʲi:s] |
| orange-cap boletus | raudonvĩršis (v) | [rɑudon'vʲɪrʃɪs] |
| oyster | áustrė (m) | ['ɑustrʲe:] |
| pâté | paštetas (v) | [paʃ'tʲɛtas] |
| papaya | papája (m) | [pa'pa ja] |
| paprika | pãprika (m) | ['pa:prʲɪka] |
| parsley | petrãžolė (m) | [pʲɛ'tra:ʒolʲe:] |
| pasta | makarōnai (v dgs) | [maka'ro:nʌɪ] |
| pea | žìrniai (v dgs) | ['ʒʲɪrnʲɛɪ] |
| peach | pèrsikas (v) | ['pʲɛrsʲɪkas] |
| peanut | žẽmės riešutaĩ (v) | ['ʒʲæmʲe:s rʲiɛʃu'tʌɪ] |
| pear | kriáušė (m) | ['krʲæuʃe:] |
| peel | lúoba (m) | ['lʲuɑba] |
| perch | ešerỹs (v) | [ɛʃɛ'rʲi:s] |
| pickled | marinúotas | [marʲɪ'nuɑtas] |
| pie | pyrãgas (v) | [pʲi:'ra:gas] |
| piece | gãbalas (v) | ['ga:balʲas] |
| pike | lydekà (m) | [lʲi:dʲɛ'ka] |
| pike perch | starkis (v) | ['starkʲɪs] |
| pineapple | ananãsas (v) | [ana'na:sas] |
| pistachios | pistãcijos (m dgs) | [pʲɪs'ta:tsʲɪjɔs] |
| pizza | picà (m) | [pʲɪ'tsa] |
| plate | lėkštė̃ (m) | [lʲe:kʃ'tʲe:] |
| plum | slyvà (m) | [slʲi:'va] |
| poisonous mushroom | nuodìngas grỹbas (v) | [nuɑ'dʲɪngas 'grʲi:bas] |
| pomegranate | granãtas (v) | [gra'na:tas] |
| pork | kiaulíena (m) | [kʲɛu'lʲiɛna] |
| porridge | kõšė (m) | ['ko:ʃe:] |
| portion | pòrcija (m) | ['portsʲɪjɛ] |
| potato | bùlvė (m) | ['bulʲvʲe:] |
| proteins | baltymaĩ (v dgs) | [balʲtʲi:'mʌɪ] |
| pub, bar | bãras (v) | ['ba:ras] |
| pudding | pùdingas (v) | ['pudʲɪngas] |
| pumpkin | rópė (m) | ['ropʲe:] |
| rabbit | triùšis (v) | ['trʲuʃɪs] |
| radish | ridìkas (v) | [rʲɪ'dʲɪkas] |
| raisin | razìnos (m dgs) | [ra'zʲɪnos] |
| raspberry | aviẽtė (m) | [a'vʲɛtʲe:] |
| recipe | recèptas (v) | [rʲɛ'tsʲɛptas] |
| red pepper | raudoníeji pipìrai (v) | [rɑudo'nʲiɛjɪ pʲɪ'pʲɪrʌɪ] |
| red wine | raudónas vỹnas (v) | [rɑu'donas 'vʲi:nas] |
| redcurrant | raudoníeji serbeñtai (v dgs) | [rɑudo'nʲeji sʲɛr'bʲɛntʌɪ] |
| refreshing drink | gaivùsis gérimas (v) | [gʌɪ'vusʲɪs 'gʲe:rʲɪmas] |
| rice | rỹžiai (v) | ['rʲi:ʒʲɛɪ] |
| rum | ròmas (v) | ['romas] |
| russula | ūmė̃dė̃ (m) | [u:mʲe:'dʲe:] |
| rye | rugiaĩ (v dgs) | [ru'gʲɛɪ] |
| saffron | šafrãnas (v) | [ʃaf'ra:nas] |
| salad | salõtos (m) | [sa'lʲo:tos] |
| salmon | lašišà (m) | [lʲaʃɪ'ʃa] |

| salt | druska (m) | [drʊs'ka] |
| salty | sūrus | [su:'rʊs] |
| sandwich | sumuštinis (v) | [sʊmʊʃ'tʲɪnʲɪs] |
| sardine | sardinė (m) | [sar'dʲɪnʲe:] |
| sauce | pādažas (v) | ['pa:daʒas] |
| saucer | lėkštelė (m) | [lʲe:kʃ'tʲælʲe:] |
| sausage | dešra (m) | [dʲɛʃ'ra] |
| seafood | jūros gėrýbės (m dgs) | ['ju:ros gʲe:'rʲi:bʲe:s] |
| sesame | sezāmas (v) | [sʲɛ'za:mas] |
| shark | ryklys (v) | [rʲɪk'lʲi:s] |
| shrimp | krevetė (m) | [krʲɛ'vʲɛtʲe:] |
| side dish | garnyras (v) | [gar'nʲi:ras] |
| slice | griežinys (v) | [grʲiɛʒɪ'nʲi:s] |
| smoked | rūkytas | [ru:'kʲi:tas] |
| soft drink | nealkoholonis gėrimas (v) | [nʲɛalʲko'ɣolonʲɪs 'gʲe:rʲɪmas] |
| soup | sriuba (m) | [srʲʊ'ba] |
| soup spoon | valgomasis šáukštas (v) | ['valʲgomasʲɪs 'ʃaʊkʃtas] |
| sour cherry | vyšnia (m) | [vʲi:ʃ'nʲæ] |
| sour cream | grietinė (m) | [grʲiɛ'tʲɪnʲe:] |
| soy | soja (m) | [so:'jɛ ] |
| spaghetti | spagečiai (v dgs) | [spa'gʲɛtʂʲɛɪ] |
| sparkling | gazuotas | [ga'zʊɑtas] |
| spice | príeskonis (v) | ['prʲiɛskonʲɪs] |
| spinach | špinātas (v) | [ʃpʲɪ'na:tas] |
| spiny lobster | langustas (v) | [lʲan'gʊstas] |
| spoon | šáukštas (v) | ['ʃaʊkʃtas] |
| squid | kalmāras (v) | [kalʲma:ras] |
| steak | bifšteksas (v) | [bʲɪf'ʃtʲɛksas] |
| still | be gāzo | ['bʲɛ 'ga:zɔ] |
| strawberry | brāškė (m) | ['bra:ʃkʲe:] |
| sturgeon | eršketíena (m) | [ɛrʃkʲɛ'tʲiɛna] |
| sugar | cukrus (v) | ['tsʊkrʊs] |
| sunflower oil | saulégrąžų aliẽjus (v) | [saʊ'lʲe:gra:ʒu: a'lʲɛjʊs] |
| sweet | saldus | [salʲʲdʊs] |
| sweet cherry | trēšnė (m) | ['trʲæʃnʲe:] |
| taste, flavor | skōnis (v) | ['sko:nʲɪs] |
| tasty | skanus | [ska'nʊs] |
| tea | arbata (m) | [arba'ta] |
| teaspoon | arbātinis šaukštēlis (v) | [ar'ba:tʲɪnʲɪs ʃaʊkʃ'tʲælʲɪs] |
| tip | arbātpinigiai (v dgs) | [ar'ba:tpʲɪnʲɪgʲɛɪ] |
| tomato | pomidoras (v) | [pomʲɪ'doras] |
| tomato juice | pomidorų sultys (m dgs) | [pomʲɪ'doru: 'sʊlʲtʲi:s] |
| tongue | liežuvis (v) | [lʲiɛ'ʒʊvʲɪs] |
| toothpick | dantų krapštukas (v) | [dan'tu: krapʃ'tʊkas] |
| trout | upėtakis (v) | [ʊ'pʲe:takʲɪs] |
| tuna | tunas (v) | ['tʊnas] |
| turkey | kalakutíena (m) | [kalʲakʊ'tʲiɛna] |
| turnip | moliūgas (v) | [mo'lʲʲu:gas] |
| veal | veršíena (m) | [vʲɛrʲʃʲiɛna] |
| vegetable oil | augalinis aliẽjus (v) | [aʊgalʲɪnʲɪs a'lʲɛjʊs] |
| vegetables | daržóvės (m dgs) | [dar'ʒovʲe:s] |

| vegetarian | vegetāras (v) | [vʲɛgʲɛ'ta:ras] |
| vegetarian | vegetāriškas | [vʲɛgʲɛ'ta:rʲɪʃkas] |
| vermouth | vèrmutas (v) | ['vʲɛrmʊtas] |
| vienna sausage | dešrēlė (m) | [dʲɛʃrʲælʲe:] |
| vinegar | āctas (v) | ['a:tstas] |
| vitamin | vitamìnas (v) | [vʲɪta'mʲɪnas] |
| vodka | degtìnė (m) | [dʲɛk'tʲɪnʲe:] |
| waffles | vāfliai (v dgs) | ['va:flʲɛɪ] |
| waiter | padavéjas (v) | [pada'vʲe:jas] |
| waitress | padavéja (m) | [pada'vʲe:ja] |
| walnut | graìkinis ríešutas (v) | ['grʌɪkʲɪnʲɪs 'rʲɪɛʃʊtas] |
| water | vanduō (v) | [van'dʊɑ] |
| watermelon | arbūzas (v) | [ar'bu:zas] |
| wheat | kviečiaĩ (v dgs) | [kvʲɪɛ'tʂʲɛɪ] |
| whiskey | vìskis (v) | ['vʲɪskʲɪs] |
| white wine | báltas vȳnas (v) | ['balʲtas 'vʲi:nas] |
| wild strawberry | žémuogės (m dgs) | ['ʒʲæmʊɑgʲe:s] |
| wine | vȳnas (v) | ['vʲi:nas] |
| wine list | vȳnų žemélapis (v) | ['vʲi:nu: ʒe'mʲe:lʲapʲɪs] |
| with ice | sù ledaĩs | ['sʊ lʲɛ'dʌɪs] |
| yogurt | jogùrtas (v) | [jo'gʊrtas] |
| zucchini | agurōtis (v) | [agʊ'ro:tʲɪs] |

| | | |
|---|---|---|
| česnãkas (v) | [tʃʲɛsˈnaːkas] | garlic |
| įdaras (v) | [ˈiːdaras] | filling |
| šáldytas | [ˈʃalʲdʲiːtas] | frozen |
| šáltas | [ˈʃalʲtas] | cold |
| šáukštas (v) | [ˈʃɑʊkʃtas] | spoon |
| šãmas (v) | [ˈʃaːmas] | catfish |
| šafrãnas (v) | [ʃafˈraːnas] | saffron |
| šakùtė (m) | [ʃaˈkʊtʲeː] | fork |
| šampãnas (v) | [ʃamˈpaːnas] | champagne |
| šokolãdas (v) | [ʃokoˈlʲaːdas] | chocolate |
| šokolãdinis | [ʃokoˈlʲaːdʲɪnʲɪs] | chocolate |
| špinãtas (v) | [ʃpʲɪˈnaːtas] | spinach |
| šùngrybis (v) | [ˈʃʊngrʲiːbʲɪs] | death cap |
| šviežiaĩ spáustos sùltys (m dgs) | [ʃvʲiɛˈʒʲɛɪ ˈspɑʊstos ˈsʊlʲtʲiːs] | freshly squeezed juice |
| šviesùs alùs (v) | [ʃvʲiɛˈsʊs aˈlʲʊs] | light beer |
| ūmėdė̃ (m) | [uːmʲeːˈdʲeː] | russula |
| žą̃sinas (v) | [ˈʒaːsʲɪnas] | goose |
| žalià arbatà (m) | [ʒaˈlʲæ arbaˈta] | green tea |
| žalumýnai (v) | [ʒalʲʊˈmʲiːnʌɪ] | greens |
| žėmuogės (m dgs) | [ˈʒʲæmʊɑgʲeːs] | wild strawberry |
| žėmės riešutaĩ (v) | [ˈʒʲæmʲeːs rʲiɛʃʊˈtʌɪ] | peanut |
| žìrniai (v dgs) | [ˈʒʲɪrnʲɛɪ] | pea |
| žuvìs (m) | [ʒʊˈvʲɪs] | fish |
| žvė́ríena (m) | [ʒvʲeːˈrʲiɛna] | game |
| ántis (m) | [ˈantʲɪs] | duck |
| áustrė (m) | [ˈɑustrʲeː] | oyster |
| ãctas (v) | [ˈaːtstas] | vinegar |
| ãvižos (m dgs) | [ˈaːvʲɪʒos] | oats |
| abrikòsas (v) | [abrʲɪˈkosas] | apricot |
| agrãstas (v) | [agˈraːstas] | gooseberry |
| aguřkas (v) | [aˈgʊrkas] | cucumber |
| aguròtis (v) | [agʊˈroːtʲɪs] | zucchini |
| alkohòliniai gérimai (v dgs) | [alʲkoˈɣolʲɪnʲɛɪ ˈgʲeːrʲɪmʌɪ] | liquors |
| alùs (v) | [aˈlʲʊs] | beer |
| alývuogės (m dgs) | [aˈlʲiːvʊɑgʲeːs] | olives |
| alývuogių aliėjus (v) | [aˈlʲiːvʊɑgʲu aˈlʲɛjʊs] | olive oil |
| ananãsas (v) | [anaˈnaːsas] | pineapple |
| angliãvandeniai (v dgs) | [anˈglʲævandʲɛnʲɛɪ] | carbohydrates |
| anýžius (v) | [aˈnʲiːʒʲʊs] | anise |
| apelsìnų sùltys (m dgs) | [apʲɛlʲˈsʲɪnu: ˈsʊlʲtʲiːs] | orange juice |
| apelsìnas (v) | [apʲɛlʲˈsʲɪnas] | orange |
| aperitývas (v) | [apʲɛrʲɪˈtʲiːvas] | aperitif |
| apetìtas (v) | [apʲɛˈtʲɪtas] | appetite |

| | | |
|---|---|---|
| arbūzas (v) | [ar'bu:zas] | watermelon |
| arbãtinis šaukštẽlis (v) | [ar'ba:tʲɪnʲɪs ʃɑʊkʃ'tʲælʲɪs] | teaspoon |
| arbãtpinigiai (v dgs) | [ar'ba:tpʲɪnʲɪɡʲɛɪ] | tip |
| arbatà (m) | [arba'ta] | tea |
| artišõkas (v) | [artʲɪ'ʃokas] | artichoke |
| atidarytùvas (v) | [atʲɪdarʲiː'tuvas] | bottle opener |
| augalìnis aliẽjus (v) | [ɑʊɡalʲɪnʲɪs a'lʲɛjʊs] | vegetable oil |
| avíena (m) | [a'vʲiɛna] | lamb |
| aviẽtė (m) | [a'vʲɛtʲeː] | raspberry |
| avokãdas (v) | [avo'kadas] | avocado |
| báltas vỹnas (v) | ['balʲtas 'vʲiː:nas] | white wine |
| báltymas (v) | ['balʲtʲiː:mas] | egg white |
| bármenas (v) | ['barmʲɛnas] | bartender |
| bãras (v) | ['ba:ras] | pub, bar |
| baklažãnas (v) | [baklʲa'ʒa:nas] | eggplant |
| baltymaĩ (v dgs) | [balʲtʲiː'mʌɪ] | proteins |
| banãnas (v) | [ba'na:nas] | banana |
| baravỹkas (v) | [bara'vʲiː:kas] | cep |
| bazìlikas (v) | [ba'zʲɪlʲɪkas] | basil |
| bè gãzo | ['bʲɛ 'ga:zɔ] | still |
| bekònas (v) | [bʲɛ'konas] | bacon |
| bifštèksas (v) | [bʲɪf'ʃtʲɛksas] | steak |
| brãškė (m) | ['bra:ʃkʲeː] | strawberry |
| briedžiùkas (v) | [brʲiɛ'dʒʲʊkas] | morel |
| briùselio kopūstas (v) | ['brʲʊsʲɛlʲɔ ko'pu:stas] | Brussels sprouts |
| brokolių kopūstas (v) | ['brokolʲu: ko'pu:stas] | broccoli |
| bruknės (m dgs) | ['bruknʲeːs] | cowberry |
| bulvė (m) | ['bulʲvʲeː] | potato |
| bulvių kõšė (m) | ['bulʲvʲu: 'ko:ʃeː] | mashed potatoes |
| cinamònas (v) | [tsʲɪna'monas] | cinnamon |
| citrinà (m) | [tsʲɪtrʲɪ'na] | lemon |
| cùkrus (v) | ['tsukrus] | sugar |
| džèmas (v) | ['dʒʲɛmas] | jam |
| džìnas (v) | ['dʒʲɪnas] | gin |
| džiovìntas | [dʒʲo'vʲɪntas] | dried |
| dantų krapštùkas (v) | [dan'tu: krapʃ'tukas] | toothpick |
| daržóvės (m dgs) | [dar'ʒovʲeːs] | vegetables |
| datùlė (m) | [da'tulʲeː] | date |
| dešrà (m) | [dʲɛʃ'ra] | sausage |
| dešrẽlė (m) | [dʲɛʃ'rʲælʲeː] | vienna sausage |
| degtìnė (m) | [dʲɛk'tʲɪnʲeː] | vodka |
| desèrtas (v) | [dʲɛ'sʲɛrtas] | dessert |
| dietà (m) | [dʲiɛ'ta] | diet |
| druskà (m) | [drus'ka] | salt |
| dúona (m) | ['duɑna] | bread |
| ešerỹs (v) | [ɛʃɛ'rʲiː:s] | perch |
| eršketíena (m) | [ɛrʃkʲɛ'tʲiɛna] | sturgeon |
| fáršas (m) | ['farʃas] | hamburger |
| figà (m) | [fʲɪ'ga] | fig |
| gãbalas (v) | ['ga:balʲas] | piece |
| gaivùsis gérimas (v) | [ɡʌɪ'vusʲɪs 'ɡʲeː:rʲɪmas] | refreshing drink |
| garnỹras (v) | [gar'nʲiː:ras] | side dish |

| | | |
|---|---|---|
| garstyčios (v) | [gar'stʲiːtsʲos] | mustard |
| gazuotas | [ga'zuɑtas] | carbonated |
| gazuotas | [ga'zuɑtas] | sparkling |
| gervuogės (m dgs) | ['gʲɛrvuɑgʲeːs] | blackberry |
| geriamas vanduo (v) | ['gʲærʲæmas van'duɑ] | drinking water |
| Gero apetito! | ['gʲæro apʲɛ'tʲito!] | Enjoy your meal! |
| grūdas (v) | ['gru:das] | grain |
| grūdinės kultūros (m dgs) | [gru:'dʲinʲeːs kulʲ'tu:ros] | cereal crops |
| graikinis riešutas (v) | ['grʌikʲinʲis 'rʲiɛʃutas] | walnut |
| granatas (v) | [gra'na:tas] | pomegranate |
| greipfrutas (v) | ['grʲɛipfrutas] | grapefruit |
| grikiai (v dgs) | ['grʲikʲɛi] | buckwheat |
| griežinys (v) | [grʲiɛʒʲɪ'nʲiːs] | slice |
| grietinė (m) | [grʲiɛ'tʲinʲe:] | sour cream |
| grietinėlė (m) | [grʲiɛtʲɪ'nʲe:lʲe:] | cream |
| grybas (v) | ['grʲiːbas] | mushroom |
| gvazdikas (v) | [gvaz'dʲɪkas] | cloves |
| ikrai (v dgs) | ['ɪkrʌɪ] | caviar |
| imbieras (v) | ['ɪmbʲiɛras] | ginger |
| jūros gėrybės (m dgs) | ['ju:ros gʲe:'rʲiːbʲe:s] | seafood |
| jautiena (m) | ['jɑutʲiɛna] | beef |
| jogurtas (v) | [jo'gurtas] | yogurt |
| juoda arbata (m) | [juɑ'da arba'ta] | black tea |
| juoda kava (m) | [juɑ'da ka'va] | black coffee |
| juodieji pipirai (v) | [juɑ'dʲiɛjɪ pʲɪ'pʲɪrʌɪ] | black pepper |
| juodieji serbentai (v dgs) | [juɑ'dʲiɛjɪ sʲɛr'bʲɛntʌɪ] | blackcurrant |
| karštas | ['karʃtas] | hot |
| karpis (v) | ['karpʲɪs] | carp |
| kalafioras (v) | [kalʲa'fʲoras] | cauliflower |
| kalakutiena (m) | [kalʲaku'tʲiɛna] | turkey |
| kalendra (m) | [ka'lʲɛndra] | coriander |
| kalmaras (v) | [kalʲ'ma:ras] | squid |
| kalorija (m) | [ka'lʲorʲijɛ] | calorie |
| kamščiatraukis (v) | [kamʃ'tsʲætrɑukʲɪs] | corkscrew |
| kapučino kava (m) | [kapu'tʂɪno ka'va] | cappuccino |
| karšis (v) | ['karʃɪs] | bream |
| kartus | [kar'tus] | bitter |
| kava (m) | [ka'va] | coffee |
| kava su pienu (m) | [ka'va 'su 'pʲiɛnu] | coffee with milk |
| kepenys (m dgs) | ['kʲɛpe'nʲiːs] | liver |
| keptas | ['kʲæptas] | fried |
| kivis (v) | ['kʲɪvʲɪs] | kiwi |
| kiaušiniai (v dgs) | [kʲɛu'ʃɪnʲɛɪ] | eggs |
| kiaušinis (v) | [kʲɛu'ʃɪnʲɪs] | egg |
| kiaušinienė (m) | [kʲɛuʃɪ'nʲɛnʲe:] | fried eggs |
| kiauliena (m) | [kʲɛu'lʲiɛna] | pork |
| kmynai (v) | ['kmʲi:nʌɪ] | caraway |
| kokoso riešutas (v) | ['kokoso 'rʲiɛʃutas] | coconut |
| košė (m) | ['ko:ʃe:] | porridge |
| kokteilis (v) | [kok'tʲɛɪlʲɪs] | cocktail |
| konditerijos gaminiai (v) | [kondʲɪ'tʲɛrʲijɔs gamʲɪ'nʲɛɪ] | confectionery |
| konjakas (v) | [kon'ja:kas] | cognac |

| | | |
|---|---|---|
| konsèrvų atidarytùvas (v) | [kɔn'sʲɛrvu: atʲɪdarʲi:'tuvas] | can opener |
| konsèrvai (v dgs) | [kɔn'sʲɛrvʌɪ] | canned food |
| kopùstas (v) | [kɔ'pu:stas] | cabbage |
| krãbas (v) | ['kra:bas] | crab |
| krãpas (v) | ['kra:pas] | dill |
| kramtomoji gumã (m) | [kramto'mojɪ gu'ma] | chewing gum |
| krèmas (v) | ['krʲɛmas] | buttercream |
| krevètė (m) | [krʲɛ'vʲɛtʲe:] | shrimp |
| kriáušė (m) | ['krʲæuʃʲe:] | pear |
| krienaĩ (v dgs) | [krʲɛ'nʌɪ] | horseradish |
| kruõpos (m dgs) | ['kruɑpos] | cereal grains |
| kukurūzų drìbsniai (v dgs) | [kuku'ru:zu: 'drʲɪbsnʲɛɪ] | cornflakes |
| kukurūzas (v) | [kuku'ru:zas] | corn |
| kukurūzas (v) | [kuku'ru:zas] | corn |
| kumpis (v) | ['kumpʲɪs] | ham |
| kumpis (v) | ['kumpʲɪs] | gammon |
| kviečiaĩ (v dgs) | [kvʲɛ'tʂʲɛɪ] | wheat |
| lėkštė̃ (m) | [lʲe:kʃ'tʲe:] | plate |
| lėkštėlė (m) | [lʲe:kʃ'tʲælʲe:] | saucer |
| lęšiai (v dgs) | ['lʲɛ:ʃɛɪ] | lentil |
| lašišã (m) | [lʲaʃɪ'ʃa] | salmon |
| lašišã (m) | [lʲaʃɪ'ʃa] | Atlantic salmon |
| láuro lãpas (v) | ['lʲɑuro 'lʲa:pas] | bay leaf |
| lãkštiniai (v dgs) | ['lʲa:kʃtʲɪnʲɛɪ] | noodles |
| langùstas (v) | [lʲan'gustas] | spiny lobster |
| lẽdas (v) | ['lʲædas] | ice |
| lẽpšis (v) | ['lʲæpʃɪs] | birch bolete |
| ledaĩ (v dgs) | [lʲɛ'dʌɪ] | ice-cream |
| lìkeris (v) | ['lʲɪkʲɛrʲɪs] | liqueur |
| liežùvis (v) | [lʲɛ'ʒuvʲɪs] | tongue |
| limonãdas (v) | [lʲɪmo'na:das] | lemonade |
| lúoba (m) | ['lʲuɑba] | peel |
| lydekã (m) | [lʲi:dʲɛ'ka] | pike |
| mėlỹnės (m dgs) | [mʲe:'lʲi:nʲe:s] | bilberry |
| mėsã (m) | [mʲe:'sa] | meat |
| mėsaĩnis (v) | [mʲe:'sʌɪnʲɪs] | hamburger |
| mángo (v) | ['mango] | mango |
| majonèzas (v) | [majo'nʲɛzas] | mayonnaise |
| makarõnai (v dgs) | [maka'ro:nʌɪ] | pasta |
| mandarìnas (v) | [manda'rʲɪnas] | mandarin |
| margarìnas (v) | [marga'rʲɪnas] | margarine |
| marinúotas | [marʲɪ'nuɑtas] | pickled |
| marmelãdas (v) | [marmʲɛ'lʲa:das] | marmalade |
| ménkė (m) | ['mʲɛŋkʲe:] | cod |
| medùs (v) | [mʲɛ'dus] | honey |
| meliònas (v) | [mʲɛ'lʲonas] | melon |
| meniù (v) | [mʲɛ'nʲu] | menu |
| mìltai (v dgs) | ['mʲɪlʲtʌɪ] | flour |
| miẽžiai (v dgs) | ['mʲɛʒʲɛɪ] | barley |
| migdõlas (v) | [mʲɪg'do:lʲas] | almond |
| minerãlinis vanduõ (v) | [mʲɪnʲɛ'ra:lʲɪnʲɪs van'duɑ] | mineral water |
| moliū̃gas (v) | [mo'lʲu:gas] | turnip |

| | | |
|---|---|---|
| morka (m) | [mor'ka] | carrot |
| musmirė (m) | ['musmʲɪrʲe:] | fly agaric |
| nealkoholonis | [nʲɛalʲko'ɣolonʲɪs] | non-alcoholic |
| nealkoholonis gėrimas (v) | [nʲɛalʲko'ɣolonʲɪs 'gʲe:rʲɪmas] | soft drink |
| nuodingas grybas (v) | [nuɑ'dʲɪngas 'grʲi:bas] | poisonous mushroom |
| ōtas (v) | ['o:tas] | halibut |
| obuolys (v) | [obuɑ'lʲi:s] | apple |
| omletas (v) | [om'lʲɛtas] | omelet |
| paštetas (v) | [paʃ'tʲɛtas] | pâté |
| pādažas (v) | ['pa:daʒas] | sauce |
| paprika (m) | ['pa:prʲka] | paprika |
| pātiekalas (v) | ['pa:tʲiɛkalʲas] | course, dish |
| padavėja (m) | [pada'vʲe:ja] | waitress |
| padavėjas (v) | [pada'vʲe:jas] | waiter |
| papaja (m) | [pa'pa ja] | papaya |
| persikas (v) | ['pʲɛrsʲɪkas] | peach |
| peilis (v) | ['pʲɛɪlʲɪs] | knife |
| petrāžolė (m) | [pʲɛ'tra:ʒolʲe:] | parsley |
| pienas (v) | ['pʲiɛnas] | milk |
| pieniškas koktelis (v) | ['pʲiɛnʲɪʃkas kok'tʲɛɪlʲɪs] | milkshake |
| pica (m) | [pʲɪ'tsa] | pizza |
| piētūs (v) | ['pʲɛ'tu:s] | lunch |
| pipiras (v) | [pʲɪ'pʲɪras] | bell pepper |
| pistācijos (m dgs) | [pʲɪs'ta:tsʲɪjos] | pistachios |
| plēkšnė (m) | ['plʲæk ʃnʲe:] | flatfish |
| porcija (m) | ['portsʲɪjɛ] | portion |
| pomidorų sūltys (m dgs) | [pomʲɪ'doru: 'sʊlʲtʲi:s] | tomato juice |
| pomidoras (v) | [pomʲɪ'doras] | tomato |
| prieskonis (v) | ['prʲiɛskonʲɪs] | condiment |
| prieskonis (v) | ['prʲiɛskonʲɪs] | spice |
| prieskonis (v) | ['prʲiɛskonʲɪs] | aftertaste |
| pudingas (v) | ['pʊdʲɪngas] | pudding |
| pupos (m dgs) | ['pʊpos] | beans |
| pusryčiai (v dgs) | ['pʊsrʲi:tʃʲɛɪ] | breakfast |
| puodukas (v) | [pʊɑ'dukas] | cup |
| pupēlės (m dgs) | [pʊ'pʲælʲe:s] | kidney bean |
| pyrāgas (v) | [pʲɪ:'ra:gas] | pie |
| pyragaitis (v) | [pʲɪ:ra'gʌɪtʲɪs] | cake |
| rūkytas | [ru:'kʲi:tas] | smoked |
| raudonas vynas (v) | [rɑʊ'donas 'vʲi:nas] | red wine |
| raudonieji pipirai (v) | [rɑʊdo'nʲiɛjɪ pʲɪ'pʲɪrʌɪ] | red pepper |
| raudonieji serbentai (v dgs) | [rɑʊdo'nʲɛjɪ sʲɛr'bʲɛntʌɪ] | redcurrant |
| raudonvīršis (v) | [rɑʊdon'vʲɪrʃɪs] | orange-cap boletus |
| razinos (m dgs) | [ra'zʲɪnos] | raisin |
| receptas (v) | [rʲɛ'tsʲɛptas] | recipe |
| riešutas (v) | ['rʲiɛʃutas] | hazelnut |
| ridikas (v) | [rʲɪ'dʲɪkas] | radish |
| riebalai (v dgs) | [rʲiɛba'lʲʌɪ] | fats |
| romas (v) | ['romas] | rum |
| rōpė (m) | ['ropʲe:] | pumpkin |
| rugiai (v dgs) | [rʊ'gʲɛɪ] | rye |

| | | |
|---|---|---|
| ruñkelis, burõkas (v) | ['rʊŋkʲɛlʲɪs], [bʊ'ro:kas] | beetroot |
| rýžiai (v) | ['rʲiːʒʲɛɪ] | rice |
| ryklỹs (v) | [rʲɪkʲlʲiːs] | shark |
| sąskaita (m) | ['sa:skʌɪta] | check |
| sūris (v) | ['su:rʲɪs] | cheese |
| sūrùs | [su:'rʊs] | salty |
| saldaìnis (v) | [salʲ'dʌɪnʲɪs] | candy |
| saldùs | [salʲ'dʊs] | sweet |
| saliêras (v) | [sa'lʲɛras] | celery |
| salõta (m) | [sa'lʲo:ta] | lettuce |
| salõtos (m) | [sa'lʲo:tos] | salad |
| sardìnė (m) | [sar'dʲɪnʲe:] | sardine |
| saulégrąžų aliêjus (v) | [saʊ'lʲe:gra:ʒu: a'lʲɛjʊs] | sunflower oil |
| sausaìniai (v) | [saʊ'sʌɪnʲɛɪ] | cookies |
| sezãmas (v) | [sʲɛ'za:mas] | sesame |
| sìlkė (m) | ['sʲɪlʲkʲe:] | herring |
| skanùs | [ska'nʊs] | tasty |
| skõnis (v) | ['sko:nʲɪs] | taste, flavor |
| skùmbrė (m) | ['skʊmbrʲe:] | mackerel |
| slyvà (m) | [slʲi:'va] | plum |
| smìdras (v) | ['smʲɪdras] | asparagus |
| sóra (m) | ['sora] | millet |
| sojà (m) | [so:'jɛ ] | soy |
| spagečiai (v dgs) | [spa'gʲɛtʂʲɛɪ] | spaghetti |
| spanguolė (m) | ['spaŋgʊalʲe:] | cranberry |
| sriubà (m) | [srʲʊ'ba] | soup |
| starkis (v) | ['starkʲɪs] | pike perch |
| stìklas (v) | ['stʲɪklʲas] | glass |
| sù ledaìs | ['sʊ lʲɛ'dʌɪs] | with ice |
| sùltys (m dgs) | ['sʊlʲtʲi:s] | juice |
| sultinỹs (v) | [sʊlʲtɪ'rʲnʲi:s] | clear soup |
| sumuštìnis (v) | [sʊmʊʃ'tʲɪnʲɪs] | sandwich |
| sutírštintas píenas (v) | [sʊ'tʲɪrʃtʲɪntas 'pʲɛnas] | condensed milk |
| svíestas (v) | ['svʲɛstas] | butter |
| svogūnas (v) | [svo'gu:nas] | onion |
| tamsùs alùs (v) | [tam'sʊs a'lʲʊs] | dark beer |
| taurė̃ (m) | [taʊ'rʲe:] | glass |
| tirpì kavà (m) | [tʲɪr'pʲɪ ka'va] | instant coffee |
| tòrtas (v) | ['tortas] | cake |
| trẽšnė (m) | ['trʲæʃnʲe:] | sweet cherry |
| triùšis (v) | ['trʲʊʃɪs] | rabbit |
| trupinỹs (v) | [trʊpʲɪ'nʲi:s] | crumb |
| trynỹs (v) | [trʲi:'nʲi:s] | egg yolk |
| tùnas (v) | ['tʊnas] | tuna |
| ùžkandis (v) | ['ʊʒkandʲɪs] | appetizer |
| úoga (m) | ['ʊaga] | berry |
| úogos (m dgs) | ['ʊagos] | berries |
| ungurỹs (v) | [ʊŋgʊ'rʲi:s] | eel |
| uogiẽnė (m) | [ʊa'gʲɛnʲe:] | jam |
| upétakis (v) | [ʊ'pʲe:takʲɪs] | trout |
| vėžiãgyviai (v dgs) | [vʲe:'ʒʲægʲi:vʲɛɪ] | crustaceans |
| válgomas grýbas (v) | ['valʲgomas 'grʲi:bas] | edible mushroom |

| | | |
|---|---|---|
| **valgomasis šáukštas** (v) | ['valⁱgomasⁱɪs 'ʃɑʊkʃtas] | soup spoon |
| **várpa** (m) | ['varpa] | ear |
| **vãfliai** (v dgs) | ['va:flⁱɛɪ] | waffles |
| **vaĩsiai** (v dgs) | ['vʌɪsⁱɛɪ] | fruits |
| **vaĩsius** (v) | ['vʌɪsⁱʊs] | fruit |
| **vakariėnė** (m) | [vaka'rⁱɛnⁱe:] | dinner |
| **valgis** (v) | ['valⁱgⁱɪs] | food |
| **vanduõ** (v) | [van'dʊɑ] | water |
| **vèrmutas** (v) | ['vⁱɛrmʊtas] | vermouth |
| **vegetãras** (v) | [vⁱɛgⁱɛ'ta:ras] | vegetarian |
| **vegetãriškas** | [vⁱɛgⁱɛ'ta:rⁱɪʃkas] | vegetarian |
| **veršíena** (m) | [vⁱɛr'ʃiɛna] | veal |
| **višta** (m) | [vⁱɪʃ'ta] | chicken |
| **vìrtas** | ['vⁱɪrtas] | boiled |
| **vìskis** (v) | ['vⁱɪskⁱɪs] | whiskey |
| **virtùvė** (m) | [vⁱɪr'tʊvⁱe:] | cuisine |
| **vitamìnas** (v) | [vⁱɪta'mⁱɪnas] | vitamin |
| **voveráitė** (m) | [vove'rʌɪtⁱe:] | chanterelle |
| **vyšnià** (m) | [vⁱi'ʃnⁱæ] | sour cherry |
| **vỹnų žemėlapis** (v) | ['vⁱi:nu: ʒe'mⁱe:lⁱapⁱɪs] | wine list |
| **vỹnas** (v) | ['vⁱi:nas] | wine |
| **vỹnuogės** (m dgs) | ['vⁱi:nʊɑgⁱe:s] | grape |

Printed in Great Britain
by Amazon

71297554R00120